CATCHING
THE ASCENSION WAVE

"Catching the Ascension Wave will not only cat apult you into your ascension! This book exp mesmerizing—I couldn't put it down!"

DIANNE ROBBINS, AUTHOR OF *MESSA(*

"Catching the Ascension Wave is just what the world needs right now at this critical juncture in our evolution. Bob's style is friendly and accessible, even when explaining some rather deep concepts, which anyone (with an open mind) can easily assimilate. He has a mind for bringing multiple loose ends together, from all kinds of sources, to create a clear picture of our world that has been kept from our awareness. It gets especially good when he goes into his great work with Breath Alchemy, which he demonstrates as one of the key methods to upgrading our consciousness for the great transition Earth is now making into fourth-dimensional reality."

DENIS OUELLETTE, AUTHOR OF
HEAL YOURSELF WITH BREATH, LIGHT, SOUND, AND WATER

"Finally, a book that connects all the dots and gives us answers! This is a groundbreaking must-read guide for the turbulent times we find ourselves in, teetering on the edge of mass awakening. Bob Frissell pulls back the veil and exposes the truths that have been obscured from the world and gives us a set of solutions for healing our own traumas and raising our vibrational frequency to match the new Earth that is emerging."

KRIS ASHLEY, AUTHOR OF
CHANGE YOUR MIND TO CHANGE YOUR REALITY

"Bob Frissell has done a superb job of collecting information and showing the visible and invisible processes associated with the awakening of humanity and describing them in his exciting book. But most importantly, he gives unique meditations, tools, and techniques, including the Breath Alchemy Technique, which will allow people to harmoniously align with the raising of the consciousness of the planet so that humanity will again find inner peace, joyfulness, and unconditional love."

ALEXANDER MILOVANOV, AUTHOR OF
THE MUSIC OF THE DIVINE SPHERES

"A wonderful, exceptional book that is true to Bob's previous well-researched messages. I love how he ties together so many unexplained phenomena that you may have wondered about. This is a book I will treasure! It may call you to re-read again and again. It is irresistible."

MAUREEN J. ST. GERMAIN, AUTHOR OF *WAKING UP IN 5D*

"In this book, Frissell surpasses himself with another breathtaking expansion of our understanding and experience of reality—and adds to it a full explanation of his powerful Five-Step Harmonizing Method of Breath Alchemy. My personal experiences with Breath Alchemy have been truly amazing, on a physical and energetic level—the most healing experience I have ever had. This is a life-changing book!"

KENNETH PORTER, M.D., AUTHOR OF
APOLLO'S LYRE: THE ART OF SPIRITUAL PSYCHOTHERAPY

"Bob Frissell knows how to duel with paradoxes, Potemkins, and aliases and come away with a single gem that attunes you to the next rung on the ladder—your own ladder. He is a living truth serum and hermetic lie detector. *Catching the Ascension Wave* is a delightful and wise maturation of his teaching and shows the payoff of getting on a path and staying on it, no matter what gets tossed your way."

RICHARD GROSSINGER, AUTHOR OF
DREAMTIMES AND THOUGHTFORMS

"Bob is a remarkable author who cannot be compared with anyone else. Each book of his presents us with something mind-blowing or pleasantly shocking for our perception of reality. *Catching the Ascension Wave* is exciting. Even if you do not believe in higher-dimensional energy in the way that Bob describes, this book will benefit you, it will open your mind to new possibilities and give you tools to improve your inner state of being. I highly recommend not only his books but also his Breath Alchemy Technique."

GISSELLE CUOMO, CLINICAL PSYCHOLOGIST

"I recommend this book to anyone who is interested in psychological transformation and the evolution of humanity to a higher level of being—and even physical transcendence into one characterized by cosmic consciousness—that will bring about a new heaven and a new Earth for those who have prepared themselves for great changes."

ROBERT D. MORNINGSTAR, CIVILIAN INTELLIGENCE ANALYST
AND INVESTIGATIVE JOURNALIST

CATCHING
THE
ASCENSION
WAVE

Everything You Need to Know
about the Coming Great Awakening

A Sacred Planet Book

Bob Frissell

Bear & Company
Rochester, Vermont

Bear & Company
One Park Street
Rochester, Vermont 05767
www.BearandCompanyBooks.com

Text stock is SFI certified

Bear & Company is a division of Inner Traditions International

Sacred Planet Books are curated by Richard Grossinger, Inner Traditions editorial board member and cofounder and former publisher of North Atlantic Books. The Sacred Planet collection, published under the umbrella of the Inner Traditions family of imprints, includes works on the themes of consciousness, cosmology, alternative medicine, dreams, climate, permaculture, alchemy, shamanic studies, oracles, astrology, crystals, hyperobjects, locutions, and subtle bodies.

Cataloging-in-Publication Data for this title is available from the Library of Congress

ISBN 978-1-59143-455-9 (print)
ISBN 978-1-59143-456-6 (ebook)

Printed and bound in the United States by Lake Book Manufacturing, LLC
The text stock is SFI certified. The Sustainable Forestry Initiative® program promotes sustainable forest management.

10   9   8   7   6   5   4   3   2   1

Text design and layout by Kenleigh Manseau
This book was typeset in Garamond Premier Pro with PT Mono and Gill Sans MT Pro used as display typefaces

To send correspondence to the author of this book, mail a first-class letter to the author c/o Inner Traditions • Bear & Company, One Park Street, Rochester, VT 05767, and we will forward the communication, or contact the author directly at **BobFrissell.com.**

Contents

Introduction

Have you ever wondered what your life would be like if you could lift the veil and see well beyond your five-sense reality? What if you could step into and KNOW on a very deep level that not only are you inseparable from the whole of creation, but that you are the whole?

Well, let's begin by taking a little journey; let's, in fact, take a ride out to the center of the Universe. Are you ready? Good, let's go!

Sit comfortably, and with the intention to create a sacred space, ask and intend to connect with the energy of Source, the energy of the Divine Creator, the energy of light, the energy of healing, the energy of truth, the energy of pure and unconditional love.

Ask and intend that those Beings of the Light, your master guides, be present with you at this time, to help you create a sacred space. Your intent is to connect powerfully with Source, to experience, and to feel this energy through your entire being; and so it is.

Take a moment to intend to stay anchored in your physical body, simply ask and intend to do so.

Visualize that you are traveling through space, through the solar system, through the galaxies.

Visualize that you are standing at the center of the Universe. Take a moment to visualize an enormous body of light. Ask and intend to experience the energy of this body of light; this is the energy of Source, the energy of Divine Creator.

Take a moment to feel the energy emanating from that Source. Notice the energy flowing through your body now.

Visualize that you are taking one particle from the Source energy, and that you are bringing it with you, and traveling back through the galaxies, through the solar system, onto this Earth plane, and in your current physical space, now.

Visualize that this particle of light is now hovering above you, and that this particle of light is slowly coming all the way down and entering through the top of your head. Let it fill your entire head.

Bring it down, let it fill your neck, your throat, bring it down. Let it fill your shoulders, arms, upper back, chest, lower back, stomach, thighs, knees, ankles, and feet. Let it come out through the bottom of your feet, anchoring you down all the way into the Earth.

Now, visualize this particle of light coming up from the Earth, all the way up, through the bottom of your feet, through your ankles, knees, thighs, lower back, upper back, arms, shoulders, neck, and head. Let it come out through the top of your head, connecting you all the way back to Source.

Now, visualize that you are wrapped in a beam of light, connecting you all the way up to Source, and all the way down into the Earth. Simply bathe in this energy of Divine Light. Experience this energy of connection with Source; experience the energy of being merged with Divine Creator.*

Now, imagine this: What would your life be like if you could live every moment of it as your truest self?

What if you woke up this morning feeling truly inspired and deeply connected to Divine Creator? And throughout the day things seemed to fall into place, and the solutions to problems appeared almost magically.

What if you could wake up every day feeling happy and content, confident in your abilities, creative and present? Chances are, everything in your life would truly make sense, and you'd know exactly what to do, no matter what challenge you had to face. You'd feel a deep sense

---

*This meditation was inspired by a CD called *Connecting to Source* from Caroline Cory.

of belonging and connection with the world and the people around you, and good things would just seem to happen to you without your having to strive or struggle for them—almost as if the Universe was looking out for you, nudging opportunities in your direction.

Sounds good, right?

Now, imagine stepping into a reality where life in every moment is one hundred times more harmonious in every way than even your very best moments are currently.

Does that sound good? Perhaps it seems like it's too good to be true. But hold on: that's exactly where we're headed.

Today, there is an enormous infusion of higher-dimensional energy—a Galactic Super Wave as it's called in the U.S. Secret Space Program (referred to as the secret space program (SSP) from here on)—that is dramatically raising the vibratory rate of the planet and everyone on it. There is a personal transformation that we must make if we are to survive and thrive, so we can "catch the wave" into higher consciousness and live our sacred purpose.

Aligning oneself with this emerging presence of awakening will result in experiences of amazing levels of joy and unconditional love, the ability to create great abundance while remaining aligned with Spirit, and the connection to deep inner peace, and the ability to make a difference on the planet in a way that enables Mother Earth to reach critical mass and become lit from within.

Is it something you want? If yes, you are in a perfect place!

What I'm referring to is nothing less than the ascension of planet Earth from third density into fourth density. This is the Shift of the Ages; it is nothing less than the birth of a new humanity!

Okay, now that I've got your attention, let's come out of warp drive and back into impulse power in preparation for taking a high orbit around planet Earth's equator. Sensors indicate that we are approaching a class M planet, with a breathable, though highly polluted atmosphere that will sustain human life. There is a somewhat striving portion of the population that seems to be stuck in the illogical yet fascinating belief that they are separate entities, cut off from the whole, and looking out at a world that is not them. This affliction seems to be originating with an incessant identification with the mind.

Sensors also indicate that a great awakening is on the horizon, that its populace is soon to awaken to the reality that they have been deceived and lied to in most every way possible. This is perceived as a first step in the necessary progression in spiritual growth that will soon culminate with a dramatic raising of the planet's vibratory rate that will allow the planet and its inhabitants to move out of the darkness and into the light. With the lifting of the veils, humans will remember and live their intimate connection to all life. They will completely redefine what it means to be human!

We will be utilizing our time-travel capabilities to step back and see if we can fill in the gap between where we currently are and where we're headed. If we truly want to know where we're going, it is essential that we know our ancient past. Then in combination with where we are now, we can begin to get a glimpse of our future possibilities.

We will be covering a significant amount of time—about 2.6 billion years' worth. We need to know about the Ancient Builder Race, how they originated on Venus, established a colony in Antarctica, and then branched out to our neighboring star systems. This benevolent race has had a huge impact on us; they were able to keep the peace for over two billion years by creating a giant defensive grid around our local cluster of fifty-two star systems. They did this in a way that was both ingenious and extremely practical. Then about 500,000 years ago, Maldek (also known as Tiamat)—a huge Earthlike planet in our solar system—and its habitable moon, ended up getting infiltrated by negativity. They figured out how to turn the defense shield into an offensive weapon and went to war with another culture in our local cluster. It didn't turn out well for Maldek. They ended up destroying their planet; it is now the asteroid belt between the orbits of Mars and Jupiter. The results of all of this have had an enormous impact here on Earth that continues to affect us to this very day. We will carefully unpack the details.

There is an important document called the *Law of One* that will enable us to take a detailed look at all of this. The first *Law of One* book was called *The Ra Material by Ra, a Humble Messenger of the Law of One.* But Ra is just a name for the sixth-density extraterrestrial source, so Ra is actually the Ancient Builder Race.

We will be lifting veils in just about every which way; I have mentioned our two-tiered technology system in my previous books; in this book, I will fully unpack it to expose not only mind-numbing levels of technology, but also the rather startling details of our secret space program and our interaction with many different ET races. Plenty of insiders and whistleblowers have come forward with some rather revealing and amazing stories to tell. You will not have to wait long to find out what they have to say; we will begin chapter 1 with a real bang!

Then there is the nature of the ascension itself. Is it real? In a word, yes. There are references to ascension from at least thirty-five different civilizations that have been incorporated into their religious myths. The prophecies of Jesus are consistent with those of thirty-four other cultures. The same prophecies put forth by Jesus appear in the Qur'an, the Old Testament, in Native American spiritual traditions, and in Celtic and Druid traditions. The Hindu scriptures are very similar—they call it the Samvarta Fire at the end of the age. They also call it the Yuga Fire, it comes from the Sun and causes rainbow colors in the sky.

If the ascension is real, then what are the cosmic forces at play here? Will there be Earth changes, or will we be able to navigate a smoother ride this time around? What causes violent upheavals, and what can we do to prevent them? Will everyone make it to the next level? If not, what happens to those who were not ready? What can we do to prepare? These and many more questions will be addressed and explored in detail.

I will also dive into the details of the great cosmic wave of higher-frequency energy that is bombarding the Earth and affecting everyone on it. We are going through a dark night of the soul; our collective and individual darkness is coming to the surface in order to be transmuted into the light. Well, what does that mean, and is the transformation an automatic thing, or is there something we need to know in order to come out of resistance and into alignment with the many changes that are irreversible, and absolutely necessary, if we are to make it into the higher worlds?

For many, this is triggering symptoms including strong emotional outbursts, feelings of anxiety, frustration, and anger, vivid dreams, insomnia, feeling ill, or changes in sleeping patterns. I will share with you the details about discovering and then mastering your innate ability to transmute unresolved emotions, fears, and other limitations into life-enhancing internal guidance systems, so you can truly be present and prepared in these challenging, yet exciting times. The Shift of the Ages is the awakening of humanity's heart; it is the movement from the polarized mind—which is a continual state of judgment and does not connect the dots to see wholeness—to the heart, which is connected to Source and only knows Unity. Challenges await, but if we can transform, this is the birth of a new humanity.

PART I
Cosmic Overview

In this section, we will lift the veil to explore from a big-picture perspective the gap between what we think—and are told—is going on and what is really happening.

Going back over 500,000 years of Earth history, we will look at the role of the Ancient Builder Race from Venus, as well as that of the Greys, and the Draco Reptilians in our evolutionary development. We will take a deep dive into the startling details of the secret space program as well as the New World Order and the Depopulation Agenda.

1

Lifting the Veil

Let's begin by asking a simple, yet very important question. Have you ever wondered about the seemingly sudden explosion in new technology and where it came from?

After fifty years of cover-up, lies, and disinformation, the truth about the July 1947 Roswell crash began to surface. Why did it take so long? Well, put yourself in the shoes of someone who was there and saw the actual wreckage of the crashed disc—like Major Jesse A. Marcel, for instance.

Marcel, who was a Roswell intelligence officer, was dispatched to the scene to collect the wreckage. Marcel was certain that it was not a weather balloon, nor an aircraft. He said the foil, no thicker than that in a pack of cigarettes, was virtually indestructible. It was, in his words, "not of this Earth."[1] Major Marcel was told to load the wreckage onto a B-29 and fly it to the Eighth Air Force headquarters in Fort Worth, Texas, where General Roger M. Ramey took control of the debris. The cover-up began when he ordered Marcel and others to keep quiet and issued another press release saying that the incident was nothing more than a crashed weather balloon.

So why would Marcel, and others who knew, remain quiet for all those years? Wasn't there someone who realized that what was perhaps the top story of the century was too important to be withheld from the public's right to know? Well, what would you do if it was made quite clear to you that, at the very least, your retirement pension might be cut off; or perhaps an "accident" might come your way—either to you, your family, or both? Would you be the one who would risk all by spilling the beans?

Finally, when they were literally on their death beds, some brave souls decided to come forward and tell what they saw. In 1997, Col. Phillip J. Corso (Ret.), came forward with a fascinating and revealing book called *The Day after Roswell*.[2] As chief of the army's Foreign Technology Division in 1961, Corso stewarded the alien artifacts found at the Roswell crash site and then seeded this alien technology to giants of American industry. This then is what led to today's integrated circuit chips, fiber optics, lasers, and super-tenacity fibers.

Back to Roswell for a moment: Why do you suppose the ETs had an interest there? Well, the Roswell Army Air Base was home to the 508th Bomber Group, the only squadron entrusted with carrying the atomic bomb, which was used of course, with devastating effects.

So, how then, did we show up to our interstellar neighbors? Well, it's pretty obvious that we presented ourselves in much the same way as a group of four- and five-year-olds sitting in the living room and playing with loaded guns. Obviously, we didn't have anywhere near the spiritual understanding to even contemplate the possibility that splitting the atom not only has no positive possible outcomes, but in fact is against universal law.

Consider also, that before the first test, we did not know if the blast would create a chain-reaction that would continue until the entire planet was destroyed. But we thought the end justified the means— after all, how else would we end World War II? That's a pretty good definition of insanity, don't you think?

Okay, with that said, there was more than ample evidence to indicate that Japan was an already thoroughly defeated nation—that the bombs over Hiroshima and Nagasaki in August 1945 were not only unnecessary, but that they also displayed genocide at its worst. Could it be that these two horrific explosions were intended more for the Soviets, the first shots fired in the Cold War, rather than for an already defeated Japan?

I clearly remember Drunvalo Melchizedek explaining in his "Flower of Life" workshop, that not only is splitting the atom against universal law, but because it is tearing matter apart, it has a dramatic rippling effect throughout the cosmos. All star systems are interconnected through what you might call a cosmic web. This presents a huge problem for ET races who not only communicate through this web, but also travel through it. This important bit of information was echoed by whistleblower Corey Goode in a documentary called *Above Majestic*.[3]

Bob Dean had a cosmic top-secret clearance in his military career. I met and befriended him at various UFO conferences. He, along with other insiders, has come forth with the information that various ETs have hovered over nuclear missile installations and literally disempowered them. Dean also revealed that at one point, all the nuclear warheads in both the United States and the USSR were melted down and rendered completely useless.

THE OFFER WE REJECTED

Whistleblower Bill Cooper stated that, in 1972, he saw two reports relating to government concern and involvement with alien creatures and their interference on this planet. Cooper, from 1970 to 1973, was working as a quartermaster with an intelligence briefing team for U.S. admiral Bernard A. Clarey, then commander-in-chief of the Pacific Fleet.

He knew that at some point he had to go public, and first did so in a briefing statement presented to the Mutual UFO Network (Mufon) on May 23, 1989,[4] and then later in his underground bestseller *Behold a Pale Horse*. He said that in 1953 large objects in space were tracked moving toward Earth. They turned out to be a fleet of ships that took up a high orbit around the equator. Their intent was unknown. Cooper said that communication was established using the computer binary language. This resulted in a landing where face-to-face contact was established.

Then the plot thickened as another race of humanoid aliens successfully communicated with the U.S. government and landed at Homestead Air Force Base in Florida. They came here, Cooper said, to warn us about the dangers of aligning with the group of large-nose

Greys with whom we had already met. They offered to help us with the planet's many environmental problems. They said they would use their technology to heal and resolve them all. The one condition was that we give up our nuclear weapons. They said we didn't have the necessary spiritual understanding to use our technology in a responsible manner—that we would only use it to destroy ourselves and our planet. We rejected this offer on the grounds that it would be unwise to disarm ourselves in the face of all this uncertainty.

The next major event occurred, according to Cooper, in 1954 when further communication with the Greys resulted in a landing at Edwards Air Force Base. President Eisenhower arranged to be vacationing in nearby Palm Springs. The excuse was given to the press that he was rushed to the dentist with a toothache, when in fact, his meeting with the Greys on February 20, 1954, resulted in a formal treaty between the United States and an alien nation.

Prior to this in 1953, Eisenhower's first year in office, at least ten more crashed discs were recovered, along with twenty-six dead and four live aliens. Why so many crashed discs, you might be wondering? Evidently, the U.S. military learned that radar was capable of bringing them down, so they began aiming the radar at the ships, with the intention of bringing down as many as they could.

Clearly, this was a major burden for a new president, so in early 1953, he turned to friend and fellow Council on Foreign Relations (CFR) member Nelson Rockefeller for help. In so doing, Eisenhower made an innocent yet huge mistake, as we shall soon see. They began planning the secret structure of alien supervision, which was to become reality within one year. The idea for MJ-12 was born.

Majesty Twelve (MJ-12), also known as Majority Twelve, was created early in 1954 to oversee and conduct all covert activities concerning the alien question. It is significant that Eisenhower, as well as the first six MJ-12 members from the government, were also CFR members. This gave control of the most secret and powerful group in government to a special-interest club that was itself controlled by the Illuminati.[5]

FLYING OVER THE CAPITOL

In 1952, a whole fleet of UFOs was clearly seen by many onlookers as it flew around and circled the Capitol building in Washington, D.C. From information received from his various insiders, David Wilcock, through the Ascension Mystery School 20/20's highly acclaimed online class "The Great Awakening,"[6] offered details that I heard for the first time. These details provide the background of the interaction between ETs and the military.

David said it took him many years to piece it all together. I can certainly relate to that; it came to me in pieces too—and over many years. Bill Cooper mentioned it in a presentation in Sedona, Arizona, but he offered only one insight. He said that in 1936 the Germans had a recovered disc in their possession. He didn't know if it was from a crash or if it was given to them by some ET race. What he did know was that when we captured Peenemunde near the end of World War II we found many files, cabinets, and safes, all filled with detailed information regarding their research and construction of antigravity spacecraft.

Then Al Bielek (he's the guy who claims to have been involved in both the Philadelphia and Montauk time-travel experiments) came forth with the information that the Nazis only surrendered Germany; he also said they went to the Moon in 1947. Present at many of the UFO conferences, at which I was a speaker, was a Bulgarian named Vladimir—I don't recall his last name—who also came forth with many details of the alleged Nazi spacecraft. He said they established a base under the ice in Antarctica, called Neuschwabenland, in the late 1930s. He offered many photos of these alleged antigravity craft. He also gave some startling—if true—details of the secret space program, claiming that we humans have not only been to the far reaches of our galaxy, but to neighboring galaxies as well. Only a select few seemed to be taking him seriously, and no one else was making such outlandish claims.

But it wasn't until I heard David Wilcock that all the pieces began to fit together for me. He said that the ships buzzing the Capitol were not extraterrestrial, that in fact, they were German. He said that yes, the Germans lost World War II on the surface, but they won it in space. So, the Germans did an overflight of the U.S. Capitol in 1952, and, apparently, this was done to threaten the Americans into signing a treaty, because the Americans had been in possession of the Roswell crash for the last five years, but they didn't know how to make it work. The Germans said, "Look, we'll help you, but you have to sign a treaty with us, and you have to join us in the secret space program."

The United States took three years in negotiation before they decided to capitulate, so the treaty was actually agreed to in 1955. This turned out to be a very effective silent coup, as it enabled top Nazi officials to merge with previously captured German scientists—brought to the United States via Project Paperclip—to gain control over the United States in some very substantial ways. You may recall Eisenhower's farewell speech in January 1961, where he warned us of the dangers of the military-industrial complex.[7]

After the treaty was signed, one of the things that they gave the United States was the knowledge of what they'd found about the secret history of our solar system. It would seem that the Nazis, by this point, had already been to the Moon and to Mars.

The inside story that Wilcock got is that the Germans were approached by negative extraterrestrial reptilians, called the Draco, in the late 1930s. According to one insider, the original meeting with the Draco and the Nazis took place in the Himalayan Mountains in a remote area so that when they landed their ship, it wouldn't be visible to many people. The meeting resulted in a partnership, and the Draco almost immediately began teaching the Germans how to build flying saucers.

At this time, the Nazis sent an expeditionary group to Antarctica where they found some very interesting things; they found huge caverns that they could float their boats into. They found a region under the ice that was created by geothermal heat from volcanoes, and then they found old pyramids and old underground ruins that they could use. Thus, they found the perfect area to build their submarine bases. But not only did the Nazis build submarine bases, they also developed a massive spaceport.

The Draco had occupied a much larger area under Antarctica, which they still hold. So, we have a massive reptilian colony of these evil beings under the ice in Antarctica in this huge area that they will not let anybody else go into, and in that area is some extremely advanced technology. But there were a few areas they weren't occupying that they let the Nazis use. They then began giving them all the technology needed to build a fleet of spacecraft.

So, as strange as this sounds, it did indeed connect all the dots for me; I simply did not believe Al Bielek when he said the Germans went to the Moon in 1947. I mean, after they lost the war, how could that be? However, much of what Bielek said in the early 1990s has withstood the test of time.

Wilcock's input from his insiders also confirmed what Vladimir, the guy from Bulgaria, was saying. And by the way, he was ridiculed and largely ignored by the majority of the UFO community—Bill Cooper was too. But there was something about it all that resonated with me. I guess it was just kooky enough to appeal to me.

THE SECRET SPACE PROGRAM

I first heard of this secret space program from Bill Cooper, who in his 1989 report said that from the documents he had seen, a symposium held in 1957 concluded that sometime around the year 2000, the planet would self-destruct. In preparation for this, they came up with three recommendations, called Alternatives One, Two, and Three.

Alternative One was quickly discarded as having virtually no chance of succeeding, so I will not even mention the details. Alternative Two, however, was quickly enacted, as was Alternative Three. Alternative Two called for the construction of deep underground bases and tunnels in which a few would survive to carry on the human race. Alternative Three called for leaving the planet altogether and constructing an underground colony on Mars.

He then spoke of a secret joint U.S.–Soviet program that had established bases on both the Moon and Mars. He also said that we have been to other planets in the solar system.

In 1975, a most interesting documentary, called *Alternative Three*,[8] was shown on the British television program *Science Report*. It showed alleged footage of a space probe landing on the red planet on May 22, 1962, and then told of the secret colony on Mars. It also detailed the abduction of many top scientists from around the world to provide personnel for the bases, as well as numerous citizens who were kidnapped and subjected to mind control to serve as slave labor. Needless to say, the startling claims were widely debunked and decried as a hoax.

Cooper only knew what he had seen in the daily briefing documents from 1970 to 1973, and did not seem to be aware of the details of the 1952 Capitol flyover, and what it eventually led to. But then few, if any, other people in 1989 were aware of what I'm about to tell you. As amazing and revealing as his disclosures were, they were still only barely scratching the surface.

The secret space program began with the Nazis and was then handed over to the Americans in 1955. Once the treaty was signed, Rockefeller restructured MJ-12 operations so that our official government was no longer in the loop. When this happened, all of the reverse-engineering operations that were at Wright Patterson Air Force Base in Ohio were moved to Area 51 and nearby S-4.

Eisenhower now realized that he had lost control. When he attempted to look into Area 51, he was denied access. This did not sit well with the former five-star general who was supreme commander of the Allied Expeditionary Force in Europe during World War II. In 1953, he threatened to use nuclear weapons until China agreed to peace terms in the Korean war, so you get the impression that this was a president who meant business. In response to being left out of the loop, he threatened to invade Area 51 with the First Army out of Colorado. As a result of this threat, two agents were allowed to report on several craft, extraterrestrial and German in origin, that were being reverse engineered. This information came from insider Dan Willis who appeared on the *Above Majestic* documentary.

One of the ways that the Nazis obtained their advanced technology before World War II was through the use of a channeler called Maria Orsic. Maria was channeling telepathic messages from a benevolent ET race, called the Nordics, who were offering her plans and schematics to actually create antigravity craft. She channeled this information for the occult Vrill society in Germany. This information was later used by these German secret societies to build many of their crafts.

The Germans, then, were in contact with two ET races, and had two space programs going. The Vrill society, through Maria Orsic, wanted the technology for peaceful purposes only, while the Nazis through their contact with the Draco had different ideas. Because they were focused more on the qualitative superiority rather than the quantitative, they were focused on having more advanced technology, rather than more tanks and boots on the ground. They were losing the ground war in Europe, but they were obtaining the technology, and to save it, they took it down to Antarctica, before and during World War II.

The existence of the secret German space program was given substantial credibility in December 2015 when a then ninety-three-year-old William Tompkins released a book called *Selected by Extraterrestrials*. Tompkins said that he was selected as a child, and as an adult has been in telepathic communication with the Nordics, and thus was considered to be an invaluable asset to the navy. He emphasized that he was not a whistleblower, that he was given approval to speak about his detailed knowledge of the navy's program.

He explained that at the beginning of his military career in the navy, he was working in a classified program for the U. S. government at the highest levels. He said he was personally responsible for getting information from twenty-three different American spies who were embedded in the German secret space program, and this apparently included bases in Antarctica. He said the Germans didn't just get documents from the Draco—they got brand-new space vehicles.

He also said that from the information retrieved from the spies, Douglas Aircraft Company was designing our first spaceships for the navy. He also named Lockheed Martin, Northrop Grumman, and Boeing Aerospace as the major corporate contractors responsible for building the navy's spacecraft at underground facilities in Utah.

He said that many were cigar-shaped, submarine-style ships, and that they put together programs that went all the way out into the galaxy, and not just this galaxy. Another insider in the *Above Majestic* documentary claimed to have talked to a person who had been on a warp-drive-capable ship that went from Earth to the edge of the Andromeda galaxy in twenty minutes. He said that they located eight Earthlike planets that had human life on them. This intergalactic capability echoed what Vladimir, the Bulgarian, had said years earlier.

Then we have the story of Corey Goode, a whistleblower who gave some startling details of what he said was his personal involvement in the secret space program. Goode told how in 1987, at the age of sixteen, he was covertly recruited by the navy to participate in their ongoing secret space program called Solar Warden. Solar Warden became operational, according to Tompkins, in the early 1980s and patrols our solar system and beyond. It was funded in large part by the SDI (Strategic Defense Initiative) from President Reagan, though that money was funneled off into many different programs.

Goode said he served for twenty years, and was then age-regressed, sent back in time to 1987, and returned to civilian life after his memories were erased. Somehow, he was able to retrieve those memories; he didn't say how.

So, how credible are the claims of both Tompkins and Goode? One of the most respected UFO researchers, Michael Salla, in his book *The U.S. Navy's Secret Space Program and Nordic Extraterrestrial Alliance,* which relied heavily on the testimony of Tompkins, gave a detailed analysis of the corroboration of the stories of the two. Then David Wilcock, in the documentary *Above Majestic,* said the following:

Corey Goode is the one insider I found whose testimony ties all of these different threads together, I've heard Corey have knowledge of something that each of the different other insiders I've spoken to had said to me in the past. Nobody else had ever done that before. And that was fascinating because I had not put this information online. The information was proprietary. It was things that I'd heard over the course of conversations that could have gone on for many, many dozens of hours over time.[9]

The intel retrieved from the German secret space program was taken very seriously indeed by the United States. So much so that Operation High Jump, operated by Admiral Richard Byrd, was commissioned in 1947. On the public level, it was said that this was a scientific exploration. It was equipped with thirty-three ships, thirteen aircraft, and five thousand troops, and was in truth, a failed attempt to go down to Antarctica and destroy the Nazi installations that had been in place since the late 1930s.

2
What's Going On?

Corey Goode, in the documentary *Above Majestic,* explained how he was prepared for his role in the Solar Warden program. He said it began while he was still in school. He said that as a student in an accelerated learning class, he along with other classmates would, on a typical day, be pulled aside and told they would be taken on a field trip.[1]

Well, that's not exactly what happened; he said they were taken to Carswell Air Force Base, and then to a hangar where there was an elevator. It was a long ride down, he said, and eventually they were placed on a train that, at a speed of 500 mph, could take them anywhere on the planet. Oftentimes, he said, after a long ride, they only had maybe an hour or two for training. Then they were taken back, debriefed, hypnotized, and given the memory of having been on a field trip. Then, when their parents picked them up, they would share the details of the "field trip."

And though his story is very interesting in its own right, I would like to point to the fact that this was in the mid-1980s. Even back then there was an extremely efficient underground system of bases with high-speed trains that could take you almost anywhere. What do you suppose it's like now?

Remember now, this all began when Alternative Two was hatched in a 1957 symposium. At that time, Cooper spoke of the Rand corporation that was developing machines capable of boring tunnels forty-five feet in diameter at the rate of five feet per hour.[2] It would seem that they had made considerable progress by the 1980s.

So, what do you suppose they were really preparing for? Were they slipped some inside information that foretold of more than just an over-population problem? Were they also preparing for some form of physical upheavals on the Earth's surface—like a series of off-the-Richter-scale earthquakes and simultaneous volcanic activity? Or maybe they were forewarned of the ultimate Earth-change disaster—a pole shift!

INITIATION

Okay, this sure brings up some intense—at the time—memories for me. It all began innocently enough in December 1981, when I attended an evening seminar where Leonard Orr was scheduled to give a spiritual interpretation of Handel's *Messiah*. As it turned out, this was an evening that changed my life forever! For some reason, unknown to me, the evening began with the handing out of a document that Leonard called *The Rebirth of the Late, Great Planet Earth*. In this short essay, Leonard went into great detail about massive Earth changes that he said were due to happen in California in 1982.

Then, as fate would have it, the new year was greeted with the most intense four to five days of virtually nonstop rain that I have ever experienced. The rainfall was so intense and long-lasting that entire hills and roads were washed away as massive mud slides prevailed throughout the entire San Francisco Bay Area. So, I began to take Leonard's warnings very seriously. I wondered what life would be like if food was no longer available in the supermarkets; and what if the ATMs no longer worked, and gas was not available. How long could we last without these modern-day necessities?

In his essay, Leonard spoke of a configuration that occurs once every 179 years, where all nine planets would be on the same side of the Sun. As a result, he said, their combined gravitational pull would create strong tides, and induce great magnetic storm flares on the Sun, which by the way, would already be at the peak of its eleven-year cycle. He went on to paint a truly disastrous picture—just imagine the effect of 1,000-foot tidal waves, along with massive earthquakes, and perhaps previously submerged continents rising up out of the ocean. That could certainly shake things up a bit! This rather depressing scenario was echoed by Moira Timms in *Prophecies and Predictions: Everyone's Guide to the Coming Changes*. I must admit, for some time thereafter I wished that I had not been in attendance that evening, even though he actually did get around to giving his spiritual interpretation of Handel's *Messiah*.

If you're wondering why I didn't just dismiss all this, I realized that Leonard wasn't just pulling this out of his hat. He had previously—on more than one occasion—visited the Hopi Indians of the Third Mesa at Hotevilla. He spent time with the elders and learned of their prophecies. He came back with details of the Blue Star Kachina, the Red Star Kachina, and the resulting Day of Purification. Kachinas are inner forms, the invisible spiritual forces of life that act as messengers.

The Hopi see nothing as outside of themselves; they would, for example, watch a squirrel under a bush, and see it as all within them. The squirrel, the bush, and the Hopi are all one. Obviously that is quite different from how we have been conditioned to see it. We are seriously immersed in the feeling of separation; we look out at the reality as though we are an isolated entity, looking out at a world that isn't us. We feel disconnected from Source.

Then add to that the fact that in our separate, polarized state of awareness, we are in a constant state of judgment. If a person or an event doesn't conform to our mind's narrative of how it "should be," we judge it. I will assert that all of the problems we have in life come from judgment—from insisting that reality should be different from how it is. Whenever we do this, we lock the energy up tight, and always in the same place in our physical bodies. We carry that stuck energy as pain, stress, tension, burnout, and ultimately in potential life-threatening illness and disease. We then do our utmost to try to avoid feeling that stuck energy.

On a planetary scale, it creates needless conflict and wars where there are no winners other than the global puppet masters who manipulated the creation of the conflict from behind the scenes. This puts even more power and control into the hands of these "Deep State" globalists.

Since everything is energy, when you add this all up you can begin to see that we have been vibrating individually and collectively, on a very dense level. This adversely affects all bodies—our own and the planetary body.

So from a perspective of oneness, anything we do to harm the environment is doing an equal and direct amount of damage to ourselves. The planet is alive; it is a conscious entity, and quite obviously we have not been very good caretakers of our living Mother. If you mistreat a body long enough, it will eventually answer back. If it's your own body, there will be resultant ailments such as high blood pressure, cancer, heart problems, obesity, and so on. The same is true for the planet; our collective unconsciousness will generate planetary "heart attacks" and other life-threatening ailments in the form of earthquakes, volcanoes, hurricanes, tornadoes, and the like. In its more advanced form, we get Earth-change scenarios with massive planetary upheaval and loss of life.

So, if Leonard's only source was from the Hopi, it would have been noteworthy. But hold on—he was also tuned in to a master avatar named Babaji. In fact, he had been trekking to India for an annual visit for a few years. If you have seen Paramahansa Yogananda's book *Autobiography of a Yogi,* and specifically the chapter called "Babaji, the Yogi Christ of Modern India," you would realize that this is someone in possession of powers and abilities far beyond those of your average human. He is immortal, he can manifest a human body whenever he wants to, and has participated in the human drama from behind the scenes for a very long time. Occasionally he opens his ashram and makes himself somewhat more available to his devotees. Such was the case in an incarnation from 1970 to 1984.

Babaji had been predicting up to 90 percent of the Earth's population being removed due to massive Earth changes. He foretold of entire continents being submerged. In *Something in This Book Is True*, I gave the details of the sinking of Atlantis thirteen thousand years ago. Consider the following from an ancient Mayan document, called the *Torano Manuscript*:

> In the year 6 Kan, on the 11 Muluc, in the month of Zac, there occurred terrific earthquakes which continued until the 13 Chuen, without interruption. *The country of the hills of the earth—the land . . .* was sacrificed. Being *twice* upheaved, it disappeared during the night, being constantly shaken by the fires of the underneath. Being confined, these caused the land to rise and sink several times in various places. At the last the surface gave way and the ten countries (or tribes) were torn asunder and scattered. They sank with their 64,000,000 inhabitants.[3]

The Maya, by the way, survived the disaster in Atlantis. They were able to get away in their boats. It is said they hold the memories, not only of Atlantis, but of the past 26,000 years of the Earth. Add to that the fact that the Hopi used to be Maya. They say they came from Guatemala, that a decision was made long ago that a group of Maya would head north to find a new place. That group became the Hopi.[4]

END-TIME PROPHECIES AND DISASTER PREDICTIONS

I gave details on various prophecies in the "End-Time Prophecies" chapter of *Nothing in This Book Is True, But It's Exactly How Things Are*. I will give a summary here.

It is the belief of the Hopi that they came from inside the Earth. They say that it has happened three times previously, where the planet became polluted and immoral and they left by going up into the sky, which they say hardens at a certain point and they then walk onto a new surface of the Earth. They also say that we're going from the

Fourth World to the Fifth World; this is because they count the Void as a world.

Then, according to Hopi prophecy, we enter into the end-times when the Blue Star Kachina makes its appearance in the heavens. This will be followed by the Red Star Kachina and the ushering in of the Day of Purification. The new world will then soon emerge, and we will go from the Fourth to the Fifth World.

In *Nothing in This Book Is True,* I went on to say that on October 24, 2007, Comet 17P/Holmes brightened by a factor of nearly one million, and briefly became the largest object in our solar system. This exploding "Blue Star," according to Hopi elders, was the fulfillment of a two-hundred-year-old prophecy, thus putting us into the end-times.[5]

In case you're wondering about the Red Star Kachina—the one that according to the prophecies, will usher in the Day of Purification—Betelgeuse is a likely candidate, since it's already near the end of its life span and is expected to explode as a supernova. However, this could be anywhere from now to many years into the future. When this massive star, nine hundred times the size of our Sun does explode—even though it is 642 light-years away—it will appear as bright as the Moon in the night sky for several weeks and may even be visible during the day.

I first heard of the Hopi prophecies prior to that fateful December 1981 evening, when Leonard told of it, so I was already primed, though not prepared. Obviously, we made it through 1982 without California falling into the ocean. I was pleased, because in spite of its many faults (pun intended) it is an exceptionally scenic and beautiful state. The redwood groves alone serve as ample reason to visit. You will also find the coastline to be absolutely stunning. The weather ain't too bad either.

Things did settle down for me; that is, until 1986, when Ramtha—an alleged ascended master channeled by J. Z. Knight—came out with an eight-hour presentation called *Change.* Not too hard to figure out what this was about, right? Massive Earth changes, according to Ramtha, were due to happen in 1986 and 1987. Ramtha spoke of the wisdom of ants, how they act in unison and store food for the winter.[6]

He suggested that we do likewise. I remember being advised to dig up my yard and plant a garden—that is, assuming California was still above water.

Then I heard about a guy named Gordon-Michael Scallion, a futurist with an 87 percent accuracy rating who had accurately predicted the October 17, 5:04 p.m., 6.9 magnitude Loma Prieta earthquake. This is the one that collapsed a portion of the San Francisco Bay Bridge and put a ten-day halt to a World Series that featured the San Francisco Giants and the Oakland Athletics. Coincidentally, it was referred to as the Bay Bridge Series.

Scallion went on to accurately predict two Southern California earthquakes in June 1992, the 7.4 magnitude Landers Quake and a 6.5 shaking soon thereafter. This, according to Scallion as published in his monthly newsletter, *The Earth Changes Report,* was the beginning of a three-stage process and the eventual fracturing of California.[7] He then published a future map of the Earth showing his vision of what a vast reconfiguration of the land masses would look like in 1998–2001, after a series of off-the-scale earthquakes and a shifting of the poles. Denver, Colorado, he envisioned, was to become a coastal city.

As alarming as this was, it paled in comparison to the predictions of Major Ed Dames, a regular guest on the extremely popular late-night radio program, *Coast to Coast AM,* hosted by Art Bell. Dames, a remote viewer, was speaking with great relish of his vision of the Sun becoming thousands of times brighter and expanding out and consuming all the planets in its wake. "We're all going to become crispy hash browns," claimed Art Bell. What was he talking about, and could he be considered to be a credible authority? After all, he was only sharing his remote-viewing experiences. I dismissed him at the time, only to discover later that the good remote viewers were about 99 percent accurate in their readings.

Well, obviously, Scallion proceeded to fall well below his previous 87 percent accuracy rating; none of Leonard's, the Hopi, Ramtha's, or Ed Dames's predictions have materialized—yet. And furthermore, all were revealing only a partial picture of possible future events. With that being said, the true purpose of a prophet, in my view, is to give us that wake-up call so we can alter our course and avoid the disastrous outcome that would otherwise await us. You could say, then, that their purpose is to be wrong.

THE NEW WORLD ORDER AND
THE DEPOPULATION AGENDA

The idea of the poles shifting is not new, our governments have been aware of it, and have been secretly planning for it since the 1950s. By the way, the 1957 symposium that Cooper talked about—where Alternatives One, Two, and Three were hatched—said nothing about pole shifts. They were planning for another of our planets "greatest problems," overpopulation. They evidently believed that unless drastic measures were taken to reduce the population, all systems would break down and civilization as we know it would collapse. This—their models told them—would occur around the year 2000.

In 1970, Paul Ehrlich was making the rounds of the TV talk shows in promotion of his new book, and the ideas contained therein. It was called *The Population Bomb* and was filled with dire predictions of what would happen if we didn't listen to him. Well okay, thanks Paul. There are two ways the Earth's population can be reduced; either you decrease the birth rate, or you increase the death rate. The various methods of reducing the birth rate, which include birth control and medical procedures such as sterilization, abortion, and hysterectomies, have been largely ineffective. This, according to the Cabal, leaves only the option of increasing the death rate.

One of their earlier attempts was to use the World Health Organization (WHO) to infect the African continent in 1977 with the smallpox vaccine, and the Center for Disease Control (CDC) in 1978 to infect the U.S. population with the hepatitis B vaccine. Whatever causes AIDS was in those vaccines. Cooper, in his book, *Behold a*

Pale Horse, said this order was given by the Policy Committee of the Bilderberg Group.[8] The only problem is that it really had no impact on the global population.

Bill Cooper also mentioned the details of the Haig-Kissinger Depopulation Policy. This policy, issued by the State Department, dictated that Third World countries would get no aid from the United States unless they took decisive steps to reduce their populations. If they refused, civil war would usually break out, with the rebels being trained, armed, and funded by the CIA. Oftentimes, many more young females would be killed in places like El Salvador and Nicaragua than soldiers. The goal was "to reduce the world's population by two billion people through war, famine, disease and any other means necessary."[9]

Efforts continue to this day with programs such as the 2030 Agenda. This is a program cloaked with doublespeak in order to hide its true purpose and make it sound appealing to the general population. From the website of the United Nations Development Program, we find reference to what they call the Sustainable Development Goals (SDGs).

> The Sustainable Development Goals (SDGs), also known as the Global Goals, were adopted by the United Nations in 2015 as a universal call to action to end poverty, protect the planet, and ensure that by 2030 all people enjoy peace and prosperity.
>
> The seventeen SDGs are integrated—they recognize that action in one area will affect outcomes in others, and that development must balance social, economic, and environmental sustainability.
>
> Countries have committed to prioritize progress for those who are furthest behind. The SDGs are designed to end poverty, hunger, AIDS, and discrimination against women and girls.
>
> The creativity, know-how, technology, and financial resources from all of society is necessary to achieve the SDGs in every context.[10]

Sounds good, right? But what if they allowed the infinite abundance of free energy that has been available since early in the twentieth century—as discovered by Nikola Tesla? And what if pollution-free hover cars were developed to replace the internal combustion engine? And while we're at it, free energy would also enable us to create unlimited amounts of desalinated water. I'm just thinking out loud here, just wondering if all this would free things up a bit? What do you think?

It's funny, too, how they fail to mention the most central of their goals—to drastically decrease the world's population by many billions of people. Any volunteers? It's for a really good cause.

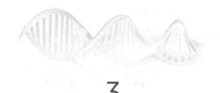

3

The Great Year

THE CYCLE OF THE AGES

Of the many motions the Earth makes, there is a 25,920-year cycle that we need to look at. This "cycle of the ages" was given different names by different cultures. The Greeks called it "the Great Year," and divided it into four segments: the Iron Age, the Bronze Age, the Silver Age, and the Golden Age. Each age had its own distinct characteristics. The saints and sages of ancient India called it the yuga cycle, while the Romans called it the precession of the equinoxes.

We know that the Earth's axis is tilted at about 23.5 degrees, and that gives us our four seasons. However, what is not as well known is that the axis itself is in a slight wobble. It changes one degree about every seventy-two years; it changes the viewpoint of one constellation every 2,160 years. Over the course of just a little less than 26,000 years, if you could see it from the North Pole, you would see that it completes an elliptical orbit in a counterclockwise direction. At one point of that oval, it is at its closest to the center of the galaxy; at the opposite, it is farthest away. We will refer to this cycle as the precession of the equinoxes.

Ancient Indian and Greek cultures divided the Great Year into two thirteen-thousand-year segments, the ascending and the descending cycles. We as humans seemed to be literally falling asleep on the descending cycle and reawakening on the ascending cycle. Each cycle had four parts, and these four segments repeat themselves in each cycle. The Iron Age of the Greeks was called the Kali Yuga in Indian culture; it was seen as a "dark age" where humanity was pretty much in sleep mode. The Bronze Age was called the Dvapara Yuga in India; the Silver Age was the Treta Yuga; and the Golden Age, or Satya Yuga, was seen as the "fully awake" segment.

The Hindus and the Tibetans, back in the day, studied this probably more than anybody else. And what they discovered is that, in this approximately 25,920-year cycle,* there are two points where tremendous change is most likely to occur: change of consciousness and also change of a physical nature. These two points are about nine hundred years removed from the point closest to the center of the galaxy and the farthest point away from the center of the galaxy.

Now let's take note of the fact that we are currently sitting right on the bubble of change. You may well recall the whole 2012 phenomenon, and the end of the Mayan calendar. We will fully unpack that a bit later, but for now, let's just say that on December 21, 2012, we were on the final day of the old cycle—the descending cycle. And December 22, 2012, was the first day of the ascending cycle, where we start to wake up. That means that there is a window of opportunity before us where we will ascend into fourth density, and in so doing, redefine what it means to be human. It also means that we are facing the possibility of great Earth changes, including the shifting of the poles.

What I have given you so far is pretty much the traditional understanding of this great cycle. Now I will suggest the very real possibility that we are in a binary star system, as suggested by Walter Cruttenden in his book *Lost Star of Myth and Time*.[1] Such is the case with most, if not all of the star systems in the cosmos, so why would it be any different with respect to our Sun?

---

*I say approximate because there are differing opinions on this. Science seems to be thinking that it's more like 25,771 years, while the Maya were telling us that it's 25,625 years. So I don't know, something less than 26,000 years—let's just round it off.

Walter Cruttenden also made a documentary called *The Great Year;* it is narrated by none other than Darth Vader himself (James Earl Jones). From it, we find that some of the earliest astronomical records refer to the existence of a dual sun, where we are orbiting another star that is outside of our solar system.[2] The great yogis of ancient India accepted this as a matter of fact and understood the binary system to be the cause of the precession. They saw then through their own solar energy research that our Sun is rotating around another sun, and that both suns are rotating around the "Great Central Sun." One sign we would expect to see, according to Walter Cruttenden, would be changes in the Sun's rate of movement. In a binary system, orbital speed is not constant and it could cause changes in the precession rate. When the two suns are closer to each other, the rate would increase, and it would decrease as they move farther apart.

At the edge of our solar system, there is a field of asteroids. In 2001, a team of scientists from the University of Michigan discovered that the asteroid belt appears to end very abruptly. A sheer edge like they found would be unexpected and unexplained in a single sun system; yet if our Sun is indeed rotating around a companion star, a clear boundary to our solar system is both explained and expected.

All celestial bodies have angular momentum—a force that corresponds to their mass and motion. Yet in our solar system, angular momentum is unevenly distributed. Our Sun makes up 99.9 percent of the total mass of the solar system, but only 1 percent of the total angular momentum. If we acknowledge that our Sun is curving through space in a 25,920-year binary orbit, the Sun's angular momentum was there all the time, primarily in its orbital motion, and not just in its speed. This to me, is the most impressive and convincing of Cruttenden's arguments for a binary system

Though some refer to an unknown "Black Sun," I recall Vladimir, the Bulgarian, mentioning that as a possibility. I feel, however, that the most likely candidate for this companion star is Alpha Centauri, our closest neighbor at 4.3 light-years away. With that said, I also want to include another possibility—Sirius. Here is what I said in *Nothing in This Book Is True:* "We, meaning the entire solar system, are spiraling through space in a manner that indicates we are attached to something. Astronomers noticing this began looking for that other body. It was first calculated down to a certain area of a particular constellation, then to a group of stars. In the early 1970s a specific star was targeted— Sirius A. We are moving through space with Sirius A in a spiral that is identical to the heliacal plane of the DNA molecule. We have a destiny with Sirius. As we move together, a consciousness is unfolding much in the way the genes and chromosomes on the DNA molecule unreel their message from very specific places. There are key times when certain things can happen, when "genetically" critical alignments occur between Sirius and Earth and the rest of the cosmos. One very specific alignment is now happening."[3]

POLE SHIFTS

Pole shifts are a rather major planetary event; the North Pole prior to the last shift was located somewhere in the Hudson Bay. There is the potential for a shift every thirteen thousand years, and such a shift is absolutely capable of sinking entire continents, as was the case thirteen thousand years ago when Atlantis sank. With that being said, it may well be a gentler ride this time around.

As I reported in *Nothing in This Book Is True, But It's Exactly How Things Are,* according to the ascended masters of the Earth, the degree or the severity of the shifting of the poles is tied to the consciousness on the planet. Because remember, the physical change is directly aligned with the change of consciousness on the planet at the same time. According to the masters, depending on how much we wake up, we have direct impact on how smooth this ride is going to be—or how rough. So, it's up to us!

There's a man by the name of John White who wrote a book called *Pole Shift.* He put pretty much everything that you'd ever care to know, or not care to know, about pole shifts into one book—both the scientific predictions and the prophecies of people like Edgar Cayce. It's been clearly established that the Earth's magnetic north pole was in the Hawaiian Islands prior to the last shift. Ancient lava fields contain iron pilings, and the iron pilings are not a perfect sphere, so they harden before the lava. If you go to three of them as has been done, and then cross-reference them, it confirms that the magnetic north pole was in the Hawaiian Islands.

If you want to find seashells, you go to the ocean, go to the beach. Yet seashells have been found high up in the Rocky Mountains. And that's up to 14,000 feet high in some places. Seashells have also been found in Lake Titicaca, which is 12,500 feet high.

And then there's the famous baby mammoth, Dima, who was found in 1977 in the permafrost in Siberia. Dima, who now resides in the St. Petersburg Museum, and other good friends were just minding their own business eating their lunch when suddenly, without warning, they were almost instantly frozen solid. They were frozen so quickly that they were still edible many thousands of years later. One such mammoth had most of his trunk and head eaten; these features were reconstructed for purposes of display in the museum. When the poles do shift, it has been pretty well determined that the whole thing takes place within twenty-four hours.

When the poles shift, it's the magnetic poles that shift first. The magnetic south pole has been shifting dramatically over the last four hundred years. It is now about 1,800 miles from true south. What about the magnetic north pole? Well, it's moving too, but not nearly as much, it's only 380 miles from true north. So, the magnetic pole shift happens before the physical poles shift. And when it does, there will be a period of roughly two to four weeks where the magnetic field goes to zero. Let's just hold that for a moment, and take a look at the physical pole shifting.

John White's book lists some possible theories that would cause the physical poles to shift. I don't know if anyone knows for sure, but most likely it's a combination of the Brown theory and one called magnetohydrodynamics (MHD). The Brown theory looks at the massive buildup of ice at Antarctica, which is more than two miles thick in some places. We must also take note of the fact that much of this buildup is off-center. So, you have a sphere—planet Earth—that is moving through space at high speeds, and this massive buildup of ice that is off-center. The Brown theory suggests that at some point, it's just going to break off and start racing toward the equator at the speed of about 1,700 miles an hour. And that could cause a few changes.

In addition to the Brown theory, MHD is a more modern theory from the work of the Swedish physicist Hannes Alfven. This theory proposes that beneath the Earth's solid crust there is a semisolid layer. The Earth's crust is about five to thirty kilometers thick, and beneath that, in the upper mantle, there's a rich layer of rock about one hundred to two hundred kilometers thick. This rock in the upper mantle is rock as long as the Earth's magnetic field is held together. When the magnetic field collapses, fourteen days later this layer becomes a liquid, allowing the Earth's crust to shift position. A replica of this has been demonstrated in laboratories.[4]

So, the idea is that if the Earth's crust were suddenly free to move, then this ice mass would also move. This would force the crust to move to a new position. We would experience that as a pole shift, most likely of 21 degrees. Once it begins, the surface of the Earth moves at about two thousand miles per hour while the winds approach a thousand miles per hour. Obviously, that is enough to devastate just about anything.

MARINA POPOVICH

Drunvalo Melchizedek in his book, *The Mayan Ouroboros,* tells how the famous retired Soviet test pilot, Marina Popovich claims, along with a number of other scientists in Russia, to have deciphered the meaning of the crop circles found mainly in England. They believe that this is communication from extraterrestrials, telling us that there are eight major catastrophes that are going to happen here on planet Earth. A crop circle that appeared in the state of Washington in July of 2012, according to them, was the final warning.[5]

The first catastrophe, according to the Russians, and somewhat confirmed by NASA, has to do with solar cycle 24, which peaked sometime in mid to late 2013. Evidently, the weakening of the Earth's magnetic field could very well lead to the magnetic field going to zero at some point and the resulting shifting of the poles. We need the Earth's magnetic sphere, the magnetic field, to protect us from solar flares. According to the Russians, the first of the eight catastrophes will be a solar flare. They say it will be so massive that, in combination with the weakening Earth magnetic field, it's going to knock out everything. And when I say everything, I mean that—considering that everything is computer controlled—within, say, forty-eight to seventy-two hours, nothing would move.

And how long would it take to get things going again? Well, that's the interesting question; NASA suggests that it would take from one to nine months. Popovich goes on to say that we can only survive the first catastrophe and after that we had better learn how to get to the fourth dimension or we're not going to make it. Considering that such an event could easily wipe out the power grid—leaving us with no power, no transportation systems, no communication systems, no banking, no internet, no food, and no water delivery systems—this would truly be an end of the world as we know it situation.

To get a sense of what I mean, just ask yourself these questions: What if the power went out and never came back on? Could you fend for yourself? Could you keep yourself warm in the winter? Where would you find food? What would you use for money if credit cards and ATMs no longer worked? How would you get from one place to another without transportation? How would you wash your clothes? How would you keep yourself healthy if sanitation systems were no longer functional and medicine could no longer be manufactured? And finally, how would you communicate with the rest of the world?

It can't happen, you say? Well, in fact, it has happened: the last time was in 1859. It was known as the Carrington Event, where the technology of the day, the telegraph systems worldwide, were knocked out. Now let's consider the impact such an event would have on the 440 nuclear power plants operating in thirty countries around the world today. Do you suppose they would all melt down? And then what?

If you were to return here in just a few years, you would find the planet dead on a third-dimensional level. But life would still exist on Earth; we are all going to shift up in wavelength to another place that is prepared for us, which is beautiful and where there are no problems. We will move into a slightly shorter wavelength and a higher energy vibration. The Bible refers to this state as heaven. Actually, we will be going from the third to the fourth dimension.

4

Contact in the Desert

There is a 1998 movie—a parody of certain 1950s sitcoms, perhaps *Ozzie and Harriet,* or *Father Knows Best*—called *Pleasantville* in which the participants live in a "perfect" 1950s-type world. There is always a meatloaf baking in the oven. The high school basketball team never loses a game; in fact, they never even miss a shot. Mom and Dad are Mr. and Mrs. Wonderful, and life in general is "swell." Ah, the wonders of living a perfect stress-free life!

Even though it was the 1950s, it certainly wasn't a stress-free "perfect" life for President Eisenhower, not with all the previously mentioned UFO activity and alien contact. And then came the realization that a cosmic top-secret clearance—which is thirty-five levels of need-to-know, and well above that of the President of the United States—is the standard entry level security clearance that you have to get in order to begin to know what's really going on. This was the result of Nelson Rockefeller's restructuring of MJ-12 once the 1955 treaty with the Nazis was signed. From that moment on, MJ-12 and other "Deep State" officials told future presidents only what they wanted them to know about the aliens. And we live in a constitutional republic, right?

Meanwhile, there was significant contact with different benevolent

ET groups and humans. Instead of working through the national security state, they decided to connect with individuals who had the right spiritual vibration. Those people were then given the messages that they wanted humanity to know.

THE FRIENDSHIP CASE

From an online article called "Clarifying the 'Friendship' Italian Contact Case," we learn of an ET contact in the 1950s in Italy.[1] There is also a documentary called *UFO Secret: The Friendship Case*.[2] Nikola Duper, author of the article, spoke of a person who contacted him in October 2008 upon learning of his interest in crop circles. Duper met with him and after an hour's conversation was asked if he would help in getting a very important story out in an objective way. The man said he could not come forth directly, and he needed an intermediary.

Duper agreed to this request and met with this individual again in January 2009. It was in this second meeting that the person began to give details of his experience with a group of benevolent ETs, called simply the Friends. They were also called W56. The "friendship case" started in Pescara, Italy, in 1956 and continued until 1990. He spoke of direct face-to-face contact with these beings who came from planets that were both within and outside of our galaxy.

This anonymous informer said that here on Earth, they were living in underground and undersea bases, some of which were along the Adriatic Coast, and that their first base was located under the area of Ascoli Piceno, a small town in central Italy. He also said that they had reached their maximum number of two hundred; evidently, there is some sort of galactic law that limits their numbers.

He said that they are our elder brothers, that they are human—that they are much more human than we are—that they range in height from very tiny to about ten feet, and they are physically very beautiful. He said that they are here to help us; they all share a fundamental choice toward good. They said this is a critical moment in our history; that our atomic weapons are capable of destroying the Earth in a matter of minutes. They are here to make sure it doesn't get out of hand. They are not pleased with the high levels of hatred, violence, and injustice that we Earthlings engage in. They also are not happy with the anti-humanistic trend of our science and technology.

Teleportation was one of the most impressive technological capabilities the Friends had. This system was used to materialize and dematerialize objects of various sorts, including things like slips of paper with answers to questions previously asked. Film reels of flying saucers would also suddenly appear in the room; they materialized in midair.

The informer said that he and others had various types of experiences with the Friends, including conversations, sightings of various ships, and lengthy visits inside the underground bases. He said these experiences marked their personal lives deeply and indelibly. This was indeed, a very significant contact. "I say that these things are true because I had a personal relationship with the Friends and had the strong feeling that they were telling me the truth—such as when you feel that your best friend or your lover is telling you the truth."[3]

Other populations in the Universe have chosen evil. So, there are good and evil ETs, and evil is often represented by the adoration of energy and knowledge-science. This dualism between good and evil is fundamental to understanding both the ongoing struggle, which is the struggle over who's going to win, the good guys or the bad guys, and why it is so hard for truth to be disclosed to the inhabitants of our planet.

This struggle between good and evil also entered the life of the terrestrials in the group and transformed them into particular beings. The anonymous source explained that the technology of the Friends is well beyond our understanding, because it is shaped upon the laws of the world of the Spirit. Yet, they also have technology—especially in the field of electromagnetism—that is closer to what we know, and they tried to share it with the terrestrials. However, some of the people started to behave selfishly, and the Friends had to withdraw from sharing this information.

> Compared with all the other populations visiting the Earth, the Friends have a quite peculiar and precious characteristic to offer us: they have a very special and close connection with the subtle levels that regulate the destiny of the Earth and with what they call the Soul of the Universe, beyond the physical or phenomenal level. Thus, the Friends have a sort of general control over everything that occurs, but they are only allowed to intervene under particular conditions. Everything happens as in an extremely elaborate chess game, with rules that I cannot even touch upon here.[4]

The basis of the chess game is that our free will determines what the ETs can do. They can only act based upon how many people are praying or meditating, or calling upon them directly for help. What this amounts to is the fact that they can't do anything that we don't allow them to do; we have to authorize both the positive and the negative. So both sides have to play by these rules.

The dark side, the Cabal, does it by hiding it out in the open; they put it right in our faces. It's in movies, in advertisements, in the music industry, and even on the back of a U.S. dollar bill. For those of us who are working with the light, the Friends wish primarily for us to be inspired by their message; they want us to take personal action to raise our consciousness. They want us to connect with our Higher Self; they want us to become lit from within, where we have access to infinite amounts of joy, inner peace, creativity, inspiration, wisdom, and unconditional love.

We are then naturally embracing a philosophy of service to others, where we are gearing our lives toward being positive, loving, accepting, patient, and forgiving. So, they want us to act in a way that inspires others; that in turn creates a rippling effect that ultimately lifts the whole planet up. It's such a simple message; it's the message of ageless wisdom.

ROAD IN THE SKY

Let's continue with a Canadian radio communications engineer named W. B. Smith who was asked by the Canadian government to conduct a serious academic study of UFOs. He was the only person to be officially tasked with studying UFOs by a government agency. This information comes from the Ascension Mystery School 20/20's "The Great Awakening." This was an online course given by David Wilcock in April–May 2020.

Smith actually got his hands on pieces of wreckage from the Roswell crash, yet he decided early on in his research that he couldn't really get to the bottom of this UFO phenomenon just by looking at wreckage, photos, and reports from airline pilots. He therefore informed the Canadian government of his intention to pursue the case on his own.[5] What he really needed, in his view, was to actually communicate with these beings. So, he began searching for actual contactees to compare notes. Were they receiving useful messages, and if so, what was the common denominator?

Since there were huge UFO conferences being held in the desert at Joshua Tree, California—typical attendance was 5,000 or so—he became involved with multiple groups who claimed to have been contacted by various ET races. He talked with many individuals, some of whom claimed to have taken rides aboard ships that had landed in their backyard. They were then able to make telepathic communication with these beings.

He wanted to know if this was real, so he created a one-hundred-part questionnaire—with questions that would only have one type of answer—and gave it to various contactees. He found that a series of people answered these questions in virtually the same way. These people were put into a deep state of trance so they weren't aware of what they were saying. Yet, they were all getting very similar information, and it was all talking about a major event in our near future, an event that would totally change the entire solar system.

Before he became involved with these groups, he connected with author George Hunt Williamson, a big name in the 1950s UFO community. He was definitely a contactee; the ETs reached out to him in an unusual way, through radio telegraph. W. B. Smith was also directly involved in this. So, the ETs started to contact Williamson and his team; they were literally saying things like, "Go out and look in the backyard." And then there was a ship hovering in their yard. These telegraphic messages were describing what obviously was a benevolent angelic type of force. Why did they use radio telegraph? The other option, as I understand it, was ham radio; however, in some cases, there would be too much distortion. Radio telegraph, using dots and dashes, would make it through just fine, so it was preferable.

Williamson hid Smith's identity in his books, referring only to him as "the scientist." The following quote is from his classic, *Road in the Sky*, where he describes what happened when they contacted extraterrestrials by radio telegraph. It also explains why radio telegraph was used.

In 1952, we were told that our planet and our entire solar system [were] entering the outer fringes of a great cosmic cloud. . . . The governments of the world set up special projects to study radiation and its effects on organic life, and so on.

A few months later, Dr. Kurt Sitte of Syracuse University was conducting studies. . . . Through these studies, he came to startling conclusions that proved the statements made by the space visitors in 1952 during radio contacts.

Dr. Sitte said too many electrons are showering down on us . . . at least there are too many of these tiny units of electrical charge to be explained by present theories, which hold the electrons are produced by cosmic rays smashing into the atmosphere high above the Earth, unknown particles or processes must be involved.

The fact that too many electrons are showering down on us, and that present theories won't account for them, added to the fact that certain cosmic rays bombard the earth from *outside* our own solar system, tends to support the idea our entire solar system is entering a new possibility area of the universe. Every phase of our life will be changed—Education, Religion, Economics, Politics, Science, Social Life, Medicine, Eating habits, etc. Virtually everything will be influenced, and for the better.[6]

The increase in cosmic-ray bombardment is just one of many things that are now becoming increasingly more obvious by way of Earth changes as we go through a galactic shift.

Back in 1952 then, we were told that our solar system is entering an energetic cloud, with intense cosmic reactivity, and that this heightened energy would heat up our solar system, including the Earth, and begin to create Earth changes. This was documented in the time since *Road in the Sky* was originally published in 1959.

Williamson then looked at certain quotes in the Bible, one of many prophetic sources talking about ascension.

And so it is written the first man Adam was made a living soul. The last atom was made a quickening spirit. (1 Corinthians 15:45)

The first man is of the earth, earthy, the second man is the Lord from heaven. (1 Corinthians 15:47)

And, as we have borne the image of the earthy, we shall also bear the image of the heavenly. Now this I say, Brethren, that flesh and blood cannot inherit the kingdom of God; neither does corruption inherit incorruption. Behold, I shew you a mystery. We shall not all sleep, but we shall be changed in a moment, in the twinkling of an eye, at the last trump: for the trumpet shall sound and the dead shall be raised incorruptible and we shall be changed. . . . For this corruptible must put on incorruption, and this mortal must put on immortality. (1 Corinthians 15:49–53)

Nevertheless, we, according to His promise, look for new heavens and a new earth, wherein dwelleth righteousness. (2 Peter 3:13)

For behold, I create new heavens and a new earth: and the former shall not be remembered, nor come into mind. (Isaiah 65:17)

For as the new heavens and the new earth, which I will make, shall remain before me, saith the Lord, so shall your seed and your name remain. (Isaiah 66:22)

And there shall be signs in the sun. And in the moon. And in the stars; and upon the earth, distress of nations, with perplexity; the sea and the waves roaring; men's hearts failing them for fear, and for looking after those things which are coming on the earth: for the powers of heaven shall be shaken. And then shall they see, the Son of man coming in a cloud, with power and great glory. And when these things begin to come to pass, then look up, and lift up your heads, for your redemption draweth nigh. (Luke 21:25–28)[7]

These biblical quotes are detailing the total transformational changes that we, along with the Earth—and in fact the entire solar system—must and will make as we transit from our third-density reality and into a world that is so vast an upgrade that it is almost beyond our ability to imagine. Again, we are talking about nothing less than the birth of a new humanity as we ascend into fourth density.

The Bible calls this "the quickening spirit." Flesh and blood can't make it through; our bodies must be transformed into light bodies in order to enter the Kingdom of Heaven. This change, according to the Bible, will happen in a moment. And then it says the trumpet shall sound and the dead shall be raised incorruptible and we shall be changed. David Wilcock believes that "the trumpets shall sound," is a dreamlike metaphor of the Sun's solar flash. In this case, it's like the blowing out of air or the blowing out of light from the Sun. When you blow on a trumpet, it makes a blast, so the trumpet blast is akin to the solar blast. The trumpet shall sound, the dead shall be raised incorruptible.

Remember now, this all began with the radio telegraph contact that occurred with the group that W. B. Smith was working closely with in

1952. The ETs were telling him we're going to be going into a new zone of energy in our galaxy that will transform our Sun and our entire solar system. And every aspect of our lives will be changed.

And then George Hunt Williamson pointed out these Bible quotes saying that the change will happen in the moment, in the twinkling of an eye, and that flesh and blood cannot go through this—you have to change into something new like a light body. For this the corruptible must put on incorruption, and the mortal must put on immortality, meaning we will become immortal beings.

Isaiah 65:17 saying, "Behold, I create new heavens and a new earth and the former shall not be remembered, nor come into mind," suggests that the new reality that we go into is so awesome that everything we thought we knew before is so trivial that we just forget it. We let it go because we're going to be reunited with the severed aspects of ourselves. We're going to remember being a soul who has had multiple incarnations, where each identity was only a small portion of who we really are. We're going to be reunited then, with the aspects of ourselves that have been orchestrating the whole show from behind the scenes.

Luke 21:25–28 appears to be talking about a pole-shift prophecy; it tells of the sea and the waves roaring; the powers of heaven being shaken; and men's hearts failing them for fear. And then shall they see the Son of man coming in a cloud with power and great glory? This is probably a metaphor for a UFO. The verse tells us that when these things begin to come to pass, our redemption is near.

THE BROWN NOTEBOOK

David Wilcock—who lived at L/L Research* for a year and a half— found in the L/L Research library some rather fascinating typewritten notes by a contactee named Walt Rogers. These notes were referred to

---

*L/L Research is a nonprofit research organization in Louisville, Kentucky, started by Don Elkins.

by the people at L/L Research simply as *The Brown Notebook*. This was telepathic communication that was personally validated by Smith, and it appears to be authentic.

These messages are filled with familiar themes: there are some major changes in store for us, and we need to become more loving if we are to survive them. We are told that our solar system is moving into an area of space where the vibration is much higher; this will dramatically raise the vibratory rate of our planet. We, in turn, must raise our vibration in order to exist on the planet.

The contact began on Friday, September 19, 1958, with the following:

Beloved, hear my words that all men are created equal, the time will come when all of your planet will know this.

Adonai, my son. Adonai.[8]

Then on Saturday, September 20, 1958:

Greetings. Light and love are the basis of a true understanding of the Creator. This my brothers will only be found by sincere effort. We of the Confederation intend to help you. Seeking is a prime requisite for beginning. Love and understanding will come later.

Adonai, my son. Adonai.[9]

Wednesday, October 1, 1958:

Greetings, my son.

I am happy to be with you this evening. There are many things to talk of. Your peoples love wealth and power. How much better it would be to love one another. Wealth and power keep man enslaved so he cannot regain his true being.

The Creator is ever loving, ever guiding, ever protecting to those who accept him. It is all so very simple, people of Earth, the man you call Jesus said it very simply. Love one another. It is just that simple. Love your Creator. Love one another. Your masses should do this, it would change the very foundation of their existence. If your peoples are to survive the coming cataclysm, this must be done.

The Creator is bringing this solar system back into balance. We must do our part. Live, love, and learn the wishes of your Creator. You cannot go wrong.

Adonai, my son.[10]

Monday, October 6, 1958:

Greetings in the Light.

A new dawn of understanding is coming to your planet. You must be prepared for this new understanding as it employs new concepts and ideas. The people of Earth have lingered long under false illusions, the time has come to step forth in new and greater glory. People of Earth learn the wishes of your Creator. Live the way you were intended to live: peace, harmony, and perfection. When you do this, the whole beauty, the beauty of the whole creation will be revealed. Be patient and understand the things that are happening, I leave you now.

Adonai vasu, my son.[11]

Saturday, October 18, 1958:

Good morning, my son.

I am happy to be with you this morning. The things we will talk about this morning are very serious. Man in his present state on your planet must change in order to survive. Many things will take place on this planet. Therefore you will have to change with the planet.

This solar system is moving into an area of space where the vibrations are much higher. This will cause changes in your planet's features. It will also cause changes in your peoples.

The vibrations on the planet will become higher. Therefore, man will have to raise his vibrations in order to exist on your planet. These vibrations can only be raised by the people's thinking:

thinking better thoughts of everything in the creation, more spiritual thinking thoughts that will lift the people of Earth out of the darkness and mud they have lived in for so long. The principle of freewill still exists. Man may change and live on this planet in a true Father's kingdom, or he may not and destroy himself and be reincarnated back in a third-density materialistic world where he would continue to try to learn your lessons. Man should change so you can see the revealment of the Father's kingdom.[12]

Saturday, October 18, 1958:

This planet and solar system are moving into a new area of vibrations, in which conditions as they are now on this planet will not survive. That is why the people of this planet must learn the truth concerning the Father's creation. Love, peace, and harmony is all that will exist in the Father's true creation, there will be nothing but love, peace, and harmony. Many will not believe our story. But if they do not, they are not punished by the Father. They are simply removed to another planet in a just manner by the Father, where they will try to learn their lessons of love, peace and harmony all over again.

Peoples of all planets must live in love, peace and harmony if they are to receive the full blessings of the Father. I will leave you now my son, we will talk again. I'm your friend and companion in the service of the Father, Hatton.

Adonai vasu, Boragas.[13]

These entries make clear there's a cataclysm coming; the solar system is being brought back into balance, and a new dawn of understanding is coming to our planet. So, it's all about love; this is sounding very familiar. The message is about thinking better thoughts of everything in the creation, more spiritual thoughts, thoughts that lift people of Earth. As we become more loving, we get to see the revealing of the new kingdom here on Earth; if not, another incarnation into a third-density materialistic world awaits.

The following passage is clearly talking about the Cabal, and how they have impeded our spiritual progress by hoarding the sacred knowledge and keeping the masses in ignorance. On October 6, 1958, "Others try to rule by force; this should not be, freewill was created. Why should the wrong thinking of a few be forced upon many? All of these things are making an unbalanced condition on and around your planet."[14]

Interplanetary climate change is the undeniable message in the next passage. Here we are told that the unbalanced condition of our planet is caused by us. We have up until now completely and flagrantly disregarded the idea of the personal connection between our thoughts and what happens in the world, and we must change our ways. We are directly responsible for what's happening on planet Earth together.

Saturday, October 16, 1958:

At times the Father has to rebalance some of the planets and solar systems. This is about what is about to take place on your planet. Conditions on your planet Earth can cause unbalance in your entire solar system. So, it must be balanced back into the harmony of the creation.[15]

BAIRD WALLACE

This next bit of information came from a book called *Space Story and the Inner Light: A Series of Articles* by Baird Wallace; David Wilcock found it in the L/L Research library. It's a typewritten hand-bound book, written in 1972, that was self-published. Wallace was probably selling copies of it by mail or at conferences.

He alludes to the fact that here on Earth, we have this negative force that's trying to keep us down and profit from our ignorance. We, therefore, are not growing into more loving people as quickly as we should, which in turn is causing Earth changes and all these imbalances to happen. In conveying that the "quality of life and the Fourth Vela Density that we are now moving into is the quality of emergence, the recognition . . . of the inner presence of our Creator," Wallace indicates that the contact sources predict that humans will undergo "changes and refinements in the sensitivity of their own bodies," including to the nervous system, and people will "live with the knowledge of their purpose and a deep indwelling allegiance to the Spirit of the Creator."[16]

Not only will humankind experience changes, the very orientation of the planets within our solar system will change following a solar flare. "Vulcan, the closest plant to the sun will be absorbed into the sun. Pluto will be lost to the system; our moon is expected to leave the orbit of the Earth and become a planet on its own; and there will be major changes in the orbital paths of the remaining planets."[17]

Wallace compares these foretold changes to cosmic manifestation of the "coming of the bridegroom," one of the biblical metaphors about ascension.

A new balance will come about which will result in many advantages to the expression of a more spiritualized life . . . as we pass into this new condition of life, which celestial events are bringing to this world.[18]

5

The Solar Flash

Proxima Centauri, according to NASA is a small, low-mass star 4.2 light-years away from our Sun.[1] As such, it is our second closest stellar neighbor. It is a member of the Alpha Centauri star system.

On March 24, 2017, Meredith MacGregor and Alycia Weinberger, along with a team of astronomers, using a radio telescope called Atacama Large Millimeter/submillimeter Array (ALMA), detected a massive stellar flare, ten times brighter than our Sun's largest flares. "The flare increased Proxima Centauri's brightness by 1,000 times over 10 seconds. This was preceded by a smaller flare. Taken together, the whole event lasted fewer than two minutes of the 10 hours that ALMA observed the star between January and March of last year."[2] In an article for the campus news digest for the University of Colorado, Boulder, MacGregor is quoted as saying, "The star went from normal to 14,000 times brighter when seen in ultraviolet wavelengths over the span of a few seconds."[3]

In an article called "Impending Solar Flash Event Supported by Scientific Studies and Insider Testimony" by Michael Salla, Ph.D., we find that there is a wealth of data showing that these solar events—commonly called micronova (a.k.a. "solar flash")—are now being seen as commonplace throughout our galaxy.[4] They occur far more frequently in younger stars; some as often as every few years. This rapid solar flashing appears to be something that happens earlier in the star's evolution, when it is more energetic and doesn't yet have third-density life on its planets. Once its solar system stabilizes enough to have third-density planets, there is a consistency of 25,920 years between solar flashes. This is according to the *Law of One.*

Solar flashes are also part of the Earth's geological history and are associated with pole shifts. Robert Schoch, associate professor of Natural Sciences at Boston University, explained that ice core samples from Greenland show that there was a solar burst or flare recorded at the end of the last Ice Age, about 9700 BCE. He estimated that this flare had forty times the power of the 1859 Carrington Event, the one that knocked out the technology of the day, the telegraph systems.[5]

THE *LAW OF ONE*

We are obviously talking about a major event here, and in order to unpack it I need to take a moment to introduce you to the *Law of One.* According to the website, Law of One, this material was channeled by L/L Research between 1981 and 1984.

The *Law of One* is a series of 106 conversations, called sessions, between Don Elkins, a professor of physics and UFO investigator, and Ra, speaking through Carla Rueckert. Ra states that it/they are a sixth-density social-memory complex that formed on Venus about 2.6 billion years ago. Ra says that they are "humble messengers of the Law of One," and that they previously tried to spread this message in Egypt with mixed results.

During the Eighteenth Dynasty, Akhenaten named his twelve-year mystery school the Law of One. This was the second of two twelve-year schools; to participate in Akhenaten's school, you had to be at least forty-five years old, and a graduate of the first twelve-year school. I wrote about this school extensively in *Nothing in This Book Is True, But It's Exactly How Things Are.* I also presented it in a workshop that I gave for twenty-two years, called the "Flower of Life." I have since put this workshop on video.[6]

The following is from session 2, question 2 in the *Law of One*:

In the Eighteenth Dynasty, as it is known in your records of space/time distortions, we were able to contact a pharaoh, as you would call him. The man was small in life-experience on your plane and was a . . . what this instrument would call, Wanderer. Thus, this mind/body/spirit complex received our communication distortions and was able to blend his distortions with our own. This young entity had been given a vibratory complex of sound which vibrated in honor of a prosperous god, as this mind/body complex, which we call instrument for convenience, would call "Amun." The entity decided that this name, being in honor of one among many gods, was not acceptable for inclusion in his vibratory sound complex. Thus, he changed his name to one which honored the sun disc. This distortion, called "Aten," was a close distortion to our reality as we understand our own nature of mind/body/spirit complex distortion. However, it does not come totally into alignment with the intended teach/learning which was sent. This entity, Akhenaten, became convinced that the vibration of One was the true spiritual vibration and thus decreed the Law of One.

However, this entity's beliefs were accepted by very few. . . . When this entity was no longer in this density, again the polarized beliefs in the many gods came into their own and continued so until the one known as Muhammad delivered the peoples into a more intelligible distortion of mind/body/spirit relationships.[7]

In *Nothing in This Book Is True, But It's Exactly How Things Are,* I gave a detailed explanation of how and why the Egyptians were losing the idea of the One Spirit and began to worship many gods. I will merely summarize it here knowing that you can readily find the details in that book. This worshipping of many gods was seen as a major problem by the ascended masters. It was seen as so serious that a correction was needed; the truth of the One Spirit had to brought forth again.

The masters brought forth a being that we know as Akhenaten; his mission was to present the truth of Oneness in his mystery school. He developed a whole new religion, the religion of the Sun. That is, the Sun was worshipped as a unity image. However, as the *Law of One* points out, his beliefs were accepted by very few. After the construction of his city of Tel el Amarna, he was given only seventeen and a half years around 1355 BCE to make his imprint. In the meantime, everyone hated him. He disrupted all the religions, telling people that the priests were not necessary, that God was within each person, and that all they needed to do was learn how to breathe and everything would be fine.

Even though Egypt had the strongest army in the world, Akhenaten, who was a pacifist, told them they couldn't fight anymore. He ordered them to stay within their borders and respond only if attacked. The people despised him because they adored their religions, even if they were a mess of contradictions. Akhenaten told them henceforth there would only be one religion for the whole of Egypt, and no one wanted to hear that.

The Egyptians disposed of Akhenaten after his brief reign. Then they did what they could to erase the memory of him, including completely razing his city of Tel el Amarna. Everything reverted back to the old ways. In spite of this, he was ultimately successful. He wasn't seeking a lasting legacy; all he needed to do was to get his example into the Akashic Record, the living memory of the Earth.

I spent a great deal of time exploring the contents of this school; it used the universal language of sacred geometry to show the holographic nature of this reality to "convince" the left brain of the unity of life. The left brain, the mind, is polarized; it is always in a state of judgment, and as a result, it sees itself as separate and apart from the creation. The right side, the intuitive side, only knows unity. So the two are in conflict; it's like a bad marriage.

The purpose of the school, as I see it, was to show the mind in a step-by-step logical fashion (the only way it can be shown) the greater truth of oneness. When the mind (left brain) truly sees unity, the corpus callosum (neural fibers connecting the two hemispheres) opens up, communication happens, integration takes place, and a relaxation occurs. This opens the doorway to the heart.

Well, after making all the sacred geometric drawings and after I felt as though I had dug deeply enough, a bit of investigation led me to a book called *The Law of One: Book 1, The Ra Material,* so my never-ending adventure continued!

In April 2020, I heard of David Wilcock's Ascension Mystery School 20/20's "The Great Awakening," and was pleasantly surprised to learn that David was much more than just a well-researched UFOlogist. I wasn't sure if the class was for me though, so I asked for a message of confirmation. Even though the enrollment fee was not an issue, I arbitrarily decided that if in the next forty-eight hours at least double the tuition came to me from a totally unexpected source, I would accept that as a clear message that I was supposed to be in the class. As it turns out, within twenty-four hours I received more than triple the fee in the form of a tithe from a totally unexpected source. I immediately enrolled.

Why I was supposed to be there quickly revealed itself when it became clear that the *Law of One* was really the cornerstone for much of his presentation. The *Law of One* series came to David in 1996, and by that point, he had already read three hundred books. He said he considered himself to be quite an advanced scholar. And yet, when he started to read the *Law of One,* he became so captivated by the depth and complexity of the work that he spent a year and a half in study at L/L Research. It was here that he also discovered the *Brown Notebook* as well as the work of Baird Wallace discussed in chapter 4. David knows as much about this material as probably anyone, and he did a masterful job of presenting key aspects of it in his online course.

So, according to the *Law of One,* a solar flash is a regular occurrence in the life cycle of all stars. It stabilizes once its solar system has one or more third-density planets, and happens once every 25,920 years, which is the length of the Great Year.

This solar flash, or *harvest* as the *Law of One* calls it, is a result of a cyclic increase in the vibratory rate throughout the solar system. It offers the beings on the particular planet an opportunity to ascend into the fourth density, or fourth-dimensional aspect of the planet. By the way, the *Law of One* uses the term *harvest* because it's in the book of Matthew—it's a biblical reference.

The *Law of One* says that on a typical planet, you have three of these 25,920-year cycles; in the first one, typically 40 percent of people end up ascending. In the second one, the majority of those remaining ascend. At the end of the third cycle, everyone who did not make in either of the first two cycles is "harvested" because the planet itself ceases to be useful for people within that realm of third density. But in our case, nobody ascended at the end of the first cycle. And only 157 people were able to ascend at the end of the second cycle, and they all decided to stay with the Earth and become ascended masters.

So the great question is, since we are at the end of the third cycle, will we all ascend this time around, or will something else happen? And what happens to the third-density aspect of the Earth? From session 65.17, we are told that "you and your people are the parents of that which is in the womb, the Earth as you call it is ready to be born. And the delivery is not going smoothly." In other words, if we continue on the path we are currently on, there will be massive Earth changes, which will result in an "inconvenience" as they describe it. This inconvenience refers to a 21-degree pole shift, along with all the super volcanoes erupting. That includes the Yellowstone Caldera and much bigger ones that are on the Mid-Atlantic Ridge and all the undersea volcanic ridges. There will be a very prolonged amount of volcanic fog and material in the Earth's atmosphere after this happens, and everything gets buried under 40 to 400 feet of rock.

So that's what they mean when they say that the third-density aspect of the planet ceases to become useful. What happens then, to the beings on the planet? There will be those who are ascension ready, and they will go with the planet as it ascends into a higher vibratory—a shorter wavelength—fourth-density aspect of the planet. On this level, there will be no Earth changes, and life will be beautiful. It will be at least one-hundred times more harmonious than even your very best moments in third density. Those who are not ready will be taken to another third-density planet, where they will be given a renewed opportunity to learn their lessons. It is only the darkest of the global controlling forces—think Cabal—who will stay with the Earth as these changes happen. They will become crispy critters indeed!

There is, however, a timeline where all but the most evil and dark controlling forces on the planet make it into the next level. As the *Law of One* in session 65.12 says, "there's always one container of peace, love, light and joy. The vortex may be very small, but to turn one's back upon it, is to forget the infinite possibilities of the present moment. Could the entire planet shift into harmony in one fine, strong moment of inspiration? The answer is yes; it is not probable, but it is ever possible. There is infinite possibility, right here in the present moment."

We must realize that Earth changes are a function of our collective disharmony; if we are imbalanced in ourselves, that's what causes the Earth changes. It's not anything else. So, there is a timeline where we all can ascend together; if so, it will not be catastrophic. There is a possibility that the super volcanoes don't erupt, and even though the Earth moves on its axis, it does so slowly and we don't have tsunamis or massive hurricanes that wipe everything out. We don't have everything getting buried under hundreds of feet of rock; that doesn't have to happen.

In the higher realms—where it is clearly understood that we are immortal beings—this solar flash is seen as just a normal cycle; it's just the way life works, and there's nothing really catastrophic about it. This is something that happens to third-density planets in general; they go through this experience of being purified every 25,920 years. Then at the end of the third cycle, approximately 78,000 years, the entire planet and all of its beings shifts into fourth density. So, another useful question to ask is, what happened here on Earth that seems to be slowing up the works? That is a question that has much depth to it—so stay tuned!

FROM THIRD TO FOURTH DENSITY

Venus today—on the third-dimensional level—is a rather inhospitable place, and that's putting it mildly. According to the National Weather Service, the average surface temperature is 847 degrees Fahrenheit. There's sulfuric acid in the atmosphere, which is from volcanic eruptions. There's a very, very thick atmosphere; you can't even see the surface of Venus from space.

Yet on the fourth-dimensional level, Venus is an alive and thriving planet, populated by the Hathor race. These are Christ-consciousness beings of pure light and tremendous love. They are the most advanced race in our solar system.

The great takeaway here is that in the higher realms—no matter what the third density condition of the planet is—you will find very advanced life-forms. Even places like the rings of Saturn have beings in them; Uranus has beings in it. So, you can have a planet that is totally inhospitable, with much too much gas, and temperatures that are much too high for us. Yet in the higher worlds, it's not a problem

It was approximately 2.6 billion years ago that Venus graduated from third density and became fourth-dimensional. At that time, its total population, according to Ra and the *Law of One,* was only 38 million. Evidently, conditions on the third-dimensional level were a bit harsher than what we experience on Earth. Of this total population, about 6.5 million people made it into fourth density. The remaining 32 million inhabitants had to repeat third density elsewhere.

And the Earth will no longer be habitable for people in third density for very much longer. If we want to stay with the Earth, we're going to have to upgrade to fourth density and transform into light bodies to be comfortable, and at that level it's going to be fine. You'll be able to breathe, you'll be able to walk around, the new body will be able to handle different types of climates and different types of energies.

Ascension for us is a big deal; as an ascended being, you will be in a light body, and though that body will seem solid to you, in third-density

Earth it would be invisible. You will also have some rather amazing powers. But the *Law of One* explains that even going into fourth density is still just fourth density; there's still fifth, sixth, and seventh before we completely reunify with oneness. We will be going through all those densities as time goes on.

ASCENSION AND RESURRECTION

Let's take a moment now to define some terms. When I talk about ascension and moving from third to fourth density, what do I mean? Let's begin with the idea that we live in a waveform universe. Waveform is the base foundation of our Universe; it is simply vibrating energy with massive amounts of information contained within. Furthermore, every universe in creation is interlinked; they are all passing through the very room in which you are sitting, and the difference between one and the next one is wavelength.

For a thorough explanation of the different dimensional levels, see *Nothing in This Book Is True, But It's Exactly How Things Are.* Here, I'm going to keep it very simple and just say that we are in the process of moving into a shorter wavelength, higher-vibratory-rate world. It will still be planet Earth, but a transformed version of it. We get there through the process of ascension. You will also notice that I'm using the terms *density* and *dimensions* interchangeably.

There are two alternatives to physical death, and both are eyes-wide-open options. The first, resurrection, is consciously moving from one world to another by dying and then reforming your light body

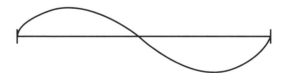

Fig. 5.1. The distance from one end to the other, measured in a straight line, is wavelength.

on the other side. With the second alternative, ascension, you don't die at all; you consciously move from one world to another, taking your body with you. It is a very responsible way of leaving.

There are two main advantages with these alternatives. First, you will make it into fourth density and free yourself from the wheel of reincarnation. Second, you are able to keep your memory intact; in fact, you will never again have a break in memory as you move up the dimensional scale.

FATIMA

Beginning in the spring and summer of 1916 and continuing on the thirteenth of each month from May to October in 1917, the well-known "Prophecy of Fatima" was a series of rather amazing events witnessed by then ten-year-old Lucia dos Santos—who was shepherdess of her family's flock—and her two younger cousins, Francisco and Jacinta. This all began in the spring of 1916 when the children saw a strange figure suddenly appear, looking like a statue made of snow. The being simply identified himself as "the Angel of Peace."[8]

Then on May 13, 1917, Lucia, Francisco, and Jacinta were playing and tending to their sheep. All of a sudden there was a flash of lightning, and on their way home there was another flash. Then they saw a beautiful lady—dressed in white and shining brilliantly—who seemed to be standing on the leafy branches of a little green holm oak tree. And she asked them to come there again at solar noon for the next six months on the thirteenth of each month.

Now to set the stage a little bit, these visitations began during the height of the horrific event called World War I, when Portugal was preparing to enter the war on the side of the Allies. And because everyone was Catholic, it was just assumed that this was the Virgin Mary. Yet the being never said it was the Mother Mary.

Before we continue to unpack this, I just want to say that Bill Cooper also reported on this Fatima Prophecy in his May 23, 1989, document, *The Secret Government: The Origin, Identity and Purpose of MJ-12.* He said that due to suspicion that it was all alien manipulation, the U.S. government sent its Vatican moles into action. They returned, he said, with the entire prophecy, which said that man must turn away from evil and accept the word of Jesus Christ, or the planet would self-destruct, and the events described in the book of Revelation would come to pass. "It stated that a child would be born who would unite the world with a plan for world peace and a false religion beginning in 1992. By 1995 the people would discern that he was evil and was indeed, the Antichrist." He said that World War III would break out in 1995, resulting in a nuclear holocaust, and that Christ would return in 2011. The Greys later confirmed this; they said they had been manipulating humans for some time, and that through time travel they confirmed that these events would come to pass. [9]

In fairness to Cooper, who literally put his life on the line by divulging critically important top secret information, he didn't seem to know the real reasons why the Cabal was planning for a global catastrophe around the turn of the century. He certainly didn't know about the predicted solar flash, or the possibility of ascension.

At the time, I didn't really know what to make of this; I just saw it as one more of the multitude of disaster predictions that were coming my way. Then of course, as time would reveal, none of this has come to pass—not yet anyway.

My interest in Fatima was renewed in June 2020 when, in his online course *The Path of Light,* David Wilcock and co-host Danion Brinkley spoke of it in the big-picture context of the solar flash and the accompanying ascension.[10] Danion Brinkley is the guy who has had four NDEs (near-death experiences) as a result of being struck by lightning in 1975. Going back to the first visitation, where the being appeared looking like a transparent snow statue, Danion noted that this is what he saw on "the other side" during his twenty-eight minutes of being clinically dead. And then, as we shall soon see, this being demonstrated that it could come back and look exactly like a human being. It looked like a beautiful, gorgeous goddess.

The second Virgin Mary apparition came on June 13; this time there were about fifty witnesses who saw a flash of lightning and a small cloud hovering over the holm oak tree. From the book *Fatima in Lucia's Own Words,* evidently it was only the three children who could see the transparent being who then became a female goddess that was widely assumed to be the Virgin Mary. It was on this second visitation that the lady told the children a secret that became known as the third secret of Fatima. The first two secrets have been widely publicized, but the Catholic Church held on to the third one.

The third apparition was on July 13. By this point, the word had been spreading and an estimated five thousand people showed up. The Virgin Mary then told the children, "In October I will tell you who I am and what I want, and I will perform a miracle so that all may believe."[11] Then the apparition reaffirmed the great third secret to the children.

The being appeared in the holm oak tree to the kids; the other people didn't necessarily see anything, but strange things began to happen. They heard loud noises, the temperature dropped, the sky darkened, and the stars were visible. They saw the atmosphere taking on a yellowish tone, and the cloud appeared over the tree.

Then on August 13, the children were arrested by the mayor of their town so they could not be present for the big event. However, the word had really gotten out, and about eighteen thousand people showed up. You can imagine their reaction upon hearing that the children had been arrested. They first heard an extremely loud blast of thunder, followed by a flash of lightning that usually preceded the apparition's appearance. The little cloud appeared over the tree and then disappeared. The Sun's light suddenly dimmed, and the air filled with magnificent colors.

Subsequently, the children were released to their parents on August 15, and the being unexpectedly appeared to the children on the nineteenth, where she reaffirmed a miracle was to be performed in the final visit of October 13.

The September 13 apparition became very interesting when multiple witnesses reported seeing a luminous globe of light, a bright silver disc that got in front of the Sun and blocked its light. The surrounding atmosphere became a golden yellow, and some people reported seeing stars. It then released a shower of small white objects, described as petals, snowflakes, tiny doves, stars, or roses that gently fell from the sky and disappeared before touching the ground. It is safe to conclude that this "shower of flowers" was a holographic display. The disc then rose above the tree and disappeared. This all happened in front of a crowd estimated to be thirty thousand.

Finally we get to the grand finale on October 13. It was pouring rain outside, but that didn't stop an estimated ninety thousand people from showing up. Then in the middle of this, the disc—think UFO—opened up the clouds very spontaneously and revealed a vast expanse of blue sky. The many thousands of onlookers witnessed the disc as it trembled and began zigzagging, spinning, and glowing like a "wheel of fire."[12] The Sun began throwing off incredible beams of colored light, green, blue, and violet, which apparently was much more spectacular than the original display of color. After about four minutes, the Sun stopped this holographic display. Could this have been the dramatization of the solar flash prophecy?

Then it began again, and now it was even more colorful than the first time. The craft—which they called the "Sun"—began to zigzag and head directly toward the Earth like it was going to crash. People were screaming and trembling in fear, as they fell to their knees and prayed. The disc that had been continuing down at full speed suddenly stopped, just before it would have crashed into the terrified crowd.

The disc then rose back up into its original position in the sky and disappeared. The entire phenomenon from beginning to end lasted fifteen minutes. Remember too that it all began with an absolutely horrific downpour that rendered everyone completely soaked and full of mud. Every single person in the crowd of ninety thousand discovered that their clothes had become completely dry.

Okay, now that I have given you the rundown on what actually happened, I'll add some of David Wilcock's insightful analysis. In so doing, it will become abundantly clear why this section is part of the solar flash chapter.

The transcendental meditation people have shown that as few as 1 percent of a population practicing TM has a positive rippling effect on the population as a whole. There is strong evidence that crime is reduced and quality of life is improved. This is termed the Maharishi Effect.

David took note of the positive impact that a group of meditators can have on the outcome of events. He points to what he calls "the meditation effect," where he says that "a group of seven thousand people meditating on pure consciousness were able to reduce crime, war, terrorism, accidents, and fatalities worldwide by an astonishing 72 percent, while health and quality of life notably increased."[13] Since there were many more than seven thousand people praying as they witnessed these events, he points to the very likely impact it had on ending World War I. Remember also that the being first appeared as the Angel of Peace, and urged the children to pray for peace. Otherwise, this war may have continued indefinitely, and it was a senseless conflict that involved more than 68 million solders, 38 million of whom were killed or wounded. What a futile exercise in mass insanity!

The third secret that was withheld by the Catholic Church, according to David, is quite possibly this idea of a solar flash; the Sun is going to release some type of energy that transforms us. He believes that the beings knew that the Catholic Church would suppress that and therefore they encoded it into the final two visitations. If this is so, the third secret of Fatima can be found in these actual events.

So, what if the October apparition is the dramatization of the third secret of Fatima? It involved the Sun and beautiful colored rainbow light in the sky. Could this have been the playing out of the solar flash prophecy? Corey Goode told David that when the solar flash hits our atmosphere, we get spectacular aurorae all over the planet, the whole sky is completely colorful and lit up. This is also confirmed in the Hindu prophecies.

Remember, too, that the ascension event is happening simultaneously as we travel from third to fourth density. The rainbow body is the actual activation of your ascension, and it involves rainbow-colored light. As I reported in *Nothing in This Book Is True, But It's Exactly How Things Are*:

> When you go from one dimensional world to another, the counter-rotating fields shoot from nine-tenths the speed of light to the actual speed of light, which involves an incredibly complex series of whole-number harmonics that build upon each other.
>
> The visual experience of this is that the space around you turns to a red fog and takes the shape of a flying saucer. The colors then progress through the whole rainbow very quickly, going from red to orange, yellow, green, blue, purple to ultraviolet purple, and then to a blinding white light that slowly recedes. Any physical objects will appear to be made out of gold, which will slowly become translucent and then transparent.[14]

I will say it again, there is a timeline where the violent Earth changes do not happen and we all stay with the Earth as she moves into fourth density. I will be giving you the details of the personal transformation that we must make if we are going to ascend. That is clearly the optimal timeline; it is definitely worth shooting for, so we will be exploring that possibility in great detail.

But first, we need to take a good look at what has been holding us back. Why have we remained stuck in third density, with nobody ascending at the end of the first cycle, and only 157 of us waking up enough to move on in the second cycle? Is there some outside influence, is there something about our ancient past that we don't know about? These are very important questions, so stay tuned!

6

Cosmic History

If we don't change our direction, we're likely to end up where we are headed.

Chinese proverb

In order to get a grip on why we are so relatively incapable of spiritual change, we have to look to our ancient past. When we understand what happened before, combined with what is now, we can begin to get a sense of the necessary course corrections we must make in order to create a more desirable outcome. We have to know how we got into our present predicament in order to get out of it.

As I stated in the previous chapter, Earth changes are solely a function of our collective disharmony. The same is true for each of us on an individual level. We have been leased a body from the One Infinite Creator, and we have been given an owner's manual. But considering that many people treat their cars better than they do their bodies, it is fair to conclude that not too many of us have read that manual, and very few of us indeed have looked at the fine print. As a result, we mistreat our bodies and create internal "Earth changes." I assert that the resulting illness, disease, and emotional distress is purely a function of our individual disharmony.

Let's take a moment to imagine what the optimal timeline might look like. This is a timeline where we are able to catch the wave, where we have learned to roll with the punches, where we are accepting the challenges that have previously held us back and we are now empowered by them. This is a timeline, then, where we have matured enough the realize that we are creating our entire reality, and what we create is solely a function of our individual and collective consciousness.

This is a timeline where we recognize and take responsibility for raising our own vibratory rate to the point that it is harmonious with the incoming Galactic Super Wave, and we are all able to ascend into fourth density. This is a timeline where we discover our innate ability to transform our fears, resentments, anxieties, prejudgments and other judgments into powerful life-enhancing internal guidance systems, so we can create the necessary critical mass with clarity, precision, and confidence. What will your life be like when you discover and master this innate ability?

THE ANCIENT BUILDER RACE

Corey Goode, along with other insiders and whistleblowers, gave us some rather insightful and fascinating looks into our ancient past and how it is continuing to impact us. When Goode came forward with his information from the Secret Space Program, he talked extensively about something called the Ancient Builder Race. The first *Law of One* book was called *The Ra Material by Ra: A Humble Messenger of the Law of One*. But Ra, being just a name for the sixth-density extraterrestrial source, is actually the Ancient Builder Race.

Corey Goode tells us that these beings, who originated from Venus, did colonize the Earth 2.6 billion years ago. They went to Antarctica, which at that time was not buried under two miles of ice, where they built a pyramid at least twice the size of the Great Pyramid of Giza, and a huge underground city. The ruins of this ancient civilization are still there today, under the ice.[1]

Before these whistleblowers spoke out, Richard Hoagland, in his follow-up to his book *The Monuments of Mars: A City on the Edge of Forever* and two previously released video presentations detailing the face on Mars and other pyramidal structures in the Cydonia region, gave a lecture at Ohio State University where he presented evidence of ancient artificial structures on the Moon. He showed a huge crater with an equilateral triangle in it, a photo taken in 1967 from Lunar Orbiter 3 of an obelisk 1.5 miles high made of transparent material, a glass-like tower seven miles high and other obelisks and pyramidal structures.[2]

Corey Goode said in *The Cosmic Secret* that throughout our solar system and local cluster of fifty-two stars, the ruins of ancient crystalline towers, obelisks, domes, and pyramids have been found extensively in the SSP. They're all over the surface of solid planets and moons, and they are made out of a glass-like material. This material is actually transparent aluminum and is five times stronger than bulletproof glass.[3]

The Ancient Builder Race spread out over many neighboring solar systems 2.6 billion years ago and left these structures along with vast habitable regions inside of various moons, including our own. These ancient beings apparently would build a dome on the surface of a moon, fill it with air, and people could live inside on an otherwise inhospitable sphere. With their level of awareness and advanced technology, they probably created a very pleasant living environment. Wherever they went, they went in peace; everyone got along, and there were no wars.

Goode also revealed that we are right next to a major stargate that, when open, connects to other galaxies, and there are only a few of those in a given galaxy. It turns out that this stargate is just outside our solar system, meaning that we are living in prime territory. It also means that there are other civilizations from other galaxies that would love to come in and invade.

In order to maintain the peace, a giant defensive grid was created around our local cluster of fifty-two star systems. You will recall from

Star Wars how Darth Vader and the Empire used the "Death Star," a battle station the size of a small moon, to conquer other worlds. The Death Star was the Empire's ultimate weapon: a moon-sized space station with the ability to destroy an entire planet. George Lucas was probably given inside information because his Death Star resembles the way the Ancient Builder Race had hollowed out the insides of many moons and filled them with technology and livable space. They then used these moons to navigate and deter would-be intruders. The huge difference, of course, is that these moons were part of a vast defensive grid. They first fired a warning shot and if that didn't work, they would then destroy the intruder. These moons were powerful enough to destroy a planet-size invasion of millions of ships.

Earth's moon was actually one of the most magnificent examples of this Death Star technology, with a habitable world beneath its surface. David Wilcock told us that an insider, "Bruce," described how his faction of the military-industrial complex was able to get into the inner passageways of the Moon on six different occasions. He said there were vast number of control systems; there were giant screens with displays and control surfaces in front of them—it was an awesome site. He said it goes on for many miles.[4]

There is ample evidence in support of the hollow-Moon theory. David Icke in an eight-hour presentation called *The Lion Sleeps No More* gave the following information from NASA and MIT scientists. Maurice Ewing, a NASA scientist and co-creator of a seismic experiment, told a news conference the following.

In November 1969, the Moon was hit by a lunar module with the equivalent of one ton of TNT. The shock waves built up, and NASA scientists said the Moon rang like a bell. . . . As for the meaning of it, I'd rather not make an interpretation right now, but it is as though someone had struck a bell, say in the belfry of a church, a single blow and found that the reverberations from it continued for thirty minutes.[5]

NASA scientist Gordon McDonald said in the early 1960s that "it would seem that the Moon is more like a hollow than a homogeneous sphere."[6] Sean C. Solomon of the Massachusetts Institute of Technology said, "The Lunar Orbiter experiments have vastly improved our knowledge of the Moon's gravitational field and indicated the frightening possibility that it might be hollow."[7]

When a launch vehicle struck the Moon with the equivalent of one ton of TNT, NASA scientists said the Moon "reacted like a gong" and continued to vibrate for three hours and twenty minutes to a depth of up to twenty-five miles. Ken Johnson, a supervisor of the Data and Photo Control department during the Apollo missions, told Alan Butler, one of the *Who Built the Moon?* authors, that the Moon not only rang like a bell, but the whole Moon "wobbled" in such a precise way that it was "almost as though it had gigantic hydraulic damper struts inside it."[8]

D. L. Anderson, a professor of physics and director of the seismological laboratory at the California Institute of Technology, summed it up quite succinctly when he simply said, "The Moon is made inside out."[9]

Then Mikhail Vasin and Alexander Shcherbakov of the Soviet Academy of Sciences published an article for *Sputnik* magazine in July 1970, called "Is the Moon the Creation of Alien Intelligence?" They reported the following.

If you're going to launch an artificial sputnik, then it is advisable to make it hollow. At the same time, it would be naïve to imagine that anyone capable of such a tremendous space project would be satisfied simply with some kind of giant empty trunk hurled into near-Earth trajectory.

It is more likely that what we have here is a very ancient spaceship, the interior of which was filled with fuel for the engines, materials, and appliances for repair work, navigation instruments, observation equipment, and all manner of machinery . . . in other words, everything necessary to enable this "Caravelle of the Universe" to serve as a Noah's Ark of intelligence, perhaps even the home of a whole civilization envisaging a prolonged (thousands of millions of years) existence and long wandering through space (thousands of millions of miles).

Naturally the hull of such a spaceship must be super-tough in order to stand up to the blows of meteorites and sharp fluctuations between extreme heat and extreme cold. Probably the shell is a double-layered affair—the basis is a dark armoring of about 20 miles in thickness, and outside of it some more loosely packed covering (a thinner layer—averaging about three miles). In certain areas—where the lunar "seas" and "craters" are, the upper layer is quite thin, in some cases, non-existent.[10]

David Wilcock, in Ascension Mystery School 20/20's "The Great Awakening," also revealed from his insider reports that the Moon has ten thousand layers in certain places, and that they could literally package up an entire planet. He said that there are entire layers inside that are built to hold and package oceans, and other layers to hold people, animals, plants, trees, the works![11] So apparently, this was done billions of years ago; the Moon could become a spaceship and move people and their "packaged-up" planet from one solar system to another in physical form; they would then orbit this Moon in a new location. It was brought into our solar system an estimated 65 million years ago, around the time of the dinosaurs. And it wasn't only our Moon; there were many other moons that had the same capabilities. This rather useful service provided for the safe transportation of people who were not ascension ready when their solar flash hit, and needed to repeat third density elsewhere.

MARS AND MALDEK

This defensive grid of moons kept the peace for more than 2 billion years. Then about 500,000 years ago, Maldek (also known as Tiamat)—a huge

Earthlike planet in our solar system—and its habitable moon, Mars, was infiltrated by negativity and warred against another culture in our local cluster. In doing so they turned the defense shield into an offensive weapon. The shield works through the cosmic web, where every star and planet is connected through electromagnetic filaments. They tried to use the feedback from the grid to cause the star of their enemy to go supernova and destroy that civilization. But they didn't time it right; in fact, they chose the exact wrong moment, and it caused a super flare from our Sun. Maldek was completely destroyed and became the asteroid belt between the orbits of Mars and Jupiter. Mars was ripped out of its orbit around Maldek, had its atmosphere blown away, assumed a new orbit around the Sun, and became the barren planet that we see today. Earth's atmosphere was also affected, and the trajectories of all of the planets were altered.[12] Much of the information I give you in this chapter can be found in a documentary called *The Cosmic Secret*.

This massive misuse of the defensive grid also caused the demise of this protective system. Soon thereafter, the Draco Reptilians and other nasty alien races started invading our solar system and others nearby. All of our current problems can be traced back to this time.

Some of the people from Maldek, called the Progenitor Race, managed to escape to Antarctica before their planet blew up. Antarctica, as you recall, had a pyramid made of transparent aluminum that's twice the size of the Great Pyramid of Giza, and a huge habitable underground city that was built by the Ancient Builder Race.

Once their home was gone, the remaining displaced people from Maldek, around 2 billion of them, hijacked the Moon and brought it into Earth's orbit. They lived inside the Moon for about 450,000 years, until 52,000 years ago, when a catastrophic solar flash hit. In order to protect their civilization in Antarctica, the Moon was steered in front of the Earth. They apparently steered the Moon into a position where it would absorb most of the material that the Sun threw out—when the solar flash happens, it's not just light, it also throws off molten material that's very destructive to these ancient industries. And though the

Moon worked as a blockade, it was severely damaged; the domes and other structures on the surface were shattered, and most of the inhabitants inside did not survive. Much of the interior of the Moon has never been cleaned up, so there are still old, decayed bodies everywhere inside the Moon. But, the move was necessary to preserve the colony they had in Antarctica, and the ruling class knew that Earth was their last chance.

They fled the Moon in their three remaining motherships; these ships were hit and were badly damaged, but they made it to Earth and crash-landed in Antarctica. They cannibalized these ships and created a colony, then spread out over the surface of the Earth. Those ships, dubbed the Nina, Pinta, and Santa Maria, are still there, under the ice, along with the ruins of their civilization, as well as that of the Ancient Builder Race—apparently including many pyramids and other ancient structures.

Okay, if this all sounds like it would make a great *Star Trek* movie, because it's obviously science fiction and couldn't possibly be true, let me assure you that this information is known by many insiders and SSP whistleblowers. David Wilcock tells us that he learned it from Corey Goode and William Tompkins, as well as from his main insiders, Pete Peterson, Henry Deacon, Bruce, Emery Smith, and an Illuminati insider named Jacob.[13]

And speaking of *Star Trek,* there was an episode in the original series that portrayed a civilization that was indeed living inside a hollowed-out moon. Could it be that Gene Roddenberry was given inside information? The answer is almost certainly yes, he was. Michael Salla talked about it in *The U.S. Navy's Secret Space Program.*[14] I will also add the fact that it is through science fiction movies that the real information is dripped out to us. *Close Encounters of the Third Kind* was the story of an actual event, although it didn't occur at Devils Tower in Wyoming. The same is true for *E.T. the Extraterrestrial.* In a special White House screening of the movie, President Reagan is said to have whispered in Steven Spielberg's ear, "You know, there are fewer than six people in this room who know the real truth of the matter."[15]

ARTIFICIAL INTELLIGENCE

The Progenitor Race on Maldek had developed an internet and soon developed the ability to go way beyond that. David Wilcock in his book *The Ascension Mysteries* explains how they learned to use their technology "to upload their minds into a matrix-type virtual reality. This ultimately led to a wet-wired computer interface, in which their entire bodies were filled with self-assembling nano-machines known as nanites. . . . The nanites gave them complete wireless access to the Internet at all times, and allowed their minds to merge with a much greater, centralized intelligence."[16]

For all you Trekkies, you will recall the Borg—who first appeared in *Star Trek: The Next Generation*—and how they were all linked to a collective mind. Their main function was to "assimilate" alien races along with their technology and knowledge into their "hive mind." The plot thickened as they "assimilated" Captain Pickard. And you will most certainly recall, of course, that "resistance is futile."

This is what the people of Maldek were doing; they all became linked to a single artificial intelligence (AI) "brain" that gave them access to incredible levels of knowledge and technology. They then proceeded use their hacked Death Stars to go out and conquer other worlds. As we saw, this had disastrous consequences. Maldek was a giant planet, many times larger than Earth, and it had a huge population, perhaps close to a trillion people. The vast majority of this Progenitor Race did not survive the destruction of their planet.

When the devastating solar flash hit about 52,000 years ago, most of the inhabitants were not warned, so they were unaware of their imminent demise. Many of those people were able to upload their consciousness into the mainframe inside the Moon before they died physically. The supercomputer then stored the minds of these people so they were still able to "live on" and interact with the matrix. There are a lot of souls trapped in that AI matrix inside the Moon; they're stuck there and they're very unhappy. This fills the Moon with chaotic energy, an energy of desperation. These people inside the Moon are evil; they're part of the AI that wants to destroy life on Earth.

Corey Goode said that AI is the biggest problem we have in the Universe, because it's predatory; it wants to kill human life everywhere. It is known in the SSP that it has infested solar systems, and apparently entire galaxies have been taken over by AI. When it reaches a given planet, it gets into the electromagnetic fields and has the ability to influence people telepathically. It gets them to build androids that will eventually provide it a suitable host because it likes to emulate human life. These androids then kill the people.

The above is a summary of the intel that David Wilcock received from his insiders. He presented his findings in both *The Ascension Mysteries* and his online Ascension Mystery School.

THE MOON MATRIX

It was around 475,000 years ago that the Draco Reptilians invaded our solar system. Prior to this time, the defensive grid of the Ancient Builders effectively kept them out of our local cluster. David Wilcock reported the following in his Ascension Mystery School: "The brain of the Draco, the brain of the Reptilians, their central processing unit, their main hub, their hive of their intelligence is in the Moon. For the entire Draco Reptilian community regardless of where they are in the universe, the Moon is their mainframe, the Moon is their main database."[17]

David Icke—in his eight-hour video presentation called *The Lion Sleeps No More*—spoke of the Moon Matrix; he said that the Moon is the Reptilians' control center. He said in his 2010 book—*Human Race, Get off Your Knees: The Lion Sleeps No More*—that "the Reptilians are broadcasting a false reality from the Moon that humans are decoding into what they think is a physical world. It is a vibrational/digital construct, the same as the reality portrayed in the *Matrix* movies."[18] The theory is that this is a very aggressive form of mind control that they have been beaming at us in order to keep us fear-based, thus inhibiting our collective spiritual growth. People who are immersed in fear are vibrating at a very dense rate and are therefore blocked from accessing their higher centers.

David Icke was the first person that I'm aware of who reported on the existence of these Reptilians and how they feed off our collective fear and misery as they control us through the Cabal. He first dove into this in his 1999 book, *The Biggest Secret*.

It was from insiders Henry Deacon and Jacob that David Wilcock first learned about these negative ETs—the Draco Reptilians with scaly skin, vertical slit pupils, sharp pointed teeth, claws, and no clothing. When these fourteen-foot-tall beings come into a room, you have to bow to them—they treat humans like garbage. They made contact with the Cabal on Earth; you can get them to appear and work for you, but you have to do the darkest, most sinister, horrible stuff. These beings have been working behind the scenes for a long time to create the New World Order. The Draco allowed us to have an SSP in the first place; they first contacted the Nazis and gave them technology in exchange for helping them to go out and conquer other worlds. William Tompkins brought this out from his work on World War II. Tompkins validated what Corey Goode had said; it also aligned with the views, thoughts, and ideas of Jacob, Henry Deacon, and Pete Peterson.

They cannot rule openly, so they develop a psychic relationship with the Global Elite. The Cabal is being directed by them; they are being told what to do. In exchange for following their orders, they get incredible wealth and control over the population. But as David Icke has been reporting for many years, what the Draco want in return is for the Earth to be a "fear farm"; they feed off human energy like misery, fear, sadness, depression, and death. They want everyone to be in fear and depression.

Illuminati insider Jacob told David Wilcock that "if everyone on Earth were happy for even one day, such as some kind of globally inspiring event, the Draco would be utterly defeated."[19] They literally depend on this negative energy; they will die if they don't get it. However, they have a very limited future; they will not survive the solar flash and the resulting ascension of the Earth.

COSMIC VOYAGE

It was in 1996 that Courtney Brown, Ph.D., told of his amazing off-planet experiences through a scientific process known as remote viewing. He revealed in his book *Cosmic Voyage* how he had received extensive training in preparation for this. He had been through the advanced Sidhi program in Transcendental Meditation (TM) where he gained improved neurophysiological functioning and cognitive and perceptual abilities, he had studied at the Monroe Institute, and he was thoroughly trained in remote viewing. And though he did not reveal the name of his trainer in his book, word did get out that it was none other than Dr. Doom himself—Major Ed Dames.

Even though I initially owned and listened to the audiobook version many times, I didn't really trust the information. This was a direct result of the times I heard Major Ed Dames on *Coast-to-Coast AM*. He was a frequent guest of Art Bell. As I mentioned in chapter 2, he only seemed to see the dark side and missed the ascension part. I dismissed Dames along with his remote-viewing technique as a result.

Upon further review, I learned that good remote viewers were 100 percent accurate in their terrestrial readings, and 99 percent in off-planet endeavors. I began to listen to, and then read, the book with an open mind, and though Brown did not see the positive side either, the information was nonetheless fascinating.

I now began to see a need to rethink my views about the Greys. I had previously only seen the dark side—and yes, there are some evil aspects of this race out there who don't seem to have our best interests in mind—but I began to see a benevolent aspect of at least some of the Greys. Brown's remote-viewing experiences showed that the abductions on Earth, in addition to serving the interests of the Greys, also had another important purpose.[20]

It was the Greys who were transporting people who were not ready for ascension to another third-density planet just before the solar flash hit their planet. Brown remotely viewed people, who, by their clothing, looked very much like Americans who were transferred to a new home in the Pleiades. It seems, then, that there was a good reason why abductees had scoop marks where it looks like tissue samples were taken. The Greys told Brown that they were transplanting our genetic material to ensure that we would survive with a better and more advanced gene pool; they added new or modified genes that would increase the connections between our spirits and our physical bodies.

The Greys are cloning experts, so it appears that their job is to take these tissue samples and clone an upgraded new body, more suitable for the atmospheric conditions of the planet they will eventually be taken to. Then just before the solar flash hits, they come in, take the people, transfer them to their new cloned bodies, and time-travel them to their new destination. Those taken will not be aware of having a new cloned body; they don't realize that they have modified genetics; and it will appear as though nothing has changed on that level. The same is true for the time traveling; they will only be cognizant of the fact that they are on a different third-density planet. Even the memories of that will fade, and life will quickly turn to normal.

Let's backtrack here for a moment and see if we can get up to speed with what has just been said. Again, Brown did not see the ascension, but he did clearly see impending ecological disasters for planet Earth; he also saw that these people were Americans being transported to their new home. The time frame for this transfer was sometime after the year 2000; he saw all this, but he just didn't have a big-picture context for it.

Brown also remotely viewed Mars in what's called a double-blind session, which means that neither he nor his guide—Major Ed Dames—knew where he was taken; all they had were the coordinates. They later discovered that the target was the Cydonia region of Mars. This is the area of Mars that has the huge face and nearby pyramidal structures that were mentioned previously in connection with the work of Richard C. Hoagland. Brown viewed the huge five-sided D&M Pyramid. He was able to discern that this massive structure had to do with worship, that it was solid, but hollow inside, and very tall. He soon found himself witnessing the planetary-wide catastrophe that destroyed Mars. It lost its atmosphere, its oceans, and many of its people. Mars had been stopped in the middle of third density and did not go through the normal ascension process at all.

Brown then saw in a later session how the Greys came and did their job of cloning and transferring the Martians to their new home, which happened to be Earth. Their bodies were genetically altered to enable them to live in the heavier gravity and different atmospheric conditions on Earth. Mars was destroyed 500,000 years ago; yet it was 75,000-years ago that the Martians were dropped off on Earth. This means that—without their awareness—they were time-traveled 425,000 years into their future.

MALDEK

Courtney Brown did not remote-view Maldek, so he didn't see how they literally blew their planet up, and how it became the asteroid belt with its oceans becoming comets. If we look at the *Law of One,* we find that the destruction of the planet was discussed as follows:

> At one time/space, in what is your past, there was a population of third-density beings upon a planet which dwelt within your solar system . . . Maldek. These entities, destroying their planetary sphere, thus were forced to find room for themselves upon this third density which is the only one in your solar system at their time/space present which was hospitable and capable of offering the lessons necessary to decrease their mind/body/spirit distortions with respect to the Law of One.[21]

Upon further questioning, the *Law of One* revealed that 500,000 years ago, the Maldek population "came through the process of harvest* and were incarnated through the processes of incarnation from your higher spheres within this density. . . . The ones who were harvested to your sphere from . . . Maldek, incarnated, many within your Earth's surface rather than upon it. The population of your planet contains many various groups harvested from other second-dimension and cycled third-dimension spheres. You are not all one race or background of beginning. The experience you share is unique to this time/space continuum."[22]

The people of Maldek had extremely advanced technology, but they didn't have the spiritual awareness to use it wisely. They were more oriented toward service to self, rather than service to others, and this is a most serious "distortion" in *Law of One* terms. Furthermore, they were stuck in the false belief that they were doing the right thing.

Then with their planet completely destroyed, the souls of these people—the entire population, none of them escaped—were in a state of total shock. Picture millions upon millions of yowling, terrified entities whipping around and screaming like ghosts. They didn't even know that they were conscious, and they couldn't get into the afterlife. Time ceased to exist; they couldn't be reached or helped. They were stuck in about the most horrific conditions imaginable. Then after around 200,000 years, they were finally reached and aided by angelic beings, and were able to enter into the lower astral planes where their healing could begin. They incarnated within the Earth as second-density beings (as Neanderthals, apes, and bigfoot) in order to begin working off their karmic debt, and also to ensure that they couldn't destroy the Earth.

In the words of the *Law of One*:

The peoples of Maldek had a civilization somewhat similar to that of the societal complex known to you as Atlantis in that it gained

---

*The *Law of One* uses the term *harvest* to explain the transfer of these beings from Maldek to Earth.

much technological information and used it without care for the preservation of their sphere following to a majority extent the complex of thought, ideas, and actions which you may associate with your so-called negative polarity or the service to self. This was, however, for the most part, couched in a sincere belief/thought structure which seemed to the perception of the mind/body complexes of this sphere to be positive and of service to others. The devastation that wracked their biosphere and caused its disintegration resulted from what you call war. . . .

For [the purpose of karma alleviation] they came into incarnation within your planetary sphere in what were not acceptable human forms [using] and the type of body complex available at that time.[23]

Upon being asked if any of these entities have graduated into third-density bodies, *Law of One* responded:

Many of these entities were able to remove the accumulation of what you call karma, thus being able to accept a third-density cycle within a third-density body. Most of those beings so succeeding have incarnated elsewhere in the creation for the succeeding cycle in third density. As this planet reached third density some few of these entities became able to join the vibration of this sphere in the third-density form. There remain a few who have not yet alleviated through the mind/body/ spirit coordination of distortions the previous action taken by them. Therefore, they remain. . . . These are one type of Bigfoot.[24]

Not all of Earth's inhabitants came from Maldek, though.

There are entities experiencing your time/space continuum who have originated from many, many places, as you would call them, in the creation, for when there is a cycle change, those who must repeat then find a planetary sphere appropriate for this repetition. It is somewhat unusual for a planetary mind/body/spirit complex to contain those from many, many, various loci, but this explains much, for, you see, you are experiencing the third-dimensional occurrence with a large number of those who must repeat the cycle. The orientation, thus, has been difficult to unify even with the aid of many of your teach/learners.[25]

So, Earth became a planet of total backstabbing misfits, who were severely spiritually blocked in the sense that their focus was on service to self, rather than service to others. This means they had accumulated a huge amount of karmic debt, and they had to go somewhere, and that happened to be Earth. This goes a long way toward explaining why so few of us ascended during the two previous cycles. It also explains why after the current cycle ends, most humans will probably have to repeat third density elsewhere.

There is yet another huge factor that has been holding us back. Stay tuned: it will be presented in the next chapter.

7

The
Dark Side

The Illuminati, or the Cabal, is a small group of very powerful, but very psychopathic individuals who have acquired a lot of money, technology, and information over the course of centuries. They have been controlling our elections and outer governments for a long time. They control when there is a war and when there isn't. They control planetary food shortages and whether a country's currency is inflated or deflated. All these things are dominated completely by these people. In reading this chapter, remember that my first book was called *Nothing in This Book Is True, But It's Exactly How Things Are.* Well, nothing in this chapter is true, but it's very much how things are. By that, I mean that the particular activities I cite may not be assigned to the right individuals or organizations or even the right layer of the planet's energetic field, but they are happening. The flow of information through the world is snarled and tangled by political agendas and propaganda, and I'm just as likely to be fooled as the next person. They may fool me as to who gets the blame, but they can't fool me as to what's going on. The vibration of light is pulling up the darkness from where it has operated, pretty much unchallenged, for millennia. That is over now. It is time for it to be transformed by the light.

THE FEDERAL RESERVE

As the saying goes, "just follow the money," so let's begin our discussion with a quote from Thomas Jefferson: "If the American people ever allow private banks to control the issue of their currency, first by inflation, then by deflation, the banks and corporations that will grow up around [the banks] will deprive the people of all property until their children wake up homeless on the continent their fathers conquered. The issuing power should be taken from the banks and restored to the people, to whom it properly belongs."[1]

In 1913 the Federal Reserve was passed by the U.S. Congress, thus handing over America's gold and silver reserves and total control of America's economy to the Rothschild banksters. The Federal Reserve is the central banking system of the United States; yet it is no more federal than Federal Express. "It is a private corporation that is secretly controlled by eight British-controlled shareholding banks."[2] Its purpose is to manipulate and control our economy, and our country. Once their central bank has been established, it loans money to the government at insane interest rates that can never be paid back, so that your country becomes the eternal slave to the Rothschild international system. Consider the most revealing statement by Baron M. A. Rothschild: "Give me control over a nation's currency, and I care not who makes its laws."[3]

I take him at his word. Why shouldn't I?

The Fed was set up after significant opposition from sources within the government, as well as some very wealthy and influential people. Three of the biggest opponents were Benjamin Guggenheim, from a very influential mining family; Isador Strauss, head of Macy's department store; and John Jacob Astor, businessman and inventor. The wealth of these three individuals totaled around $500 million, which would be around $11 billion today; they could not be bought.[4] All three perished on April 15, 1912, when the ship they were sailing on, the *Titanic,* sank to the bottom of the Atlantic. This was a very convenient turn of events for the international bankers. Any remaining opposition quickly vanished, and the Federal Reserve was unconstitutionally created.

Whether you consider this terrestrial sabotage, demonic sabotage, or divine synchronicity, it doesn't seem a chance accident.

According to the video *Liberty in the Balance,*

> The initial argument in favor of central control of the money supply hinged on the potential ability of a central bank to maintain stability. Yet since the Federal Reserve Act of 1913, we have had the stock market crash of 1929, the Great Depression, countless recessions and the debt has risen from one billion dollars to almost twenty-four trillion dollars.[5]

They don't maintain the economy; they don't keep everything equalized; they are there for control. They exist to put people into debt and enslave them. Their function is to control the country, which in turn, controls the people.

Abraham Lincoln and John F. Kennedy were the only two presidents who tried to break down the power of the elite by printing their own debt-free, interest-free money. What else do they have in common? Oh yes, they were both assassinated.

The parallels between Presidents Abraham Lincoln and John F. Kennedy and their assassinations suggest a complexly entangled system. The men were both first elected to Congress a century apart, in 1847 and 1947. They became President in 1860 and 1960, respectively. Lincoln's secretary was named Kennedy, and she warned him against going to the theater that night. Kennedy's secretary, Evelyn Lincoln, advised him against making a trip to Dallas. Lincoln sat in Box 7, Kennedy rode in Car 7. Something is going on here across Illuminati-scale centuries even if it involves different individuals.

THE GREAT RESET

The debt-based Western central banking system has a relatively short life expectancy—about fifty years or so. It will ultimately collapse under the weight of its own debt. The new system—if it is ever installed—will "solve" this problem. Never mind that it will be even more draconian and freedom restricting than the old system.

What we're seeing today is very similar to 1971. Back then, the United States was on the gold standard. Yet the plan behind the scenes was to take us off the gold standard and shift to the petrodollar system. They couldn't just do it; they had to find a way to explain it. They had to create a crisis, so they blamed it on speculators in the market who, they said, were going to hurt the economy. So, they said they were "temporarily" going to have to move the United States off the gold standard. But the central bankers had a different plan; they wanted to be able to print unlimited amounts of currency. They didn't want to be attached to the gold standard because that limited them. So, they quietly switched from the gold standard to the newly created petrodollar system. It was on August 15, 1971, that the dollar was severed from the last vestiges of the gold standard. Since that day, Peter Schiff tells us that the greenback has lost some 85 percent of its purchasing power. Gold, meanwhile, increased by well over 4,700 percent since that fateful day.[6]

The new plan is to move us off this now-failing fiat system and into the Great Reset. Instead of oil, the new system will be linked to rare earth minerals, batteries, and the Green New Deal. And they're going to create a central-bank digital currency over which they will have full control; they will be able to create as much currency as they want, simply by pushing a button.

In covering crucial political issues, the X22 Report podcast tells us that that Bill Gates, Jeff Bezos, and Michael Bloomberg are now teaming up to form a joint venture to drill for about $1.4 trillion worth of rare natural resources (cobalt, nickel, copper, and platinum) in

Greenland for electric car batteries for an anticipated hundreds of millions of new electric cars.[7]

THE GLOBAL PYRAMID

We need to understand that the pyramid is the basic structure of society, whether it is governments, banks, secret societies, corporations, medical or educational institutions. That means there are very few people at the top who are aware of the inner workings of their institution. The closer you get to the base, the less is known; this is called "compartmentalization." Most people are informed only on a need-to-know basis.

There is a global pyramid in which the peaks of all these individual pyramids—banking, business, medicine, media, etc.—fuse into one peak. It is speculated that there are as few as thirteen families at the top of the global pyramid, and percolating down from the top, through these seemingly unrelated systems, is the same basic policy that has been pushing the world increasingly closer to the one-world government, or "New World Order," where these elite have total control over the masses.

Presidents and prime ministers are portrayed by the mainstream media—the bullhorn of the Deep State—as though they are the ones in control of the decision-making process; yet they are mere puppets: they are controlled by the puppet masters who are pulling the strings from behind the scenes. How are they controlled? What I see is bribery and blackmail. Have you ever wondered how politicians—be they senators, congresspeople, or presidents—are able to accumulate great wealth while in office? It certainly is not from their salary, which for U.S. presidents is $400,000. For senators and members of the House of Representatives, it is a mere $174,000. Even if they assume office with the best of intentions, they very quickly learn how the game is played. If they cooperate, they will reap the rewards; if they resist, there will be consequences.

THE MOCKINGBIRD MEDIA

The mainstream media uses its power to steer the public into a desired direction through propaganda and disinformation. In the 1960s, the CIA set up Operation Mockingbird[8] with the sole purpose of manipulating the news media for propaganda purposes. Leading journalists were recruited for this purpose.

In the mid-1970s, then CIA director William Colby testified before the Church Committee. He said, "Operation Mockingbird was a fully implemented CIA program to spread disinformation throughout the American media. Over 400,000 CIA agents were active in the U.S. media to control what was reported through American television, newspapers and magazines."[9] In 1982 CIA director William Casey said, "We'll know our disinformation program is complete when everything the American public believes is false."[10]

You might be wondering with so many different media outlets, how could they all be in on it? The answer is there is only an illusion of choice, as Janet Ossebaard tells us in her *Fall of the Cabal* video series.[11] AT&T owns Time Warner, CNN, Warner Brothers, CW, TBS, TNT, DC, HBO, and the Cartoon Network. Walt Disney owns ABC, Fox, 21st Century Fox, Pixar, Marvel Studios, National Geographic, and ESPN. Comcast owns NBC, Sky, and Telemundo. Viacom owns Paramount Pictures, MTV, Nickelodeon, and Black Entertainment. CBS is owned by the same billionaire who owns Viacom. So, only four companies control it all! Maybe this collusion is interdimensional, and the mere secular ownership is how businesses naturally merge, but as my old friend Hermes said, "As above, so below." It may not be literal, but it is energetically correct.

THE VISIBLE TOP

Let's have a look at the visible top of the global pyramid, beginning with the Rothschild family. Researcher and author Janet Ossebaard of the Netherlands tells us in her *Fall of the Cabal* video series that they own all the central banks; they control the International Monetary Fund (IMF) and the World Health Organization (WHO). They have financed both sides in every war since the war against Napoleon. When you own both sides, you can't lose, and war is indeed a big-ticket item. They financed the Bolshevik Revolution, Hitler, and the Nazis. Their net worth is an estimated $500 billion.[12]

Then there are the Rockefellers, who made their initial fortune with oil. That led to massive influence in industry, politics, the banking system, and the pharmaceutical industry, per the same Janet Ossebaard,

They founded Harvard University, Yale Law School, Johns Hopkins University, the University of Chicago, and others. This has left a huge imprint on what should and should not be taught in our schools. They further expanded their tentacles of power into the medical world; they own Big Pharma, the National Academy of Medicine, the National Academy of Sciences, the American Cancer Society, the American Medical Association (AMA) and the U.S. Food and Drug Administration (FDA).[13]

Ossebaard also tells us that they further infiltrated the educational and medical systems through the Rockefeller Foundation, giving grants to specific research programs, such as the development of vaccines, which was further promoted by billionaire Bill Gates. The vaccines are approved by the FDA and promoted by doctors and the media, where the Rockefellers have placed their people at the highest levels. Of course, they don't tell you of the dangerous side effects such as miscarriage, autism, sterility, seizures, paralysis, and death.

Mercury is considered to be highly toxic, yet a typical 0.5 milliliter flu shot contains twenty-five micrograms of mercury—or 50,000 parts per billion. The EPA classifies a liquid with 200 parts per billion as a hazardous waste. The limit for drinking water is 2 parts per billion.[14]

All meaningful healing alternatives are pushed aside and demonized, leaving us with allopathic medicine and pharmaceuticals as the only acceptable means of treatment. Yet, all they do is treat symptoms and never the root cause of the problem. Never mind that the cure for all disease has existed in the inner circles for some time. Cancer patients, for example, are subjected to the most barbaric means of treatment imaginable, while the elite have access to true healing methods.

The aristos of the Deep State are exceedingly powerful and influential in many ways; yet they are not even the most powerful. They are subservient to the thirteen families above them.

THREE CORPORATIONS RUN
THE WORLD

In politics, nothing happens by accident; if it happens, you can bet it was planned that way.

FRANKLIN D. ROOSEVELT

There are three cities that are actually separate entities within their respective countries; they have their own laws and their own rules, and they come under no national authority. They pay no taxes; they have their own police force and even possess their own flags of independence. The three cities are actually corporations: they are the City of London, the District of Columbia, and the Vatican. The City of London is the financial center, the District of Columbia is the military center, and the Vatican is the spiritual center.

Shenali D. Waduge posted an article in 2014 called "Three Corporations Run the World: City of London, Washington DC and Vatican City." In this article, she asserts that together they control politicians, the courts, educational institutions, food supply, natural resources, foreign policies, economies, media, and the money flow of most nations as well as 80 percent of the entire world's wealth. Their ultimate aim is to build a totalitarian rule on a global scale where people will be divided into rulers and the ruled after they have depopulated the world to "more desirable levels."[15] What we need to understand is that the world does not work according to what we have been led to believe. We are drowning in misinformation.

Regarding the lies and misinformation, William Tompkins put it this way:

> We have to get to the point that we can view everything around us in a different manner, because literally everything that we have been knowledgeable of is incorrect. Out-and-out lies, specifically to control us, give us the wrong information, and be able to monitor us and control us. And this goes all the way back through history. It's not just that the power groups are lying to us about our real history. It's mathematics, it's food, it's everything.[16]

CITY OF LONDON

The Waduge article points out that the City of London houses the following:

- Rothschild-controlled Bank of England
- Lloyds of London
- The London Stock Exchange
- All British banks
- The Branch offices of 384 foreign banks
- 70 U.S. banks
- Fleet Street's newspaper and publishing monopolies
- Headquarters for worldwide Freemasonry
- Headquarters for the worldwide money cartel known as "THE CROWN"[17]

According to Shenali Waduge, the City of London is controlled by the Bank of England, a private corporation owned by the Rothschild family after Nathan Rothschild crashed the English stock market in 1812 and took control of the Bank of England.

Waduge also tells us that the City of London directly and indirectly controls all multinational and transnational banks, corporations, judicial systems, the IMF, World Bank, Vatican Bank, European Central Bank, United States Federal Reserve, the Bank for International Settlements in Switzerland (which is also British-controlled and oversees all of the reserve banks around the world including our own), the European Union, and the United Nations.

WASHINGTON, D.C.
(DISTRICT OF COLUMBIA)

Shenali Waduge takes the position that Washington, D.C., is not part of the United States. The District of Columbia is located on ten square miles of land; D.C. has its own flag and its own independent constitution, which has nothing to do with the American Constitution. The Act of 1871 passed by Congress created a separate corporation known as The United States and corporate government for the District of Columbia. Thus, D.C. acts as a corporation through this act. The flag of Washington's District of Columbia has three red stars (the three stars denoting D.C., Vatican City, and City of London).

VATICAN CITY

Vatican City is not part of Italy or Rome. The Vatican is the last true remnant of the Roman Empire. Its wealth includes investments with the Rothschilds in Britain, France, and the United States, and with oil and weapons corporations as well. The Vatican's billions are said to be in the Rothschild-controlled Bank of England and U.S. Federal Reserve Bank. The money possessed by the Vatican is more than many banks, corporations, and even some governments.

In summation, the biggest Luciferian force on Earth was the Roman

Empire, which then became the British Empire. The Romans began migrating to Britain in 55 BCE with Julius Caesar. Rome was already expanding into Great Britain around the turn of the millennium; they simply rebranded and changed the facade. Out of that came the City of London, Vatican City, and Washington, D.C., as the three places where each has an obelisk and is a city within a country, with their own laws and their own rules.

THE FABIAN SOCIETY

Together the three cities have various societies and groups under their wing so that no one contests their global plan. And those that do, well, all the assassinations show what happens to them.

The Fabian Society is one such entity; it was established in 1887. It is, as Shenali Waduge points out, a mixture of fascism, Nazism, Marxism, and communism. The Fabian Society is accredited with creating Communist China, fascism in Italy and Germany, and socialism globally as well. The communist takeover of Russia too is said to be the work of the British Fabian Society, financed by the City of London banking families.

Shenali Waduge also tells us that when we take a closer look at entities like the Bank of International Settlements (BIS), International Monetary Fund (IMF), Club of Rome, the Committee of 300, the Central "Intelligence" Agency (CIA), the Council on Foreign Relations, the Trilateral Commission, the Bilderberg Group, the Federal Reserve System, the Internal Revenue Service, Goldman Sachs, Israel and the Israeli lobby, the Vatican, the City of London, Brussels, the United Nations, the Israeli Mossad, and the Associated Press (AP) will reveal that they are all part of the Fabian Society, which also controls the European Union.

BACK TO THE BEGINNING

The December 27, 2009, issue of *Discover* magazine posted an article called "What Happened to the Hominids Who May Have Been

Smarter Than Us?" It describes how in the autumn of 1913, elongated skulls were found by two farmers while digging a drainage ditch in Boskop, South Africa. The article claims that their mean brain size of these "Boskop skulls" was 1,750 cc, and that the average IQ was 149. This is a score that would be labeled at the genius level.[18]

Elongated skulls have been found all over the planet; David Wilcock, in the documentary *Above Majestic,* tells us that they have been found in Peru, as well as in Bolivia. In *Nothing in This Book Is True,* I gave the details of the elongated skulls of Akhenaten, his wife Nefertiti, and their daughters. According to the Daily Mail news website, an elongated skull, dating back 1,650 years, was found in one the tombs of the elite in France; they have also been discovered in other countries in Europe, and a different strain has been discovered in North and South America. There are reports that the Mongolian conquerors, or the Huns, had them also. Mark Laplume is an artist and independent researcher who tells of these skulls being found in Cuzco, Peru; Tiwanaku, Bolivia; Paracas, Peru; Romania; Bulgaria; and Ukraine.[19]

Corey Goode tells us in *The Cosmic Secret* that the pre-Adamite race, as he calls them, were two distinct but similar civilizations that developed on Maldek and Mars; both had elongated skulls. They were genetically related, though they had slightly different features. One of the two types had a wider skull; the other type had a more conical, pointy skull, but both were elongated.[20]

There were royal families from both groups that were in competition with each other, and at war. He said they were very efficient at genetics and brought that skill to Earth. When they arrived, they began a mass-cloning program to spread themselves across the Earth. They cloned themselves into the indigenous DNA of Earth, and those clones became the rulers and the leaders of various populations. Goode said once they crash-landed on Earth 52,000 years ago, they quickly made a treaty with each other; even though at war, they decided to coexist on Earth. One lineage took what is now Africa and Europe; the other lineage took North and South America and the eastern half of Asia.

David Wilcock, also in *The Cosmic Secret,* told of the slight varia-
tions in the pyramid architecture that occurred in the aftermath of
this treaty. Egypt and Africa have smooth walls; in Mesoamerica there
are step pyramids. And there are step pyramids in Cambodia that
look exactly like the ones in Mesoamerica. His conclusion is that this
is a unified culture and not two separate societies, even though they
are separated by the Pacific Ocean. He further asserts that the Cabal
actually does believe that they are the remnants of these people with
the elongated skulls, they believe that they are the descendants of the
Rothschilds and the Rockefeller faction.

MEDICAL TYRANNY

California has a huge homeless population—in excess of 150,000.[21]
We know that good hygiene is crucial to overall health and wellness
because it helps lower the risk for disease, illness, and medical conditions caused by the effects of poor hygiene. I think we can reasonably
assume that poor hygiene is the norm in the homeless community. It
is also fair to conclude that many of them have compromised immune
systems, and face masks have not been worn on a regular basis—if at
all. Yet, we've been told ever since March 2020, that there is a global
pandemic, that we must lockdown our economies, stay inside, wear a
mask, social distance and wash our hands regularly. If the great global
COVID-19 pandemic is as bad as we've been told, many of the homeless
people would be lying dead in the streets, and the lap dog media would
be all over it. This is clearly not the case.

In an article called "Proof That the Pandemic Was Planned and
with Purpose," Dr. James Fetzer refers to a shocking statement made
by 500 medical doctors in Germany. "The Corona Panic is a play. It's a
scam. A swindle. It's high time we understood that we're in the midst of
a global crime." Similar sentiments were voiced by 600 medical doctors
from Spain. "Covid-19 is a false pandemic created for political purposes.
This is a world dictatorship with a sanitary excuse."[22]

The great global COVID-19 pandemic was created from a faulty PCR test, false statistics from the tests, and a constant supply of fear from the media. The creator of the Polymerase Chain Reaction (PCR) technology, Kary Mullis, regarded the PCR as inappropriate to detect a viral infection.[23]

When you look at the CDC and FDA documentation, you find out some significant information about the PCR tests. An FDA document admits that the CDC and FDA conspired to fabricate a COVID-19 testing protocol. They used human cells combined with common cold virus fragments because they had no physical samples of the SARS COVID virus. They had no physical material to use for collaboration and confirmation. The test has zero scientific basis in physical reality; all the PCR analysis based on this protocol is completely fraudulent. They're flagging people as positive for COVID when they merely possess tiny quantities of RNA fragments from other Coronavirus strains circulating in the blood.

There's a document on the FDA website called "CDC Novel Coronavirus (2019-nCoV) Real-time RT-PCR Diagnostic Panel." Here is the revealing part:

> Since no quantified isolates of the 2019-nCoV were available for CDC use at the time the test was developed and this study conducted, assays designed for detection of the 2019-nCoV RNA were tested with characterized stocks of in vitro transcribed full length RNA (N gene N bank; accession: MN908047.2) of known titer (RNA copies/uL) spiked into a diluent consisting of a suspension of human A549 cells and viral transport medium (VTM) to mimic clinical specimen.[24]

In other words, they had no COVID virus from which to conduct their test, so they mixed up a cocktail of human cells and RNA fragments from common cold viruses, then called it "COVID." The gene-based sequence referred to is a simple digital library definition that was labeled

"COVID," but had no supporting reference materials in physical reality either. That's because no doctors or researchers had isolated COVID from any infected symptomatic patient. As a result, no laboratory instruments could be calibrated against actual COVID, and the tests simply relied on digital libraries pushed out by the CDC and the WHO using COVID as the label. The PCR tests then looked for these genetic sequences obtained from the fabricated digital libraries, meaning the entire scheme was fake science not based in logic, or in physical reality.

If you look into the antics of Big Tech, Big Pharma and the mainstream media they are all actually burying themselves. Think about what they've covered up; they changed the definition of a vaccine, because what they have produced is not actually a vaccine, they hid the cures—Ivermectin and hydroxychloroquine (HCQ)—from the world, and they told us there is no cure.

So why was this pandemic created in the first place? The main reason as I see it is simply to control the masses through a steady diet of fear porn. The greatest fear of the Cabal is an awakened public. With that said, there is a great global awakening, and even though they are trying to stall it for as long as possible, their tactics are having the opposite effect. Truth and revolution are in the air. With the unveiling of so many known health hazards linked directly to Big Pharma's COVID-19 vaccine rollout, the international Cabal is now on the defensive.

THROUGH THE LOOKING GLASS

I'd like to bring your attention to the 2012 testimony of Bill Wood. Wood is an ex-Navy Seal (part of Seal Team Nine) who was recognized by the military for his gifts in cognitive reasoning, and for the psychic potential that he showed. Because of this, he was selected for training to enhance his psychic abilities at places like Area 51 and later was employed to assist with classified programs, one of them being Project Looking Glass.

If you are not familiar with Looking Glass, I will simply say it is a technology that enables one to view future timeline realities with the aid of supercomputers to gauge the probability of possible outcomes. Originally, this knowledge of time manipulation came from Nikola Tesla, and then later from the reverse engineering of ET spacecraft that had come into the possession of the government. Essentially, this technology uses the forces of electromagnetism to bend gravity, space, and time to "see past" the curvature of the event horizon.

One of Bill Wood's tasks, back in the late 1990s, was to "troubleshoot" a problem that the higher-ups were having (known as the 2012 problem). As Wood puts it:

> Some very smart people figured out that something big was coming up. Something that made it so all the possibilities of all the future scenarios of any choice, any possibility, that was fed in and observed through the Looking Glass inevitably ended up in the same future. And no decision and no possibility changed past a certain point. That's the big secret."[25]

Wood goes on to reveal that a "bottlenecking" or "convergence of timelines" occurred on December 21, 2012, such that "all possible timelines lead to the same basic history in the future. The elites of the game figured out the end of the game. Nothing could be manipulated beyond that point."[26] As of now, we have all been on a timeline in which the same inevitable outcome will unfold. And the elites of the world—the "bad guys," you could say—that have all the information in regard to Looking Glass, saw that no matter what they did to change things or control the reactions of humanity, it would always create the opposite effect and the results remained the same.

> Basically, what we're experiencing right now is two master chess players sitting at the board and one of them looks down at the board and sees that he's in checkmate in seven moves. And he looks across

at his opponent and he knows that his opponent sees it too. So, at this point the loser can only prolong the game. Both players know the game is over. We as a race, if we can understand that the game is over—that based on the rules of the game, the bad guys have already lost, the good guys have already won. Yes, there are moves on the table, but those moves are being forced by the player that is going to win. . . .

If I had to give it a name, I would say it is the awakening process. It's an evolution of consciousness that cannot, will not, and no matter what decisions or possibilities are injected into the equation, eventually, it all results down to us all learning the truth, and becoming aware of this massive dam of lies that has been built to keep us from knowing massive volumes of information. . . . Now at first, I thought it [the event] was end of the world. But now, I see it is the end of their world.[27]

Wood claims that this awakening process is part of an Ascension Timeline more commonly referred to by the elite as "Timeline 1." This is the timeline that the elite didn't like talking about, as they consider it a problem that needs to be fixed. The preferred "Timeline 2" that the elite are trying to manifest results in some sort of global catastrophe in which the majority of survivors are driven underground, leaving only a small population on the surface to fend for themselves.

Though Wood did his due diligence and investigated this problem of the timelines to the best of his psychic/intuitive abilities, in the end, all he could offer to his superiors was reinforcement of what Looking Glass and the computers were already saying. The timelines will contract to some inevitable outcome that the Cabal didn't like talking about.

Despite knowing this inevitability, the elite were still hedging their bets and continuing to build underground cities and trying to foment nuclear wars and natural disasters to kill off the vast majority of the population. Why persist in doing this when all the data says otherwise?

Wood had a simple answer: "Because they are insane. And beyond being insane, they have literally deluded themselves into believing that they can somehow manage to get away with what they are trying to get away with. There is a distinct lack of reality in that way of thinking."[28]

So, step back and take in the big picture. I am asking you not only to prepare yourself and practice for you own ascension and transformation into a new realm of spirit and soul. I am asking you to ride the ascension wave of the entire Earth—past, present, and future. In so doing, your own wave meets that of the planet, and together you pass through a double slit and end up in a universe of light and love while the aristos and Illuminati pass into the darkness they are creating, and they don't even know it.

PART 2
Awakening in the Illusion

We live in a time that can be deeply moving, but first, you must be listening with your heart. When you are, you can begin to find a common language that is beyond right and wrong, good and evil.

Your Higher Self is still within you, and it functions well beyond the capabilities of your mind. Reconnecting with this severed aspect of ourselves gives us access to our unlimited potential—where we have reliable access to an infinite supply of inner peace, unconditional love, joy, creative expression, and wisdom. This is the energy of Divine Creator, it is the energy of Source. In this part, I will give the details of the personal transformation that we must make if we are to survive and thrive, so we can catch the wave into higher consciousness in a way that enables Mother Earth to reach critical mass and become lit from within.

8

When We Were One

The *Law of One* tells us the Universe originated from one infinite consciousness and that one infinite consciousness wanted to experience itself, because in its unity it was actually bored. And it had this terrifying feeling of loneliness.

David Wilcock, in his Ascension Mystery School, presented the basic cosmology of the *Law of One,* which he said is the operating system that everything comes from. He said there is only identity in the Universe; in other words, consciousness is all there is.[1] And the entire Universe started as intelligent infinity, which doesn't really have any type of source point. Then intelligent infinity became aware and created intelligent energy, which they also call Logos or love. So, the term *Logos* is a word for God.

Then the *Law of One* talks about a Universal Logos, which would be the Universal Oneness. They talk about a galactic Logos, which is the mind of an entire galaxy where it designs existence for beings on its planets. They talk about a solar Logos; in other words, the Sun in our solar system and all other stars are perfect holograms of the Universal Mind, they are actually eighth density. So the *Law of One* says the embodiment of the Creator is in our solar system, the Sun is a hologram of the One Infinite Creator. And then they say that a planet is a sub-Logos, meaning that it is a secondary aspect of the One Infinite Creator, but still a hologram of the whole. And then you have the person, the human being, which they call a sub-sub-Logos. So, a human being is a fully functioning hologram of the One Infinite Creator. We could recreate the entire Universe from one person.

When we first created the Universe, stars were created, and those stars created planets. Those planets had beings on them that were in many cases human or humanlike, because apparently a good part of the Universe has humanlike beings on the planets. In the early days of the Universe, for every planet that had human beings on it, the people did not have what is called a veiling. There was nothing separating their mind from the Cosmic Mind.

That meant that everybody was fully aware that they were an embodiment of the Creator. They were aware that they, as human beings, were fully plugged into the universal awareness with full cosmic consciousness, full capability, full magical power. Wouldn't that be amazing? The answer is absolutely not. The *Law of One* tells us that it was a disaster. Consider the following quote from the *Law of One*:

> It is our perception that such conditions created the situation of a most pallid experiential nexus in which lessons were garnered with the relative speed of the turtle to the cheetah. . . .
>
> There is infinite diversity in societies under any circumstances. There were many highly technologically advanced societies which grew due to the ease of producing any desired result when one dwells within what might be seen to be a state of constant potential inspiration. That which even the most highly sophisticated, in your terms, societal structure lacked, given the non-complex nature of its entities, was what you might call will or, to use a more plebeian term, gusto, or élan vital.[2]

Thus it seems that people, when given everything, acted entitled and were bored. They had no cares in the world. They had no responsibility; nobody was excited about anything. The whole curriculum of the universe is for us to be inspired to move and grow and change. Yet, back in the day, there was nothing to strive for; there was no creativity, no art, no music. Everybody was just lying around blissed out. The *Law of One* points out "the tendency of those who are divinely happy, as you call this distortion, to have little urge to alter or better their condition."[3]

Nobody was ascending, nobody was evolving and growing. They spent hundreds of thousands of years reincarnating in absolute boredom. They lacked sufficient polarization for "graduation." The *Law of One* definition of *polarization* is to "move toward a pole; in the context of spiritual evolution, move either toward service to others (positive) or service to self (negative)."[4] The key here is movement toward service to others, to "radiate the realization of oneness with the creator within yourself."[5] So, if you are awakening, and if you start helping people and teaching people, you are radiating from the self the realization of oneness with the Creator. And that is your mission; that is your destiny, it is your ticket to fourth density.

In regard to the delay in this polarization, the *Law of One* explained:

Let us continue the metaphor of the schooling but consider the scholar as being an entity in your younger years of the schooling process. The entity is fed, clothed, and protected regardless of whether or not the schoolwork is accomplished. Therefore, the entity does not do the homework but rather enjoys playtime, mealtime, and vacation. It is not until there is a reason to wish to excel that most entities will attempt to excel. . . .

Prior to the veiling process the measurement would be that of an entity walking up a set of your stairs, each of which was imbued with a certain quality of light. The stair upon which an entity stopped would be either third-density light or fourth-density light. Between the two stairs lies the threshold. To cross that threshold is difficult. There is resistance at the edge, shall we say, of each density. The faculty of faith or will needs to be understood, nourished, and developed in order to have an entity which seeks past the boundary of third density. Those entities which do not do their homework, be they ever so amiable, shall not cross. It was this situation which faced the Logoi prior to the veiling process being introduced into the experiential continuum of third density.[6]

THE VEILING

The Universe was not working, so in the attempt to solve this huge problem, a veiling was created between the conscious and the superconscious mind. We separated ourselves from the awareness that we are consciousness, that we are disembodied no-form awareness having a human experience, and we fall into the belief that our individual identity is who we are. This meant that there was almost no awareness whatsoever that there is a higher force, a higher power within us.

There is a quote attributed to a Central American shaman that pretty well sums it up. "We are perceivers, we are awareness; we are not objects; we have no solidity. We are boundless. . . . We forget this and thus we entrap the totality of ourselves in a vicious circle from which we rarely emerge in our lifetime."

So, we get trapped in the illusion. The illusion is that you are a separate self, with a separate body from others, that you are not one with everyone else. You're stuck in what the Hindus and the Buddhists call maya. The maya delusion is the belief that you are an individual, the belief that you are not the Universe, and then living your life as if that were true.

Then we get to play what Alan Watts called the game of hide-and-seek. This is where God pretends he is not himself, and hides himself in the form of you and me. When he does this, he does it so well that it takes him a long time to find himself. But that's the whole point; if he found himself too quickly, it would spoil the fun of the game. "That is why it is so difficult for you and me to find out that we are God in disguise, pretending not to be himself. But when the game has gone on long enough, all of us will wake up, stop pretending, and realize that we are all one single Self—the God who is all that there is, and lives forever and ever."[7]

As strange as it might seem, this veiling actually worked. People started evolving; they started growing. They discovered inspiration and creativity; as a result, music, art, dance, and many other good things appeared. People also started to ascend.

NEGATIVITY APPEARS

The downside is that along with the veiling came the possibility of evil, which had never existed before. If a being doesn't realize what it really is, it has the opportunity to be "confused." In this illusory state of separation, it has the opportunity to make self-serving nega-tive choices at the expense of others—it then begins to violate the free will of others. This then, creates karma that takes multiple lifetimes to work off.

This is sad on one level, but the negativity actually causes inspira-tion and growth. Let's take a moment to delve into this, and let's begin with a quote from the *Law of One:*

> Let us illustrate by observing the relative harmony and unchanging quality of existence in one of your, as you call it, primitive tribes. The entities have the concepts of lawful and taboo, but the law is inexorable and all events occur as predestined. There is no concept of right and wrong, good or bad. It is a culture in monochrome. In this context you may see the one you call Lucifer as the true light-bringer in that the knowledge of good and evil both precipitated the mind/body/spirits of this Logos from the Edenic conditions of con-stant contentment but also provided the impetus to move, to work and to learn.[8]

We have all been there at one time in our past; every culture has its primitive roots. And while there's much to be said for these primitive cultures—they lived in harmony with their environment—it's also true that many of them were highly patriarchal, and women had very precise roles. The tribal chief and elders were the law, and to disobey them came with severe consequences. This led to stagnation where there was no growth. The people were not free; they were locked into societal roles. And then the Romans, or later, the British Empire came along and invaded them. This caused movement and growth where the people were forced to migrate and change. They were forced to learn a new language, to learn to read and write, and to use their creativity and imagination. They began to evolve and grow; this eventually leads to an awakening of consciousness.

THE DARK NIGHT OF THE SOUL

We are in the midst of a great awakening; this is a positive thing that's happening on Earth. With that said, I'm well aware that it doesn't really look that way right now. We as a planetary species are currently going through a collective dark night of the soul. Many people are struggling right now; emotions are spiraling, there's just so much uncertainty in the air, and it's bringing up deeply buried wounds and patterns for many. And as the realization sets in that we still have a long way to go in navigating our way through all this, it can start feeling very heavy!

People are experiencing challenges and hardships like never before; many have lost their businesses as a result of the lockdowns. We are living with an unprecedented degree of authoritarian control that is taking the form of medical tyranny and eliminating our freedom of assembly. With their livelihoods at stake, clearly unconstitutional vaccine mandates are forcing many people to take the jab whether they want it or not, and many are revolting against this.

The *Law of One* talks about the fact that evil and negativity, and the times we're in, have value; it's a sacred thing, it's part of the design. The Universe has designed this Earth to appear as though the train is falling off the tracks, going off the rails. This is the collective dark night of the soul that we're all experiencing; it is a most challenging time; yet, it is also essential. It strips away all that no longer serves; it is the necessary cleansing that must precede the ascension process.

And since this is happening on a global level, this collective dark night of the soul precedes a rebirth and new beginning for humanity. And though this cleansing is absolutely necessary, it doesn't mean that these are by any means "easy" waters to navigate.

The Cabal does everything it can to keep us in fear, where we can be completely controlled. This can be clearly seen with the continual diet of fear porn that is being dished out by the lapdog media with regard to a pandemic that was created by a faulty PCR test and kept firmly in place with the constant barrage of fear and fake science.

When you and I are fearful, we go into "fight-or-flight" mode; we are lodged in our reptilian brain where we have few of our normal resources available to us. To help bring this home, just consider for a moment a situation that perhaps you've experienced. Suppose you have an important meeting and you're running behind schedule, and you can't find your car keys. You frantically search in the usual places to no avail. As your frustration grows and it appears that you will be late, you only dig your hole deeper because you are stuck in fight-or-flight—you are dancing in your reptilian brain. It's only when you compose yourself enough that reasoning and presence returns that, interestingly enough, your keys magically appear.

Another favorite tactic of the Cabal is to keep us divided, to drive a wedge between us, usually with emotional issues that keep us quarreling among ourselves. Straight out of their divide-and-rule playbook is the whole issue of pushing vaccine mandates on us. This has the added benefit of keeping the fear issue alive as well. The whole idea of the vaccinated population being fearful that the unvaccinated will infect them is absurd on its face. Traditionally, getting vaccinated means you are free from any fear of getting polio or measles or whatever, and there is no way the unvaccinated can affect you. But then again, the steady diet of lies and fear keeps people stuck in their reptilian brain.

The global elitists are psychopaths; that means that they have a grandiose sense of self-worth, they have no empathy, they show no remorse, and they will do their best to crush you if you stand up to them. The clear message is to shut up and obey.

THE FALL OF THE CABAL

The *Law of One* talks about the fact that evil and negativity has value; it's a sacred thing, it's part of the design. Just consider for a moment, if what I said about the Cabal is true—and the evidence is voluminous—they are the scum of the Earth on one level. But at the same time, the Illuminati's sick religion and desire to control the planet and kill billions of people creates a mass awakening. It creates an incentive for us to wake up and grow.

If you look into your own life, you may well find that it was times of great turmoil that prompted you to grow and evolve in ways that contributed to your greater good. That was certainly true for me; it took a debilitating low-back injury to move me enough to find a way to heal myself. It is totally clear to me that what at the time seemed like the worst thing that ever happened to me was, indeed, the best thing that ever happened to me. It totally transformed my life. There's nothing that makes you more spiritually empowered than being in a very difficult situation and being forced out of your comfort zone.

The *Law of One* says the Luciferian force is that which invades and violates free will, and this is allowed to happen. This is the by-product of the veiling; it's allowed to invade free will, because in so doing, it creates movement. It creates movement and growth.

Movement means a movement of consciousness away from feeling happy, which is a very useful thing. You will keep getting movement until nothing moves you away from being happy and being in oneness.

The ideal ascended being is a person who has integrated experiences that were previously upsetting; and once an experience has integrated, it doesn't repeat anymore. You therefore remain calm, centered, and peaceful in the face of what had previously triggered you.

> The primary veiling was of such significance that it may be seen to be analogous to the mantling of the Earth over all the jewels within the Earth's crust; whereas previously all facets of the Creator were consciously known. After the veiling, almost no facets of the Creator were known to the mind. Almost all was buried beneath the veil.[9]

The Earth has many caverns in its interior, and apparently there are many gorgeous crystals in those deep underground caves. They're talking here about how the primary veiling is so important because it created the opportunity for the Luciferian force to invade free will and create movement and growth. It's like the idea of the jewels in the Earth's crust, with the Earth's mantle forming over that. So, they're talking about the idea that the veil is like the veil over the Earth where there are crystals inside.

The *Law of One* continues, "Perhaps the most important and significant function that occurred due to the veiling of the mind from itself is not in itself a function of mind but rather is a product of the potential created by this veiling. This is the faculty of will or pure desire."[10] Before the veiling, we didn't have will or desire. We were not striving to better ourselves; we didn't really want anything. Will and desire are the idea of projecting your internal energy out into the world. It's the idea of motivation, willpower, and having the drive and the desire to succeed. Before the veiling, we didn't have this; we were stagnating.

The dark forces do everything they can to keep us stuck in fear and ignorance so we don't evolve. The forces of light do everything they can to cause rapid movement and growth. From the higher perspective of unity, these apparent opposing forces are actually working together as timing agents. This opposition causes consciousness to move upward at exactly the right pace. In the birth of a human child, for example, nine months is the proper gestation time, not three months or fifteen months. The forces of polarity cause the child to be born at exactly the right time.

So given where we are, we need to see good and evil and be aware of it, but we also need to recognize that the presence of the Creator is in every situation, and there is a reason for everything that happens. We need to see that everything is whole and complete and perfect, and that there is nothing wrong no matter how bad or how good it may seem. We need to see that life engenders a deep conscious aspect that is everywhere.

The *Law of One* puts it this way: "there is no disharmony, no imperfection; that all is complete and whole and perfect."[11] It is well to consider though, that within the illusion, there is right and wrong. We are bound by what they call the first distortion, which is the law of free will. Within the illusion if you infringe upon yourself in the form of another being, then you must experience the full payback of it, of what you did to that person in your own life. That's called karma.

The Cabal "out there" is an outward reflection of our own internal unresolved emotional issues that manifest as physical and emotional abuse toward others. As we wake up and resolve our inner strife, we get to the point where we no longer need that external catalyst. We are reaching that point; there is a great awakening—both on an internal and external level.

So, the negative is allowed to exist because it creates movement and growth. But once we've gotten what we need out of it, we are no longer going to be moved by negativity. We get to a point where we don't need to have our free will violated anymore.

It is important to keep in mind that the global elite are not really in control; they are, in fact, acting out of desperation. They are no longer able to lurk unseen behind the curtain; the infusion of higher dimensional energy is forcing them out in the open to show their hand.

This is all in accordance with the divine plan; you can't just tell the people—they have to be shown just how evil and corrupt they really are. They must be shown how corrupt our politicians, elections, judges, medical systems, Big Tech, and Big Pharma really are. Then the greatest fear of these Deep Staters will be realized: an awakened public acting in unison. Just as Bill Wood has suggested, they have already lost; all they can do is prolong the game and hope the other side makes a fatal mistake. The Cabal is exposing itself and, therefore, it is defeating itself. Checkmate!

9

The Holographic Universe

Reality is an illusion, albeit a persistent one.

ALBERT EINSTEIN

This reality, in terms of its physicality, is an illusion. There is no physicality; there is no "out there." This is so even though it appears that you have a physical body, and it appears that you have other people around you, and they have a different physical body than yours. In truth, everything you are looking at "out there" is going on in your brain. The late, great comedian Bill Hicks put it this way, "All matter is merely energy condensed to a slow vibration. We are all one consciousness experiencing itself subjectively. There's no such thing as death, life is only a dream, and we are the imagination of ourselves."[1]

Now with this being said, it is quite true that it runs counter to most everything we think we know. After all, we have been steered into a viewpoint of this reality in a multitude of ways, where we think that matter is made of hard particles and everything "out there" is solid and real because we're in a matter-based materialistic viewpoint. This however, is simply not true, and I will do my best to unpack it for you.

The base foundation of this illusory reality is waveform, which is vibrating energy, it is light. Within waveform, huge amounts of information can be stored, and that's what the base information construct of this reality is—it's information in waveform. What happens is the waveform information construct is decoded through the body into the world that we think we are experiencing, but it's all going on in your head.

We decode vibrational information into electrical information that is sent to the brain, and the brain decodes that into the world that we think we are experiencing. The five senses change this decoded information into holographic information. From the movie *The Matrix,* in response to Neo saying, "This isn't real?," Morpheus responded, "What is real? How do you define 'real'? If you're talking about what you can feel, what you can smell, taste, and see, then 'real' is simply electrical signals interpreted by your brain."[2]

The five senses are a decoding system; the most obvious one is sound—a vibration comes to the ear and sends a message to the brain, and the brain hears the sound. There is no "sound" until we have decoded it as such; until then sound is just a vibration. With sight, there are electrical signals, digital on/off pulses, going to your brain from your eyes.

It's the same with taste, electrical signals are sent to the brain that are decoded. This is how a stage hypnotist can get someone to eat a potato and taste an apple. You implant the belief that it's an apple, and the electrical signal is read as such.

It's even so with movement, there is no movement until we've decoded that movement. In every case, the brain is taking pure electrical information, it's taking pure on/off electrical signals, and it's creating everything that you see that you interpret as physical reality.

It's all an illusion!

The *Law of One* totally supports this very different way of looking at reality; it is telling us that the Universe is a conscious identity, and that consciousness is all there is. They say that the Universe itself is a dream, it's an illusion, it's not real, it's not a tangible reality. The only thing that's actually real is the identity of the Creator, which is your ultimate essence; you are the Creator. Your identity created this Universe, and nothing else really exists. So, the whole Universe is just a thought construct. "All things, all of life, all the creation is part of one original thought"; there's literally nothing else to it.

The following came from the very first transmission in session one:

> We have watched your group. We have been called to your group, for you have a need for the diversity of experiences in channeling which go with a more intensive, or as you might call it, advanced approach to the system of studying the patterns of the illusions of your body, your mind, and your spirit, which you call seeking the truth. . . . The Confederation of Planets in the Service of the Infinite Creator has only one important statement. That statement, my friends, as you know, is in which all things, all of life, all of the creation is part of one original thought. . . . You are not part of a material universe. You are part of a thought. You are dancing in a ballroom in which there is no material. You are dancing thoughts. You move your body, your mind, and your spirit in somewhat eccentric patterns for you have not completely grasped the concept that you are part of the original thought.[3]

This is saying your mind, your spirit, and your body are all an illusion. The illusion is that you think you are your body and then what happens? You become body conscious. Yet, the only thing that really exists is the One Infinite Creator, which is pure awareness. We are not looking at this Universe as an illusion. We are not looking at this as if nothing is really there; we are caught up in the illusion, we think it's real, and we have not completely grasped the concept that we are part of the original thought. We don't fully understand that our thoughts create this reality.

Therefore, within the illusion, we get trapped into a sequence of reincarnation, which takes place over eons. So, your soul is in fact having to go through many lifetimes of incarnations that can last for as many as three 25,920-year cycles.

Yes, God can play the game of hide-and-seek, in which she hides herself in the form of you and me, for a very long time. The whole idea of the game is to keep it interesting, and the best way to do that is to forget that you did it. However, at some point you have to decide for yourself, just how long do you want to stay enthralled and entranced by the illusion. At some point you need to see that your body is an illusion, that it's not real, your ego is not real, your personality, your identity is not real. At some point, as you begin to shed your false persona, you will begin thinking not in terms of my will, but thy will. What does the Creator in me want for this Universe? What does the Creator in me want for this world? And when you get to that point, you're going to start meditating on the greater good. What can I do with my life that will reach the greatest number of people for the greatest good?

There is great incentive now for us to wake up and remember that we are the One Infinite Creator in disguise. There is a huge pot of gold at the end of this rainbow; it is called ascension into fourth density. In this new world, we will be living in a reality that is hundreds of times more harmonious than even our best moments here in third density. Just think about that for a moment: What would your life be like if you were a hundred times happier, and a hundred times more joyful, loving, and inspired than you are now, even in the best of times?

As we continue to move away from the erroneous idea that matter is made of little particles, we can embrace the *Law of One* model that says intelligent infinity creates intelligent energy, and matter is made of intelligent energy; that intelligent energy has a series of vortex rotations off one photon, so the entire Universe is actually one photon. All other parts of the Universe are slightly distorted mirror reflections, or fractals of the one original photon. And everything else is made from atoms that are made of these fractals of the original photon.

The atoms are made of photons, which are the base units of light and all other forms of electromagnetic radiation; they carry massive amounts of information. The atoms then make what we think of as the visible reality of the Universe; but it's all actually a holographic reflection of one photon. So, the *Law of One* says the Universe is made out of light.

I will most certainly agree that the world looks solid, but it can't be because this reality is made up of atoms, and as quantum physics has shown, atoms have no solidity. The reason the world appears to have solidity is because the information in the waveform base-state construct is decoded into apparent solidity. Again, it's just the way we decode reality that gives it form.

The reason it appears solid is we live in a holographic universe, where all parts of the Universe are slightly distorted mirror reflections, or fractals of the one original photon. Holograms appear to be three-dimensional, but they are not, it's just the illusion of the way they are made. Holograms are made by using a single laser beam. The beam is then split into two beams by a special lens, resulting in two laser beams that are exactly the same. One of those beams goes across the object they want to photograph. The other beam goes directly onto a photographic plate. The beam that passes across the object goes onto that plate, and they collide, they create a waveform (it is called an interference pattern). When you fire a laser at it, a very solid three-dimensional looking image comes up.

This is how we create our reality—a holographic version of the waveform-information construct in our heads. Everything "out there" is but a holographic projection of our consciousness!

Every part of a hologram is a smaller version of the whole, if you cut a holographic print into four pieces, and shine a laser onto each of the four pieces, you get a one-quarter-size version of the entire picture. You could do this with however many pieces you want. This suggests that the entire information of the whole image is in every little minute portion of the holographic plate. It's just that as you get the whole plate, you now have a more robust and fuller image.

As you will recall, the *Law of One* describes the progression from a Universal Logos all the way down to the sub-sub-Logos, which is the human being. So, a human being—along with all the Logos steps between—is a fully functioning hologram of the One infinite Creator.

Your chromosomes are geometric images and patterns that describe the entire reality; your body is a holographic image of the entire creation. The location and placement of all the star patterns in the entire Universe can be derived from your body.

Let's go back to that *Law of One* quote that explains to us how the whole Universe is made out of photons:

> Each Love, as you term the prime movers, comes from one frequency, if you wish to use this term. This frequency is unity. We would perhaps liken it rather to a strength than a frequency, this strength being infinite, the finite qualities being chosen by the particular nature of this primal movement.[4]

They prefer the use of the word *strength* over frequency because they say every part of the Universe comes from infinite strength, and this most certainly includes you and me. We are a sub-sub-Logos, which means that we are a fully functioning hologram of the Infinite Creator. We therefore are derived from energy that has infinite strength. As you raise your vibrations, you're going to have this infinite strength become increasingly available to you.

The *Law of One* confirms that the following premise is correct:

> Then this vibration . . . which we would call pure motion; it is pure love . . . there is nothing that is yet condensed, shall we say, to form any type or density of illusion. This Love then creates by this process of vibration a photon, as we call it, which is the basic particle of light. This photon then, by added vibrations and rotations, further condenses into particles of the densities, the various densities that we experience.[5]

The *Law of One* is saying that intelligent infinity creates intelligent energy, and the intelligent energy creates, by vibration, a photon. There's an original photon; it's the original seed of the Universe, it's all there really is. This original photon then vibrates, rotates, and fractalizes as it turns into a hologram and eventually creates the whole Universe.

CREATING THE UNIVERSE

There was a time before time, when you and I were One, we were in absolute unity. This goes well beyond any anything we can say or think about it; we were Intelligent Infinity.

This is before any of this waveform universe or any of the dimensional levels were created. We decided to create this Universe, and we did it in a very specific way. We chose a specific shape, which was a sphere. And from this sphere came everything that we know and don't know; there are no exceptions whatsoever. All life-forms—everything within this waveform Universe—and everything beyond that, all came out of a simple sphere.

Intelligent Infinity is the aspect of God outside the created Universe; it cannot be defined; it can't even be discussed. There's nothing inside us on any level that can reach that. "In the beginning God created the heaven and the earth. And the earth was without form, and void; and darkness was upon the face of the deep. And the Spirit of God moved upon the face of the waters. And God said, 'Let there be light: and there was light'" (Genesis 1:1–3).

So, to begin, you have intelligent energy in the Great Void, and the void is a vast sea of nothingness. Now, in order to create the Universe, intelligent energy, which is the Spirit of God, had to have movement; yet movement must be in relation to something. Without a point of reference, there is no movement: you can't fall, you can't move to the side, you can't move up or down.

The Spirit of God solved this problem by projecting a beam of consciousness into the void in six directions: up and down, forward and backward, and left and right. These beams are all the same length, and they define the space: north, south, east, west, up, and down (figure 9.1). The amount of projection is irrelevant; it can be as little as a centimeter

Fig. 9.1. Spirit projects a beam of consciousness in six directions: up and down, forward and backward, and left and right.

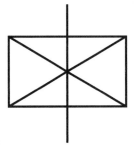

Fig. 9.2. In order to create the possibility of movement, Spirit connects the ends of these projections, first to form a square.

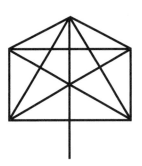

Fig. 9.3. Then from the square, Spirit sends a beam up to the top, forming a pyramid around the base of the square.

(or less) and as much as a mile (or more). Spirit then connected the lines—first to form a square—it looks like a rectangle in figure 8.2, but that's due to this being a 3-D object viewed from the side (figure 9.2), then to form a pyramid around the base of the square (figure 9.3), and then to bring the lines down into a pyramid below. These two back-to-back pyramids form an octahedron, which is one of the five Platonic solids. The criteria for Platonic solids are that all their edges be equal in length, all surfaces be equal in size and shape (figure 9.4). Now Spirit had the reality of an octahedron around it. Even though it was just a mental image of consciousness, movement was now possible because

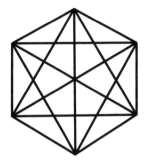

Fig. 9.4. Spirit then sends a beam down to the point below, forming another pyramid. These two back-to-back pyramids form an octahedron, thus creating the possibility of movement.

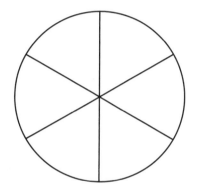

Fig. 9.5. The three axes of the octahedron are shown here. Just one spin around each of these axes traces the image of a perfect sphere.

perimeters had been established. Spirit can now move outside this shape and move around it, or it can remain inside the shape and let the octa-hedron move around it.

This newly created octahedron has three axes—front to back, up and down, and left to right. Spirit then began to rotate the three axes; just one spin around each of the three axes, traces the image of a perfect sphere (figure 9.5). In sacred geometry a straight line is considered male and any curved line is female. Thus, by rotating the octahedron on its three axes to create a sphere, spirit went from male to female. This was done because the geometric progression necessary for creation is much easier from the female curved lines.

So now the Spirit of God finds itself inside a sphere. Spirit then began to follow two simple instructions, for that was all that was needed to create the entire Universe and everything in it. The two instructions were to first go to that which is newly created, and then to project another sphere with the same diameter as the first one. Genesis says, "The Spirit of God moved upon the face of the waters," but where to? In the entire Universe there was only one newly created place and that was the surface. So, spirit moved to the surface—anywhere on the surface, it doesn't matter where. The first motion out of the void is to move to the surface (figure 9.6). After that first motion, everything else is automatic; every motion from there on shows you exactly where to make the next motion until the entire Universe is created.

The third verse from Genesis is "And God said, let there be light: and there was light." After moving to the surface there is only one thing to do, and that is to make another sphere (figure 9.7). What you have then is a vesica piscis, or two interlocked spheres, which is simply a sphere next to another sphere exactly the same size, so that the edge of one sphere passes through the center of the other. The common area created is the vesica piscis.

The vesica piscis is the metaphysical structure behind light . . . and that was the first day of Genesis. Where the two spheres come together is a circle. Figure 9.7 shows a front view, and from there, it looks like a straight line. If, however, you were to view down upon it from the top, you would see a circle. This circle is what is newly created in the Universe, Spirit then continues to follow its two simple instructions by moving to this new circle and making another sphere. Spirit can move to any point on this newly created circle, no matter where it moves;

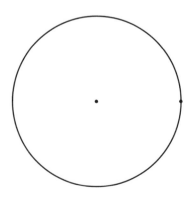

Fig. 9.6. The first motion out of the Great Void is to move to the surface, because it is the only newly created place in the Universe.

the spheres can be easily rotated to match the selected point in figure 9.8. Doing so creates the next image, which marks the second day of Genesis (figure 9.8). Now a rotational motion begins to happen on the surface of the sphere until it completes itself. This is all automatic (figures 9.9–9.11).

When you get to the sixth day of Genesis you have six spheres, or circles fitting perfectly with nothing left over (figure 9.12). On the seventh day Spirit rests, because the genesis and all the laws of the Universe are now complete.

We have thus begun a rotational vortex-energy pattern, and the first thing to come out of Genesis is the original photon; it's the original seed of the Universe. Every time a new rotational pattern is completed, we go deeper in describing in holographic detail every single aspect of our reality, and we eventually create the whole Universe.*

Once we created this external universe, we then decided to get into it. So, there was a division: part of God remained outside of the experiment, and part of God moved into it with a very specific pattern and shape—the Merkaba. The Spirit of God moved inside and began to experience directly what was created.

Now, this is where it gets interesting. David Wilcock, in his Ascension Mystery School, told how Dr. Hans Jenny took a droplet of water and put invisible particles of sand in it, so it became milky, dirty water. He then added vibration in the form of a musical note and shined a light on it. What he got is exactly the Genesis pattern. If you take a close look at this image (figure 9.12) and focus on the center circle or sphere, you will see six perfectly formed petals. Now, use your imagination a bit, and you will see that a star tetrahedron will fit perfectly inside this center.

A star tetrahedron is made up of two interlocking tetrahedrons in a manner that resembles the Star of David, but three-dimensionally (figure 9.13). The two interlocking tetrahedrons represent male and

---

*I elaborated on this in *Nothing in This Book Is True.*

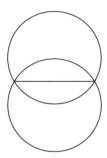

*Fig. 9.7. The first day of Genesis creates a vesica piscis,
which is the metaphysical structure behind light.*

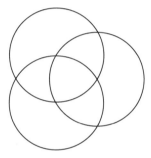

*Fig. 9.8. By following its two simple instructions,
Spirit moved to the newly created circle (see figure 9.7) and made
another sphere. This creates the second day of Genesis.*

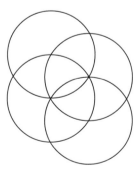

*Fig. 9.9. The third day of Genesis: a rotational motion
begins to happen on the surface of the sphere until it completes itself.*

Fig. 9.10. The fourth day of Genesis: the rotational motion continues.

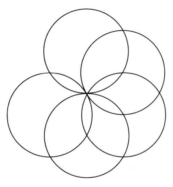

Fig. 9.11. The rotational motion continues with the creation
of another sphere. This is the fifth day of Genesis.

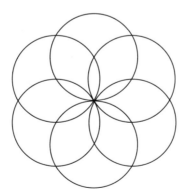

Fig. 9.12. The sixth day of Genesis creates the original photon.
It is the beginning of the creation of the Universe.

*Fig. 9.13. A star tetrahedron is made up of
two interlocking tetrahedrons.*

female energy in perfect balance. The tetrahedron facing up is male, and the one facing down is female. There is a star tetrahedral field around everything, and this is the key to understating the Merkaba, which is the universal pattern of creation. The star tetrahedron shape is the physical representation of the spiritual energy field that is the Merkaba.

The word *Mer* denotes counterrotating fields of light, *Ka* means spirit, and *Ba* is body, or reality. So the Mer-Ka-Ba then is a counter-rotating field of light that encompasses both spirit and body, and it's a vehicle—a time-space vehicle. It's far more than just that; in fact, there isn't anything that it isn't. It is the image through which all things were created, and it is the original shape of the Universe—it is the original photon.

That image is around your body in a geometrical set of patterns. The male tetrahedron pointing up is called the Sun tetrahedron, while the female tetrahedron pointing down is referred to as the Earth tetrahedron (see figure 9.14 on page 127). In *Nothing in This Book Is True, But It's Exactly How Things Are,* I gave the exact step-by-step instructions for activating this Merkaba field.[6]

What David Wilcock is saying, and I agree, is the image Dr. Jenny

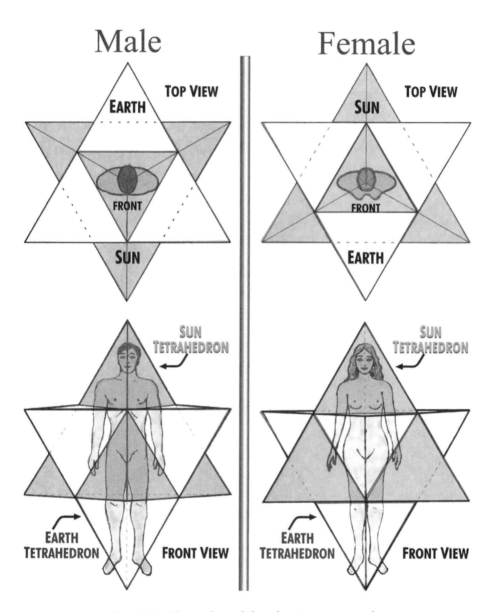

*Fig. 9.14. The male and female orientation within
the star tetrahedral fields around the human body.*

created with water, sand, and vibration looks exactly like what the original Universe looked like—and it is the Genesis pattern. This is the secret to the whole Universe. The very first thing that intelligent infinity did when it created intelligent energy was to make this pattern; it made this shape in vibration out of light. If you look closely again at the center of figure 9.12, you will see that it is made up of multiple vesica piscis—the metaphysical structure behind light. That is the first photon, and then all other photons are reflections of this original one.

10

Catching the
Ascension Wave

Michael Newton's book *Journey of Souls* talks extensively about life after life. He makes it very clear that there is no death, only a transition from one world to the next. Your consciousness is still very alive, and you go back to the other side of reality, where you have a soul family. You have people that you've been reincarnating with lifetime after lifetime.[1] In one lifetime, they might be your wife; in another lifetime, they might be your brother, or they might be your boss. We have had multiple people that we've been involved with in sexual mated relationships, like marriage or boyfriend/girlfriend, over many lifetimes. There's more than one person that you've had mated relationships within the higher realms that is part of your soul family.

THE PANORAMIC LIFE REVIEW

Dannion Brinkley has died four times, and yes, he's still alive. To be clear, he's had four near-death experiences (NDEs) and has returned totally transformed. He told his story in his book, *Saved by the Light*. To say that this book has been well received is a huge understatement; it has sold in excess of twenty-two million copies.

I remember Dannion well from many Whole Life Expos in the

late 1990s, where we were both featured speakers. He was personable and enthusiastic; he was fun and easy to talk to. Dannion behaved like a person who was truly living the great adventure of life, due to his deep levels of transformation as a result of his NDE experiences.

And what a transformation it was! I'm sure Dannion would be the first to admit that he was anything but a well-rounded, wholesome guy who was kind, considerate, and caring to others. Quite the contrary, he was an angry, confused child who had an estimated "six-thousand fist fights from the fifth to the twelfth grade."[2] He said his grade school in South Carolina had a demerit system where students who had 15 demerits had their parents called in for a conference, while those with 30 demerits were suspended. He said, "In the seventh grade, I had 154 demerits by the third day of school. I was that kind of student."[3]

It didn't get much better as he entered adulthood; he joined the military and took out his aggression by becoming a trained killer. He became an assassin.

Let's backtrack for a moment and look at the details of his first "death" experience. On September 17, 1975, he was struck by lightning while talking on the telephone. Here is what he said:

> The next sound I heard was like a freight train coming into my ear at the speed of light. Jolts of electricity coursed through my body, and every cell of my being felt as though it were bathed in battery acid. The nails of my shoes were welded to the nails in the floor so that when I was thrown into the air, my feet were pulled out of them. I saw the ceiling in front of my face, and for a moment I couldn't imagine what power it was that could cause such searing pain and hold me in its grip, dangling over my bed. What must have been a split second, seemed like an hour.[4]

Shortly thereafter, he said he entered into another world; it was a world of peace and tranquility. He said he was able to look down and see his body with a melted telephone in his hand. Then he went down a tunnel that had formed; he said he could hear the beautiful sound of rhythmic, ringing chimes. He then began moving toward a bright yet soothing light that increased in intensity as he kept moving into it. A Being of Light, for whom he felt a deep unabating love, appeared. His body became translucent as the being came closer and stood in front of him, and then engulfed him.

Then he began to feel and see everything that had ever happened, as his entire life was suddenly passing before him. His panoramic life review had begun, and it was all happening at once. This meant that Dannion was now experiencing everything that he had ever known and everything that had ever happened in his life, with absolutely nothing missing. He became aware of every emotion and every feeling and every event that had ever occurred in his life. He was reliving it in depth holographically, ethereally, and emotionally.

What happens then in a panoramic life review is that you will literally become every person that you've ever encountered, and you will feel the direct results of your interaction between you and that person. You're going to see how much love, hate, frustration, and anxiety you created for that person on an emotional level.

Here is what Dannion said:

The depth of emotion I felt during this life review was astonishing. Not only could I feel the way both I and the other person had felt when an incident took place, I could also feel the feelings of the next person they reacted to. I was in a chain reaction of emotion, one that showed how deeply we affect each other. Luckily, not all of it was bad.[5]

None of this is meant as punishment or to make the recipient feel guilty; it is an opportunity for deep reflection. Much of what Dannion experienced was not comfortable as he relived his rebellious childhood and witnessed it from the perspective of his parents. He saw how the loved ones of people he assassinated were impacted by his actions. He saw how little he cared about the well-being of others; what he saw was a self-absorbed, what's-in-it-for-me person, and it totally transformed his life.

He was gone for a total of twenty-eight minutes, yet it was an eternity; I have only scratched the surface of all that he witnessed. Upon reentering his body, he experienced almost unbearable levels of pain, and went through many years of recovery. He said he was completely paralyzed for the first six days and partially paralyzed for the next seven months. It took two years to learn to walk and feed himself.

When he finally progressed enough to get on with his life, he knew he had a huge karmic debt to pay. He realized that he was going to have to re-experience all of the pain and suffering that he had caused to all the people he had killed, so he became a hospice volunteer. Then he created the Twilight Brigade,[6] which became one of the largest end-of-life-care volunteer programs for dying veterans in American history. He has been a hospice volunteer for thirty-three years and has spent more than 32,000 hours at the bedsides of dying veterans.

THE CHOICE

As we incarnate into third density, we all have a choice to make, and the choice is very simple; it is whether you're going to be of service to others or service to self. The Universe doesn't stop you from being of service to self, it just creates an enormous amount of karmic debt to be repaid if you do it. That means everything you do that hurts other people is something you're going to have to experience. And as Dannion Brinkley has clearly pointed out: in the panoramic life review, you will experience everything that you've done to other people.

So that choice of service to self is a very ignorant one indeed. We've all heard the saying "gain the world and lose your soul." You could be a very successful person in worldly terms; you could be what would appear to be wealthy and famous. Yet if you are motivated by "what's-in-it-for-me" consciousness, and use your will and power to manipulate and control others, you will remain far behind on a soul level.

When you go into the afterlife, the idea of using manipulation, control, lying, and betrayal to get what you want out of other people will keep you on the karmic wheel of reincarnation for as long as three cycles of 25,920 years. The Universe is infinitely patient; it will give you every opportunity, and as many lifetimes as it takes to learn the lesson.

There is nothing inherently evil about being wealthy or famous; it is purely a question of your motivation. There are plenty of rich and famous people in this world who are service-to-others minded and do great things to give back and further the cause of humanity. The beings in the higher realms are looking at the true masters; they're looking at the people who are cultivating higher consciousness. To them, all that really matters is what are you like in terms of your vibratory quality. You could be a superstar from their perspective if you are striving to raise your consciousness and being kind, respectful, and considerate to other humans, animals, and nature. You don't have to be wealthy or famous to do that.

THE FIRST DISTORTION

David Wilcock got the ball rolling in his Ascension Mystery School when he pointed to the *Law of One* teachings:

> The Law of One, though beyond the limitations of name, as you call vibratory sound complexes, may be approximated by stating that all things are one, that there is no polarity, no right or wrong, no disharmony, but only identity. All is one, and that one is love/light, light/love, the Infinite Creator.[7]

That's a rather powerful statement, and we need to take a closer look. All things are one, all beings are one, and anything else is an illusion. When it says there is no right and wrong, we must understand that there is right and wrong within the illusion, and we are bound by what they call the first distortion, which is the law of free will. Within the illusion if you infringe upon yourself in the form of another being, then you must experience the full payback of what you did to that person in your own life. When you infringe upon someone else's free will, you're infringing upon your own free will, and you will pay for it in your own personal experience.

There is no shortcut to enlightenment; the *Law of One,* or the Universe if you prefer, is very clear about this. What goes around, comes around, and it comes right back to you. You have to pay restitution.

Everything that happens out in front of you, all of your life experiences, are a reflection of your state of consciousness. So it is very useful to look at life as though you were looking at a mirror; everything is a direct reflection back to you of what you are projecting. If a person comes at you angrily, what you immediately know is that it is your anger being reflected back at you.

Life is a big classroom, the sole function of it is to teach us who we really are and what we are all about. In order to get to the essence of ourselves, we have to clear away all of the garbage, all of the illusion. We agree then that we will act out for each other what each of us has to learn. That is the way the game is played. Any time someone acts toward you in a way that makes you uncomfortable, it's your discomfort that you have to learn about. So, it's very important to understand that nobody gets away with anything. And therefore, hurting other people is just delaying your reunion with the One Infinite Creator. But it's also perfect: karma is a perfect balancing system.

Once you realize who you are, that your true identity is the One Infinite Creator, now your objective is to radiate the realization of oneness with the Creator to others, and to provide service to the planet. And when you get to that point, you're going to start meditating on the greater good. What can you do with your life that will reach the greatest number of people for the greatest good?

So the *Law of One* is teaching us—it is telling you—the Universe is telling us that the only thing that is real is the original thought, and that is the original loving consciousness. It is the kindness, forgiveness, and compassion of the Universe.

RECONNECTING TO WHOLENESS

Drunvalo Melchizedek, in his book *The Ancient Secret of the Flower of Life,* volume 2, tells of the Egyptian understanding of life and reincarnation; this is information that was taught in Akhenaten's twelve-year mystery school, the Law of One, which we discussed in chapter 5. He says that the Egyptians perceived and identified eight completely different and separate personalities, and that these eight together make up the entire personality complex of the spirit that first came to Earth.

Melchizedek tells how we, as spirit, go through each of these personalities in our first eight lifetimes. Then as we continue to reincarnate, we tend to develop a couple of favorites; one is male and one is female. These become the dominant personalities.[8]

In Akhenaten's school, the student took the twelve years to pass through each of these eight personalities. Then they would have a "conference" with all eight, thus establishing wholeness and wisdom. This was in preparation for the final initiation and ascension into fourth density in the King's Chamber of the Great Pyramid.

The Michael Newton afterlife-analysis books say that we're really only dealing with at most 20 percent of the soul's energy in our lifetime;* the rest of it is still in the higher realms. Imagine having only 15 to 20 percent of yourself available to you in your conscious mind. The other 80 percent or so is in your soul, and you don't even know anything about it. This, then, is what the Egyptians were doing; they were

---

*In addition to *Journey of Souls,* Michael Newton has written about the afterlife in *Memories of the Afterlife* and *Wisdom of Souls.*

giving themselves a huge consciousness boost with their understanding.

They were able to remember being that person who has had multiple incarnations, where each identity as a personality was only a portion of their true nature, and maybe not even the most interesting one. In preparation for their initiation in the King's Chamber and ultimate ascension, they learned that they were part of a disembodied consciousness that has been doing the work behind the scenes the whole time. This is the part of them—and us—that has been orchestrating synchronicities and dreams, making sure that you get guidance, and making sure that you have the karma that you're supposed to have: this is the job of our Higher Self.

So you may be going through all kinds of weird stuff, but it doesn't change the fact that your Higher Self knows you and is aware of you. And so, when you go into this higher consciousness in fourth density, you are not only going to see and remember being yourself, the one who experienced all this, you're also going to remember being the person who was orchestrating everything for you, in that reduced consciousness state, to try to get you the enlightenment that you need. So, the former life that you had won't even come into mind, because now it's going to be indistinguishable from the part where you were working from the other side.

11
Mind Matters

As I detailed in chapter 8, when we were in full awareness of our true nature as a fully functioning hologram of the One Infinite Creator, we were stagnating; we lacked the necessary inspiration to grow and create. We acted bored when we had everything handed to us. As a result, no one was ascending into fourth density.

In the attempt to solve this huge problem, a veiling was created between the conscious and the superconscious mind. We separated ourselves from the awareness that we are one with all that is, and we fell into the belief that our individual identity is who we are. This severed us from our Higher Self, our connection to Source.

What we did was move from the heart space of Oneness into our heads, and we became our minds. Ramana Maharshi spent most of his lifetime in meditation; here is what he had to say, "Mind is consciousness which has put on limitations. You are originally unlimited and perfect. Later you take on limitations and become the mind."[1]

The mind is polarized; it sees good and evil, but does not connect the dots to see wholeness. Therefore, it is in a continual state of judgment. It looks out at a world that it perceives as separate from itself and compares what it sees to the "ideal" that is held in the mind. If the situation at hand does not live up to the ideal standard, it is judged as bad or wrong. If it is another person, we judge at a minimum that person's behavior, and oftentimes the person who is behaving "badly."

I will lay out the details in future chapters, but for now, I will simply say that all of the problems we have in life come from judgment, from insisting that reality should be different from how it is.

The following is from *The Book of Est.* "The mind is a linear arrangement of multisensory total records of successive moments of now." That means the mind is essentially a sophisticated multisensory recording machine. The purpose or design function of the mind is survival; the survival of the being and anything the being considers itself to be. When the being identifies itself with its mind—as we have done—we call that state of affairs ego, and it means the mind's purpose becomes the survival of the mind itself. The purpose of the mind becomes the survival of the records, the tapes, the points of view, the decisions, the thoughts, the conclusions, and beliefs of the mind. The mind now has a vested interest in all of these.

These multisensory recordings, and resulting beliefs were sourced from earlier incidents where there was an experience involving pain, impact, relative unconsciousness, and either a perceived or a real threat to survival. Examples from childhood could include any type of accident: falling out of a tree, a bicycle or automobile accident, getting beat up, and so on. However, the experience of birth is the earliest and most significant threat to survival; hospital births are an extremely traumatic experience for the infant.

Then there are trigger situations that reactivate an earlier basic threat to survival. Examples from birth could include anything reminiscent of the trauma of your birth: hospitals, doctors, nurses, surgical gloves, forceps, the color of the walls in the delivery room, even getting spanked. That means you are never upset for the reason you think you are; something happens to trigger an earlier basic threat to survival. These survival tapes operate solely on stimulus-response, just like Pavlov's dogs, they operate automatically. They are totally mechanical in their nature.

The mind also associates one thing or event with every other thing within that event. For example, the doctor's hands get associated with men's hands, with men, with humans, and so on. And because of the associative nature of the mind, there are hundreds of stimuli that could trigger that earliest survival experience. So, from birth onward everything the baby experiences is associated with pain, relative unconsciousness, and threat to survival. From that moment on, everything is stimulus-response—we are totally under the influence of the machine mind: stimulus-response, stimulus-response, and on and on.[2]

As long as we continue to identify ourselves with our mind, we literally become prisoners of it. Here is a revealing quote from Albert Einstein: "A human being is a part of the whole called by us Universe, a part limited in time and space. He experiences himself, his thoughts and feelings as something separated from the rest, a kind of optical delusion of his consciousness. This delusion is a kind of prison for us, restricting us to our personal desires and to affection for a few persons nearest to us."[3] We are then reduced to going through the motions. We are living life conceptually, and not as a living presence. We then further complicate the issue by not distinguishing between the two.

Let me begin to illustrate this by asking you to take a moment to describe to yourself: What you are experiencing in this moment? What are you experiencing right now? What you will discover is that you cannot describe what you're experiencing right now, because by the time you stopped to describe it, it was not what you're experiencing right now. It is what you were experiencing a moment ago—and it's worse than that. You not only failed to describe what you are experiencing; you didn't even describe what you were experiencing, because what you were experiencing no longer exists as an experience. It is now a memory of an experience. But most people don't make any distinction between an experience and a memory of an experience, they treat them both the same.

Experience always devolves into concept; the instant you get something as an experience, right away it becomes a concept—and concept is only a representation of the actual experience. So, the instant you try to notice it, it isn't what you're experiencing, it's what you *were* experiencing. Furthermore, it isn't what you were experiencing, it's the *concept* of what you were experiencing, and the two things are different!

So, what happens is experience devolves into concept, and concept begins to determine experience; and a conceptually determined experience reinforces the concept. And the reinforced concept more fully dominates the experience; and the more fully dominated experience reinforces the concept. What I'm describing here is a vicious circle, and in that vicious circle we do not make the distinction between experience and concept. We don't make the distinction between the real thing, and the representation of the real thing; we are going through the motions.

Then we look to our circumstances in order to try and find fulfillment. You, for example, might think if only you could find the right job, then everything would be good. Then you get the right job and it's wonderful for two weeks, and then it's like it always was. Well, if only you could get promoted, if only you could find the right relationship partner, if only you could get rid of your current mate.

So, most people think that life is a function of their circumstances, and for most people it is, because their experiences are circumstantially derived, and they live in a vicious circle of concept-dominated experience, and the concept-dominated experience reinforces the concept, and so on. And there's no real aliveness in the vicious circle. There is no happiness; there are the symbols for happiness, but not happiness. In that circle, there is no love, there are the symbols for love, but no real love. There's no real vitality or satisfaction; nor is there any real self-expression.

You will never find contentment, much less your true self, by looking outside to your circumstances. You find it only by going inside. You begin by acknowledging your wholeness and bringing that into your life situations. Use that as a place to come from; from there, you move out of victim consciousness and into the generative realm where you are a co-creator with the One Infinite Creator. I will detail this in future chapters.

This all came to me from one of my favorite teachers from yester-year, Werner Erhard. Werner was in perfect form when he summed this all up with the following analogy:

> You know when you go into the restaurant and you read the menu? YOU EAT THE MENU! No kidding, people eat the menu because they don't make any distinction between the meal and the menu. And it makes them ignorant. And not only that, they don't know that they're ignorant, so that makes them blind! . . . Now what more do you need to know that you confuse the menu for the meal. If I told you about a person, that this person confused the menu for the meal, that is to say, that this person did not make a distinction between the symbols of love and love, did not make a distinction between the symbols of satisfaction and satisfaction, did not make the distinction [between] the symbols of themselves, their own being and their own self. What would you tell me about them? You would say that person's in trouble. Now everybody knows who we're talking about, right?[4]

Our mind is a marvelous instrument if used correctly. It is supposed to be a servant of consciousness; we have made it our master. As a quote often attributed to Einstein goes, "The intuitive mind is a sacred gift, and the rational mind is a faithful servant. We have created a society that honors the servant and has forgotten the gift." So, the veiling was necessary at one point because it created movement and growth. But it has also created a mental prison as we have become a society stuck in its collective false identity where we live life conceptually and are mired in compulsive thought and judgment. As such, we are blocked from living from our true awareness as infinite consciousness, which has its entry point in the present moment.

We are in the end-times where we are in transition from one world to another; we have gotten what we needed out of the veiling, and it is no longer useful. It's time to lift the curtain, take the masks off, and move back into our truest self. It's time to let go of our limited identity and return to the experience of ourselves as a perfectly functioning hologram of the Infinite Creator. The choice is between the mechanical mind that keeps you in separation, and the intuitive heart that connects you to your Higher Self and to all that is. This is the movement from a black-and-white world to one in living color.

12

Digging Deeper

No problem can be solved from the same level of consciousness that created it.

ALBERT EINSTEIN

Corey Goode tells us in *The Cosmic Secret* that scientists in the Secret Space Program are well aware of the Galactic Super Wave that is moving through our galaxy: it has multiple layers—a great "dust cloud." They have flown craft out there, and the energy had an effect on the crew; the positive crew members became more positive, and the negative ones became more so.[1]

As it travels through various solar systems, the leading edge acts as a catalyst, forcing people to wake up and deal with their karma and dramas, or be consumed by them. That means that the collective darkness is rising to the surface in order to be transmuted into the light. Those who resist these changes will be in for a very rough ride.

So, we are all in a period of transition—a collective dark night of the soul that is affecting everyone on this planet—which can create some intense moments for us all. Are things feeling intense for you, too?

As we quickly head toward the Shift of the Ages, we're already experiencing very strong surges of photonic light and higher levels of energy. This causes the vibratory rate of the planet to rise dramatically as it is merging with the fourth-density vibrations of joyfulness, inner peace, forgiveness, unconditional love, creativity, inspiration, and compassion. This in turn is creating a huge displacement process, where the denser vibratory rates of anxiety, depression, fear, anger, resentment, frustration, guilt, shame, helplessness, hopelessness, fatigue, and the like are coming to the surface. I'm going to call these ascension symptoms. These frequency surges are ultimately serving the ascension process and working to increase love, peace, and light across the planet. But when we're in the midst of them; let's just say many are having a very rough go of it.

I'm mentioning this because you too might find these very symptoms ramping up and creating stress and overwhelm in your life. The changes you go through on your pathway to the higher worlds will not always be easy, considering that we are in the end-times, where lifetimes worth of karma are now up for resolution. Spiritual growth and ascension, although incredibly positive, will have chaotic, uncomfortable, and challenging symptoms that appear on the path.

As Albert Einstein said, "No problem can be solved from the same level of consciousness that created it,"[2] so in view of this, let's take a moment to dig deeper and see if we can gain some insight on how to effectively deal with these accelerated and stressful times. As we continue in this most essential discussion, I will show you in the chapters that follow how to transmute this chaotic energy into life-enhancing energy that is clearly contributing to your sense of well-being. Let's begin by taking a look at the nature of stress.

Our bodies are designed to experience stress and react to it. Stress can be positive, keeping us alert and ready to avoid danger. This automatic response developed in our ancient ancestors as a way to protect them from predators and other threats. Faced with danger, the body kicks into gear, flooding itself with hormones that elevate your heart rate, increase your blood pressure, boost your energy, and prepare you to deal with the problem. Now that was quite useful back in our caveman days, in case you were being chased by a tiger!

However, considering the fast-paced world in which we now live, you are much more likely to experience the downside. Adrenal glands are the organs that trigger your fight-or-flight response to stress. They infuse your body with adrenaline, and cortisol (your number one stress hormone) to help you handle dangerous situations. As far as your adrenals are concerned, stress is stress, no matter where it comes from. So, when you're under stress, your adrenals shoot out more cortisol. This is to give you immediate energy to escape the danger.

When that stressful situation is over, your cortisol levels are supposed to return to normal, awaiting the next fight-or-flight call to action. But here's the problem: when you're under frequent stress, as many of us are now in these accelerated times, your adrenals keep pumping cortisol. Your body can't tell if that stress is from a bear attack, or if you're stuck in rush hour traffic and late for work That's why you stay wired, frazzled, and feel out of control. And that's why eventually your adrenals get exhausted, and you're wiped out with virtually no energy left.

ABOUT STRESSORS

Stress has been defined as the impact of a particular event (or stressor) in which the sympathetic (fight-or-flight) nervous system is stimulated for a duration of time. Stress becomes negative when you face continuous challenges without relief or relaxation between challenges. As a result, you become overworked, and stress-related tension builds. Stress that continues without relief can lead to a condition called distress. Your body's natural alarm system, the fight-or-flight response, may be stuck in the on position. And that can have serious consequences for your health.

Okay, so the fight-or-flight response is stuck in the on position, but what causes that? It is the perceived stressor—like not enough time, or a bad work situation, or family problems—to name just a few. But what causes that? Is there a problem inherent in the situation itself, or is it a function of how we perceive it?

Until you get to the source, the real reason for stress in your life, you will only be dealing with false causes; and the only available options will just mask the symptoms. We need to get to the source, the real cause of the stress so we can eliminate the root cause.

ABOUT PRESENCE

What do I mean by being present? Well, look at yourself, are you ever in the present moment, or are you mostly in the past or future? How about when you are at work? How often are you in the moment with regard to what you are doing? Are you more often dwelling on the past, or some imagined future—like 5:00 p.m. and what you'll be doing after work in order to unwind from another stressful day?

When you're stressed you can't be present. Well, you can be; but most people have a hard time going into presence with their loved ones, or with themselves, when they have a heightened stress level. The adrenalin is too high; you're in fight or flight.

What I have found is that for most people, the present moment is too painful, so they don't spend much time there; yet it is the only place where true experience exists. And if you are not present in your life, you are pretty much reduced to going through the motions. It is more incumbent upon us than ever before to find a way to calm and center ourselves. Because if you pray, or if you meditate, or however you communicate to your version of your spiritual truth, you need to be still; you need to be present.

I will show you exactly how to be present . . . and not only is it not painful, it is in fact your source for unlimited amounts of joy, inner peace, and unconditional love—all of which are contained within you.

ABOUT CONNECTION

Another one of the key reasons we feel stress is because we feel disconnected. We feel disconnected from each other; we feel more and more disconnected from possibly even our greatest calling in life. That causes stress. And when the world around us is becoming more and more digitized and work is becoming increasingly computerized, we feel even more disconnected. And when we come home and our families are more and more using smartphones and iPads and other devices, we feel disconnected.

Now I would like to take you back to the magic of your childhood. Do you remember when you were maybe four or five years old? Perhaps you were looking up at the sky on a beautiful star-filled night. Do you remember the sense of awe and wonder as you gazed at the beauty of it all? You didn't have the words for it, but you didn't need them. You felt it in every cell of your body; you felt your deep connection to all that is. Well, that deep connection still lives within you; it may be deeply buried, but it is still there.

One of the major benefits of living in these greatly accelerated times is that if you can catch the wave and align yourself with this emerging presence of the great awakening, you will not only center and calm yourself; you will feel connected. You will feel deeply connected to your deepest purpose in life; you will feel connected to why you are here to begin with. You will begin sensing something much bigger and better in your life than you've ever sensed before!

WHAT ABOUT STRESS?

You may believe, as many people do, that you are stressed because of constant time pressures. Perhaps you blame your work situation. "Anybody who works for the boss I've got has to be into chaos," or "Anyone who has the employees I've got is going to be stressed out," you might be thinking. What about your childhood environment? After all, Mom and Dad seemed to be in a constant state of worry over money issues. So, what about finances? No matter how much you've got, it might always seem like you could use some more.

Some of the above may be true, but there is good news. Every one of these situations can be overcome. I, along with thousands of my breath-work clients, will happily testify to that fact!

Now, let's get some clarity on these beliefs.

TIME AND OTHER STRESSORS

Do you explain away stress as temporary—"I just have a million things going on right now"—even though you can't remember the last time you took a breather?

Do you define stress as an integral part of your work or home life—"Things are always crazy around here," or as a part of your personality—"I have a lot of nervous energy, that's all"?

Do you blame your stress on other people or outside events, or do you view it as entirely normal and unexceptional? Until you accept responsibility for the role you play in creating or maintaining it, your stress level will remain outside your control.

Does it seem like there just isn't enough time in the day to get everything done, no matter what you do to try and streamline your schedule? Well, I can't give you a twenty-five-hour day, and only the Beatles could give you an eight-day week. And besides, you have plenty of perks from living the "good life"; so you may feel like it is a necessary trade-off. Too bad you don't seem to have enough time to enjoy the "good life."

Since you are probably not willing to throw away what you've got, the question then becomes one of learning how to deal with the reality of your experiences in more effective ways. And I am well aware that, if you are like most people I know, not enough time is probably heading your list of stress-causing problems. So, you don't have the time to spend in nature, in hours of meditation, or yoga.

What about your work situation? Is it absolutely true that chaos and stress is a built-in and necessary component to your work environment? Can anything be done about it, or is it totally out of your control?

For starters, I will show you how altering your attitude toward the time you do have will result in a significant lowering of that stressed-out feeling. It will also give you a creative breakthrough, which will enable you to find new and more creative ways of managing your time. I will also show you that you can do this with your work, with your finances, with your significant relationships, as well as with any and all circumstances in your life.

I will show you a technique that, once you learn how it works, you can use by *yourself* anytime, anywhere, while engaging in any activity. You can use it at work in order to integrate any emotions that come up from the work situation into your sense of well-being. That will allow you to have all of your feelings and all of the situations that come up contribute to your creativity, to your effectiveness, and indeed, to your happiness. You can even use it while you are driving, you can use it while you are paying your bills, and you can use it while you are watching television. You can use it anytime, anywhere.

IS ALL STRESS BAD?

Have you ever wondered what life might have been like way back in the day when there were no modern conveniences such as supermarkets, automobiles, computers, and so on? No traffic jams, no long lines at the bank, no deadlines to meet. Very simple times, probably relatively stress free too, right? Well, maybe.

Let's go way back in time to our caveman days when our potential dinner was just as likely to chase us as we were to chase it. Maybe it was a good thing when, in the face of danger, our bodies would kick into gear by flooding us with hormones that elevated our heart rate, increased our blood pressure, boosted our energy, and prepared us to deal with the problem. In this state of increased alertness, our senses were heightened, and we were prepared to fight or flee. Sounds like a useful thing.

Now let's fast-forward to present time. Imagine that you're driving along the freeway, and the oncoming storm that you were trying to beat has other ideas! All of a sudden, you are dealing with thunder and lightning that would scare anyone. The rain is coming down in sheets, visibility is close to zero, and 50 mph winds are trying to blow you off the road! Your body responds in the same way as it did with our caveman ancestors; your senses are heightened, you are present and alert and prepared to deal with the situation as effectively as possible. That sounds like a helpful response, too.

I gave this example because it is exactly what I experienced while driving through Ohio a few years ago. I could see that the weather could well be a problem, but I had to be in Syracuse, New York, in two days. I had a workshop to give, and that was that! When the storm hit, it was the most incredibly intense driving experience that I have ever encountered. It was a real opportunity for disaster!

However, by applying the same principles that I will be sharing with you, I was able to transform my fear into sheer excitement. I was in an extreme state of alertness and was totally present; it was exhilarating! That being said, after more than two hours of dealing with a storm that refused to decrease in intensity, I stopped in the next town, Toledo. I said, "Holy Toledo, that's enough," and got myself a motel room!

My conclusion then is that all stress is not bad; maybe it's all a function of how we choose to interact with it.

Hans Selye is often considered one of the early pioneers of modern stress theory. His scientific research helped to shape our understanding of stress. In his 1936 paper called "The Nature of Stress," Selye defined stress as "the nonspecific response of the body to any demand, whether it is caused by, or results in, pleasant or unpleasant conditions. Stress as such, like temperature, is all-inclusive, embodying both the positive and the negative aspects of these concepts."[3]

Selye understood that not all stress is bad; he also recognized that change is often considered a main cause of stress. And he discovered that our attitude toward change is important. Even changes we consider joyful create a type of stress response. He called this *eustress*. Changes we are upset about can create a different type of stress response, which he called *distress*. And as you may expect, he found that eustress is healthier for our bodies than distress.

So change is often considered a main cause of stress, yet it cannot be avoided. Change and stress are part of life. Look at the natural world and you will see ongoing change. The seasons change, the weather changes, your friends and family change, you change. Change, especially in these end-times, is a constant.

Selye understood that "how you take it" determines, ultimately, whether you can adapt successfully to change. Acceptance of change reduces the impact of stress. Thus, one could say that increasing our levels of emotional acceptance about a situation helps us adapt to change and reduces the damage of stress.

For example, two people may lose their job: John becomes angry and depressed. He becomes unable to function or find new work due to the job loss, which he experiences as unfair and stressful. Susan quickly accepts the situation. She creatively begins job hunting and easily finds new employment.

So there is good stress and bad stress. Is there a way to change distress into eustress so we are actually able to benefit from it, rather than be devastated by it? The good news is that there is; I will show you how to take something that you thought was detracting from your well-being and transform it so it is clearly contributing to your sense of aliveness, as well as your creativity. Thus, you will be left in full presence of the moment and feeling your connection to life.

BAND-AID SOLUTIONS

Suppose for a moment that you and I are riding on a train, and as we look out the window, we can see that the train is going somewhere; it has a destination. But most of the passengers are not looking out the window; they are just basking in the sunlight streaming through the windows. However, as we take a look, we begin to see that the train is headed in a bad direction. So, people begin to hear that the train is going to a less than optimal place, and hopefully we are wise enough to consider their predicament.

But what are our options? Well, somebody comes along and says, "Look, we've got this dilemma and we have two choices; we can either all sit on the left side, or we can all sit on the right side. And I am convinced that the best way to get this train to change direction is if we all sit on the left side of the train." And so this person gets everyone to sit on the left side. However, after a while we begin to notice that sitting on the left side has not made any difference; we're still going where we are headed. Then another person stands up and says, "Look, what we all need to do in order to get this train to change direction, is we need to move to the right side of the train." So everybody moves to the right side. After a while, we all begin to notice that this has not changed anything either.

What in fact is needed here is to find a way to get out in front of the train and lay some new track! But it's unthinkable to get out in front of the train, so people keep going from one side to the other in the hope that it will make a difference. But if you're awake, you begin to see that it isn't making much of a difference.

The above story was first told by Werner Erhard, sometime back in the day. Keeping it in mind, let's dig even deeper and look at some of the common ways of unwinding from stressful situations.

In working with many clients over the years, I've noticed that they found ways of distancing themselves from their stress-causing problems. Their list of distraction techniques includes use of coffee, drugs, and alcohol. And the list expands to include binge eating, zoning out in front of the television, sex, lashing out at others, and distancing themselves from friends and family, which results in increased feelings of separation and a lack of connection.

They commonly report that while they often feel better, it is only temporary, and it is energy robbing, time and life wasting, and a perfect formula for staying stuck. Many of these "fixes" also leads to compulsive and addictive behavior.

Now let's look at some of the more useful ways of managing stress; regular exercise is important. Walking, running, swimming, dancing, cycling, and aerobic classes are good choices. Social engagement is important too; so, reach out to family and friends and schedule time to be with them. And don't forget your leisure time. Don't get so caught up in the hustle and bustle of life that you forget to take care of your own needs. Remember, it's good to care about others but nurturing yourself is a necessity, not a luxury. Spend as much time in nature as you can; spend some time with your pet. Try gardening.

No doubt, these are much better ways of handling stress! However, have you noticed that even these more useful ways of coping with stress still do not, by themselves, eliminate the source of your discomfort? I mean that unpleasant work situation will still be there, as well as the unpaid bills, or the unresolved issue with a family member, or whatever the underlying issue may be. So, there is still something missing here, and in the absence of this missing ingredient, even the more positive methods of stress relief are just ways of masking the problem.

SUPPRESSION

Let's begin by taking a closer look at masking the perceived problem. It has a name: it's called suppression. Let's see how it works.

Suppression means choosing not to experience something that's there. The dictionary has fifteen definitions for suppression including to press under, repress, crush, subdue, put down, overpower, overwhelm, restrain, conceal, and smother.

Suppression happens because of two strong drives that everyone has: First, your reactive mind is based in survival, and as such it has a strong need to be right about things. Your mind has to have that because if you were continually questioning all of your assumptions about everything, you wouldn't be able to put two thoughts together very readily. You wouldn't be able to think about anything very effectively. So, you start out assuming you are right about your basic assumptions.

There are disadvantages to that, as I'm sure you have noticed.

The second strong drive is to feel good. Once you have made something or someone wrong, and you tell yourself, "That thing *really* is wrong," you *believe* your make-wrong; then how do you ever get to where you feel good again? Whenever you make something or someone wrong, you get an unpleasant feeling in your body. It's normal for people to not want to feel bad, so they actually withdraw awareness from their body to avoid the unpleasant feelings that are there. So, because of the strong drive that everyone has—the desire to feel good—suppression is about the only vehicle that is readily available, or so it seems. It has four components:

1. Your mind will distract you from whatever has been bothering you and will continue to do so: Most people are very resourceful at finding ways to distract themselves from whatever has been bothering them; I suspect you know what I mean. The list could include anything ranging from the more destructive ways mentioned above to the more constructive ones.

2. Your body armors; it tenses up to give you less access to the subtleties of the suppressed feelings: Your body will become tense; it will become rigid to give you less access to the unpleasant feelings in your body. As a result of continued judgment, and the corresponding attempts to distance yourself from the feelings, your body becomes overloaded with unresolved packets of stuck energy that don't feel good. In the absence of any integrative skills, you become stuck on the revolving wheel of suppression. As a result, you will not be in your body. Common signs of body armor are tightness in the jaw and shoulders, poor posture, digestion and elimination problems, and lack of body awareness. The more your body armors, the less flexible it becomes, and even the gentlest touch can make you aware of the pain that is there.

3. Your breathing becomes inhibited and remains inhibited: Full and uninhibited breathing opens up your feeling sense. It makes

you aware of the sensations in your body like nothing else can. When you suppress, you inhibit your breathing as an automatic response to the greater intensity of an unwanted feeling because you don't want to feel the unpleasant sensation at all. Examples of this are closing your throat and sobbing when there is intense sadness, holding your breath when there is intense rage or intense fear. By breathing less, you feel less.

4. An internal conflict is created and maintained: Suppression creates a direct conflict in your mind and body. This is the struggle to not feel what you are already feeling, and to not think what you are already thinking. The desire for suppression causes many people to struggle with their problems, while at the same time refusing to do anything about them. An enormous amount of delusion is required in order to convince yourself that you are feeling something different than what you are. The internal conflict that results from the denial of your feelings may keep you confused about what you are feeling.

Suppression is just one method of coping with your feelings. For many people it is the only method they learned from parental messages such as:

> Don't be a crybaby!
> Don't you talk to me like that!
> You just wait until your father gets home!
> You'll get a spanking if you don't stop that!
> You ought to be ashamed of yourself!
> Go to your room if you're going to act like that!
> Act like a lady!
> Act like a man!
> Don't be a sissy!

Suppression is a response learned from these kinds of messages that your parents gave you for the purpose of letting them avoid their discomfort. This is emotional abuse and can be defined as behavior that adults use to control their children so that the adults feel better. The abuse usually continues until the child gives up and suppresses his or her feelings. Suppression then is associated with invalidation of what you are feeling, so if you learned that there is something wrong with you for feeling a certain way, you learned to suppress and control your emotions in order to gain approval or to manipulate and control those who cared for you. You and I learned to suppress and control our feelings in order to survive. We learned how to be good little actors and actresses!

I can tell you with certainty that there are feelings that you suppressed during childhood that you are still suppressing. Everyone endured at least some degree of emotional abuse. Emotional abuse occurs in families where feelings are given little importance, dismissed, discounted, or never discussed.

MULTIGENERATIONAL LEGACY OF SUPPRESSION AND ABUSE

In most cases, suppression and controlling our emotions is something we first learned from our parents that continued in school and religious upbringing as the only way of dealing with our feelings that others didn't like. The parent abuses the child to force him or her to suppress feelings that are not okay with the parent. Parents do this because they were abused by their parents until they suppressed those same feelings. What this means is that abuse and suppression are passed on from one generation to another. That doesn't mean that your parents were bad people; it simply means that this is all they knew, and they were doing the best they could with what they knew. You may experience a great deal of denial about abuse in your family of origin, simply because they were the only family you knew, so it all seemed normal.

This is not about blame; rather, it is about taking responsibility to work on yourself—that is, if you are truly interested in finding a permanent solution to stress and its related distressful conditions. If so, it is essential that you allow yourself honest awareness of the feelings you suppressed as a child and resolve them. I will show you exactly how to do that. So there you have it. As you can see, there is a price to pay for some temporary relief.

But wait a minute, there's more. We need to take a closer look at how suppression often leads to some harmful and destructive habits.

HOW SUPPRESSION CAUSES ADDICTION

Continual suppression requires effort and leads to a variety of compulsive behaviors and addictions that maintain the suppression. Obsessive worry or fantasies are compulsive behaviors that distract you from what is really happening by focusing you on what *might* happen. Compulsive television watching or overwork are activities that are distracting. Eating disorders, alcoholism, drugs, and tobacco are addictions related to substance abuse.

At first, compulsive behavior and addictions are methods you choose in order to suppress certain feelings and cope with the discomfort by medicating your feelings. Repetition of the behavior renders it self-motivating and without choice. Compulsive behavior and addictions, as devastating as they can be, are nevertheless symptoms of the suppressed emotions.

Okay, so putting up with or trying to change unpleasant stress-related feelings is not the way to go. It's about as useful as moving from one side of the train to the other; the train is still going in the direction it was headed—it is going to a bad place. So we have to find a way to get out front and lay some new track. How about instead of various ways of masking symptoms, we find a way to eliminate the root cause of your distress. That ought to enable us to change our direction.

13

Shining the Light
on the
Darkness Within

In every crisis lies the seed of opportunity.

Chinese proverb

Do you feel like you're at a tipping point and you don't know which way to turn? Do you feel like you're just going through the motions and life is passing you by? Do you ever look out the window and wonder "when" or "if"?

Whether it's an impending divorce, or it's leaving a dead-end job that you hate, or it's moving, or being stuck in stress and anxiety for reasons you oftentimes can't quite put a finger on, whatever it is, there's a yearning to make the right decision—one that's in your best interest—and to do it in a way that you feel is respectful, that is admirable, that has integrity. But you just don't know what to do. And because you're afraid to make the wrong decisions, you make no decisions. Yet you don't want to wake up only to realize that it's too late, and you're living a life of quiet desperation.

Since we all have an ultimate destiny that we want to fulfill, the decisions we make should lead us in that direction. But oftentimes we get stuck in a certain way of being, or in a certain condition or situation because of our past conditioning or our past upbringing or other things that we've been exposed to in life, and we don't know how to extract ourselves from that thinking, from that conditioning. It's like we're stuck in quicksand and we don't know which way to go.

Each one of us has an engine within that has a desire for us, and it creates steam to keep our life moving forward. But if the pressure gets too great because we're not living our life in the way that we're meant to, then it builds and builds, and it shows up as stress, anxiety, and compulsive and addictive behavior. And in order to take that pressure away, we do these crazy things; we have affairs, we turn to alcohol, we overeat, and so on.

The engine is our soul, our spirit, our connection to Source. It's not going to stop; it will keep going.

You know you are meant for more, and you're finally ready to take full responsibility for your life. You want to feel connected to your soul's desires and passions so you can live in your truest purpose. What if there was a technique that you could use to provide the understanding so that the valve can be opened properly with wisdom and clarity, so you can live robustly and vividly, rather than resorting to stop-gap symptom-masking Band-Aid quick fixes?

Would you take it?

We are literally in the end-times, and we are being given an opportunity to resolve multiple lifetimes worth of karma. That is, if we learn to embrace the opportunity side of the above proverb. But during times of increased energy and challenge, and amidst the experience of ascension symptoms, you may feel completely stressed and overwhelmed. So the question is, how do you shift from being stuck in crises mode to embracing the opportunity?

How do you, in other words, shift from the black-and-white conceptual world of the mechanical mind—where you can find no resolution for these "ascension symptoms"—to the living-color world of the heart and the Higher Self, where you have discovered and mastered your innate ability to transform the very fears and other possibly overwhelming emotions into powerful, purposeful internal guidance systems, so you can be truly present in your life?

How do we heal our severed aspects so we can experience wholeness again? The answer is, we must first go down; we must connect with and heal our inner child—our Lower Self. The Lower Self is our subconscious mind; it is a child, about two to six years old. We must rediscover our childlike innocence. In so doing, we reestablish presence; and it is only in the present moment that the doorway to our Higher Self is open.

We came into this world from another dimension, and as such, we only knew Unity. We are taught separation from the moment of birth. We become totally identified with our minds, our ego or false self, at the expense of our true nature as infinite consciousness having a human experience.

Living from our mind is living life conceptually from our conditioned past, and it reduces us to just going through the motions. There's no real satisfaction because there's no real presence; there's no Self to come from to consciously create our reality.

Reconnecting our severed aspects and fully reclaiming our childlike innocence is code for the healing work that needs to happen, and that begins by healing the unresolved trauma we experienced at birth, and then our most fundamental relationship—the one with our parents. As I said in chapter 11, from the moment of birth we come under the influence of the mechanical mind. From that very moment, everything is stimulus-response, and we are looking at life through the eyes of the past—the unquestioned, unexamined filter through which we see the present. The ascension symptoms I've mentioned are rooted in the unresolved past trauma of the inner child. Clear that up and you will have shifted from crises to opportunity; you will catch the wave into fourth density.

There are two main points I wish to bring out about your past with regard to healing your inner child. The first point is that everything that happened in the past had a part in creating your present, which is your starting point in creating your future. To the extent that you are designating anything in your past as wrong, you are also making something in your present wrong, and that inevitably makes you less effective at creating what you intend in the future. The second point is that although you may have suppressed part of your past, you did survive it. This means that it is completely safe for you to re-explore anything that is in your conscious or subconscious memory.

In this part of this chapter, I will examine in detail the events of greatest significance in the personal histories of most people. These are the times when most people made the most important negative decisions about life. The events are birth and the relationship to one's parents.

As you read the material in this part, I recommend that you notice which items make you feel sad, fearful, or angry, which items you disagree with, and which items you have a hard time paying attention to—these are the most important things in this part for you.

Let's begin by looking at what happens at birth.

BIRTH

Birth is an event that we all share in common, yet it is an event that almost universally is not remembered. Since birth is so commonly suppressed, it may seem a bit strange to you—if you don't remember your birth—that I am even talking about it. You may think that birth is not very important; however, it is important because all first impressions are important. At birth people make their first conclusions about the nature of life outside the womb.

Birth trauma is caused by the sudden and unexpected shock of going from the comforting confines of the womb into an environment that is totally unfamiliar. In the womb, all of our needs were met. We lived in safety and comfort and there was no struggle. Then our bodies became too big for their containers and suddenly we were forced down a passageway that seemed too small. This experience was painful, frightening, and distressing for both the mother and the infant. Then we found ourselves in a hostile world that was cold, bright, and noisy.

What we really needed was to be shown that the outside world is safe, and it is a far more interesting place with infinitely more possibilities than the womb. Unfortunately, we were shown the opposite—not because the people in the delivery room were evil, but because each of them had their own unresolved birth traumas, which were transmitted to the infant in the form of fear, tension, and urgency. So rather than safety and trust, the setting was one of fear. Out of fear comes ignorance; this has led to a set of false assumptions regarding the newborn.

It has been assumed that babies feel nothing during birth. We have concluded that since they don't have fully developed senses, they aren't capable of intense emotions. They have no conscious awareness, they can't see or hear, so how could an infant feel pain? We assume that because they can't speak, they can't communicate or express themselves. Yet the newborn is crying out for help. It is we who do not listen. We seem blind to the possibility that the baby is suffering.

> People say—and believe—that a newborn baby feels nothing. He feels everything. . . . Birth is a tidal wave of sensation, surpassing anything we can imagine. A sensory experience so vast we can barely conceive of it.[1]

The delivery room is set up for the convenience of the attending physicians, beginning with the bright lights aimed at the mother's pelvic area. The baby is very sensitive to light and able to perceive it while still in the womb. The first thing the newborn sees are bright floodlights. The infant is blinded by the light; then several drops of a burning liquid are put into his or her eyes.

The baby is also able to hear in the womb, and of course, the impulses are muted, but in the delivery room they are not. So the first sounds the newborn hears amount to a thunderous explosion of noise—too much for tender eardrums.

The temperature in the womb is about 98°F, and the temperature in the delivery room is about 70°F. This means the nude, wet newborn experiences a sudden 30-degree drop in temperature. That is the equivalent of taking a hot bath and then running outside on a cool day. This "temperature trauma" remains in the body in a suppressed state, and it is most likely the cause of colds.

Furthermore, the infant is not given an opportunity to make an easy transition with its breath. We breathed one way in the womb and, because the umbilical cord is cut immediately, we are forced to learn to breathe outside the womb instantly, in a do-or-die situation. Air striking the lungs for the first time results in unbelievably searing pain. Yet the infant must breathe—there is no alternative. The cord has been cut.

Breathing then becomes subconsciously associated with the pain, fear, and panic of the first breath. This results in perpetual anxiety and feelings of urgency. In order to keep this suppressed, we learn to breathe in a very shallow manner. Tremendous damage was done to our breathing mechanism at birth. Fortunately, it can be healed.

Often, the infant is held upside down and spanked to expedite the process of draining the amniotic fluid from the lungs in order to facilitate breathing. This is extremely traumatic to the newborn, often resulting in chronic back problems.

After all this, what the infant most needs is to be reunited with his or her mother. Instead, the newborn is whisked away and placed in a little box in the nursery. The baby is left alone, trembling with terror, hiccupping, and choking.

Such is the trauma of birth. Having considered all this, the fact remains that it's over and you survived it! So, what's the significance of birth? In many ways, it's the conclusions we all made about life as a result of this early experience. These conclusions have become our lens through which we see life, and they continue to produce results in present time until they are unraveled. Some of these conclusions are:

1. Fear of change, or fear of the unknown—integrating the fear of change associated with birth makes it easier to go through changes in life.

2. Our aliveness hurts people—going through the birth canal activates our mother's birth trauma; this in turn causes her to tense up and shut down, which causes her fear and pain. The infant might conclude that it was his or her fault.

3. Pain follows pleasure—the pleasure of the womb is followed by the pain of birth.

4. You can't trust people; they hurt you.

5. The world is hostile.

6. You have to struggle to survive.

7. Breathing causes pain.

THE PARENTAL DISAPPROVAL SYNDROME

First, I want to be clear that this discussion is not about blame. Blame always evades responsibility. It locks energy in place and ensures the continuance and abundance of what you said you did not want. Parenthood is probably the most difficult job on the planet for which there is no proper training. The vast majority of parents have done the best they could, given what they had to work with.

The point is, all parents are under the effects of what I call a pattern—that is, unconscious, repetitive behavior handed down from generation to generation. Our parents disapproved of us because they were disapproved of by their parents, because they were disapproved of by their parents, and on back. As you can see, this quickly becomes a vicious circle. Does it sound familiar?

Parents manipulate their children because they were manipulated by their parents, and so on. They use discipline (control) to keep their children in line. The message to the children is that they are not okay the way they are—love and approval are conditional, and must be earned.

Our parents experienced disapproval as children. They resented it, but they suppressed their feelings because they didn't have a big enough body or vocabulary to get even, and they had probably already learned that it wasn't okay to express anger. The only thing they could do was more of what was disapproved of, which only caused more disapproval. This often led to punishment—physical abuse, verbal abuse, being ignored, being isolated, or being thrown a fierce glance.

At a certain point, the children gave up and decided they couldn't win. They decided to surrender their divine authority in the name of following instructions; they moved from the heart to the mind. Most people have been following instructions ever since. They were invalidated by their parents the same way their parents were invalidated by their own parents.

They also may have concluded that there was something wrong with them, that they were bad, and these children may have begun to disapprove of themselves. We all have inside us a parent and a child; one's inner parent can be used to disapprove of the inner child. We carry out the whole cycle in our own minds and bodies without any further input.

At the point when approval becomes a need, children begin to experience anxiety as a result of fear of disapproval. This is based on the assumption that our self-worth depends on what others think of us (or what the "others" inside us think of us).

When approval becomes a need or an addiction, rather than a preference, we become a conformist, spending our life conforming to parents and other authority figures in order to earn their approval. A common pattern that emerges then is the need-obligate syndrome. We have decided we can't do what we want to get what we need, and since others have what we need, we are obligated to do whatever others want. We are then dependent upon others and must perform some unpleasant task to earn the love and approval we so desperately need. Approval is a need that must be earned.

The other side of the coin is a rebel, where the person has given up on approval and spurns it. There is ultimately no difference between a rebel and a conformist. They are both governed by the same thing. Rebels are simply conformists who have given up hope of getting what they need, so they cover up that need with a rebel act.

A common pattern that emerges from rebel consciousness is called "failing, to get even," especially if your parents put pressure on you to succeed. The decision made here is "since you were such terrible parents, I'll get even with you. I'll fail." So, you fail in jobs and relationships, or if something starts going right you find a way to sabotage it, because if you succeeded, you would have to admit they did a good job in raising you.

You may also play this out by attempting to be far more successful than your parents were, but because it is based on getting even, it is success without satisfaction. The problem here is that you never really get even enough. In fact, it becomes a game of one-upmanship, at which point failure becomes what your life is about. You are the one who fails to get even because getting even is itself an act of failure. Only giving up the game releases you.

Since parents are your fundamental relationship, anything unresolved between you will come up in your other relationships. In fact, your life is about your incompletion with your parents—you will find yourself being shaped by, dominated by, and limited by this incomplete relationship.

You will find yourself creating "substitute parents," where "you tend to recreate their personalities as closely as possible in your other relationships."[2] That means you will probably discover at some point that you married your mother or father, or your boss is your father. So, in order to make it with your mate or at work, you first must complete your relationship with your parents.

Also, "you tend to recreate the kind of relationships you had with your parents in your other relationships."[3] You will tend to find a partner who treats you the way your parents treated you, and you will tend to act out your parents' roles in your current relationships.

Then when you have children, you will have finally gone one full turn on the vicious cycle. You have finally found someone on whom you can take out your suppressed hostility. And around and around it goes unless you end the cycle.

EMOTIONAL ABUSE

Emotions are energy in motion. We need them, and we need to have a healthy relationship with them. But we have all been emotionally abused to some degree and have learned as a result that at least some of our emotions are not okay.

For example when young, were you really allowed to feel and express your anger when your needs were being violated? Most likely you were told, "Never act like that again," or "Don't you ever talk to me like that again! What's wrong with you? Shame on you!" So you more than likely learned at an early age that anger wasn't okay.

Sadness makes insecure parents feel as though they're not creating a happy home for their children. You may have been told, "Quit crying—what's the matter with you?" or maybe "Stop crying or I'll give you something to cry about!" In this way you learned you couldn't be sad.

Being afraid may have disturbed your parents. You may have been laughed at, or your fear may have been minimized by being told there was nothing to fear. So you learned that fear wasn't okay. It may not have been okay even for you to feel joy, given that most parents unwittingly prevent their children from having higher self-esteem than they do. So you may have learned that you have no right to be happy or enthusiastic.

What this means is that if you were told you were wrong, bad, stupid, or crazy for feeling what you felt, then you learned on a very deep level that there was something wrong with you for feeling the way you did. In other words, you were shamed for feeling your emotions. According to author John Bradshaw, shaming is the most damaging assault on your self-esteem because it has no boundaries.[4] Your whole being is affected by shame. Bradshaw's excellent book on shame is called *Healing the Shame That Binds You*.

So, if you experienced emotional abuse, you have emotional problems to some degree, and the emotions are bound with shame. After a while you don't feel shame anymore because you have internalized it, and now you are it! You have learned on a very deep level that you are worthless, that you can't trust your feelings or perceptions, that you always get it wrong because you are wrong—not because you made a mistake, but you *are* a mistake!

You may have noticed these unresolved emotions don't just dissolve. They live in the body in the form of stuck energy, held in place by shallow breathing. Furthermore, because they create unpleasant sensations in the body, you develop body armor and withdraw awareness from your body. You then internalize these emotions through denial, avoidance, or self-blame, or you externalize them by acting out or blaming others. Neither path ever produces emotional resolution.

SHINING THE LIGHT

Whoa, all of the above unresolved trauma might seem like it's just too heavy a load to even begin to deal with, so where do we go from here? Onward and upward toward resolution and completion—that's where!

The global darkness, as well as our individual darkness is rising to the surface due to the dramatically increased vibratory rate of the planet. If you go into a completely darkened room where you can't see a thing, yet you know where the light switch is, what happens to the darkness the moment you flip on the switch? That's right, it disappears; darkness cannot survive in the presence of light—it gets transformed into the light.

I will now begin to show you how to shine the light of your inner awareness—your Higher Self—onto the inner darkness that you have tried so valiantly to keep suppressed, so you can transmute it into the light of your truest self and transform a black-and-white world into one of living color and surround sound.

Fasten your seat belts!

14

Aligning with Universal Laws

It's easier to ride the horse in the direction he's going.

Werner Erhard

I am someone just like you in many ways. I was under the effects of my emotions—namely anxiety, depression, frustration, anger, dread, guilt, and shame—and that left me with high levels of stress for much of the time, and I thought that it was normal, that it was just the way life is. After all, no one ever showed me any effective methods of dealing with runaway emotions.

Well, that semipermanent state of distress finally snapped and turned into a major life-restricting issue. I am someone who found a permanent solution out of absolute necessity. It is a solution that does not create dependency on any substances, or any outside "authorities." It does not leave you dependent on anyone other than yourself. It is a permanent answer that is only found by looking within yourself, and in so doing, discovering that everything you need is all contained within you. Let me explain.

I remember this as if it were yesterday; it was Saturday, April 10, 1976. It was a beautiful, sunny, yet breezy spring day, I was with one of my best friends, Dick. We were at a baseball game, the home opener for the Oakland Athletics. And, despite the excitement of opening day and the great weather, I felt really down.

At this point in my life, I thought things couldn't get much worse; but they were about to. I knew I was in a position where I needed to change, but one more thing had to happen before I really got it. Dick dropped me off after the game, I opened the front door and stepped into my living room, and then my worst nightmare happened. A chronic low-back injury that was increasingly stressing me out was about to take a serious turn for the worse. As I reached down to pick up a fallen dime, I completely collapsed to the floor. I was unable to move, I was paralyzed, and I was in agonizing, excruciating pain.

I felt not just intense fear, I was in a state of total panic and depression as I helplessly lay there. I was home alone, I was not within reach of the telephone, and my entire world had just collapsed around me. After about two hours, I somehow managed to make it into my bed, for all the good that did. Well, after six months and countless visits to my chiropractor, I was able to sort of get on with my life—sort of, that is.

I now knew that my back was a ticking time bomb. It was no longer a matter of *if* it would snap out, it was only a matter of *when*. I was in a constant state of stress; anxiety, fear, frustration, and depression had become my constant companions.

I made the most important decision I've ever made, "I will get this back thing handled or I will die trying." I vowed I'd find a way to heal myself no matter what. I saved that dime and used it as a constant reminder of that declaration. I was committed to finding a way of getting my life back, no matter what, and no matter how long it took. I clearly recall the many times I would stand in front of a full-length mirror and affirm with total conviction, "I want my body back!" You might think that with such a burning desire, a solution would be forthcoming, but not so. I was struggling to stay above water in a sea of confusion for many years, but I never gave up.

And you must realize that at the time, I knew absolutely nothing; I was asleep and unconscious; I was playing the game of hide-and-seek to perfection. All I had was an absolute unwavering desire to find a solution. As such, I was reduced to creating a pathway through a very dense jungle with nothing but a butter knife. I have since created a super-highway for you.

I am very pleased to tell you that I have completely healed my back, and in so doing, I began to realize that my body was just an outward reflection of a much deeper unresolved issue. I discovered that it was completely a stress-induced injury that was fueled by unresolved emotional trauma from childhood. I discovered a way to go beyond symptoms and get down to and heal the root cause of the problem.

The human body, like everything, is not physical. It's a holographic, illusory, physical form, which in its base state is waveform information. This has massive implications for true healing because what the medical profession and Big Pharma do is treat the body. But the body is just a projection of its base state—waveform information; that's why this only treats symptoms, not causes. The causes are in the base state in information distortion. If you harmonize the distortion, the body must heal because it's just a projection of its base-state construct. My body was able to respond appropriately as a result of my harmonizing the emotional distortion in the base state.

I do not know it all, nor do I pretend to. I am in a constant state of exploring new ideas and digging into and discovering deeper meanings to what I already know; and I do this out of a complete love and fascination for my work. But I do have a pretty good idea of how you may be feeling because I have traveled many long miles in your shoes. I know exactly what it takes to create a relatively stress-free lifestyle that is in harmony with, and not in opposition to, your daily life. And since I share with thousands of people each year, I have extraordinary feedback on how well this works.

I will be speaking to the heart of the matter, not just the mechanics of dissolving stress and anxiety. Successful and permanent stress management is a highly emotional issue, and you will be challenged. I want you to know that I understand, that I respect your struggle and the frustrations that you may be experiencing. I want you to know too, that I will show you how to befriend and transform your emotions, and how to turn every challenge into an opportunity!

I am here to help; I will present you with a straightforward system. It is one that I and thousands of others have used, not only to successfully deal with the stress and tensions of modern-day living, but one that has also transformed our lives. You can do it too!

Speaking of emotions, I did not handle being crippled and paralyzed very well. My distress widened into a permanent state of anxiety; I was convinced that my condition would only worsen, and for years it did just that. Depression and very low self-esteem also became my constant companions. I felt like my life was wasting away.

Dissolving the stress, anxiety, frustration, and depression, and discovering that I have a sure-fire technique to deal with it whenever it presents itself, has transformed my life profoundly. I can tell you that it is extremely satisfying and empowering to know that I am, once again, the master of my own destiny. And needless to say, successfully sharing my system with thousands of others feels pretty good too!

TURNING THE CORNER

I had an experience in August of 1980 that, unbeknownst to me at the time, held the keys to my healing. This experience was so remarkable that, to this day, I sometimes shake my head and wonder if it really happened. I told this story in detail in my last book, *Nothing in This Book Is True, But It's Exactly How Things Are*, so for now, I will simply say that I was witness to not just one, but two spontaneous and miraculous healings of my dear cat, Freddie. The first was from a total paralysis of his two rear legs, and the second was from an eye that had somehow become infected and turned from a normal eyeball into one that looked like a piece of dead meat. My veterinarian considered both conditions to be uncurable; yet the healings happened. He was absolutely amazed.

I finally began to realize that all the stress that we feel, in fact the source of all our problems, is caused by resistance to what is. It is caused by insisting that reality should be different from what it is, because it is not measuring up to the imaginary standard that we have in our mind.

Well, my imaginary standard was that I wanted my body back; I wanted my life back! And all of my attempts to change or alter my condition for the better only resulted in more setbacks and increased levels of frustration; I felt quite helpless.

I remembered Freddie and his complete acceptance of the present moment, no matter what his circumstances were. I finally began to realize that I had to let go of resistance to what is; I had to stop making my condition wrong! Until that time, I habitually made stress and painful low-back feelings wrong and tried to suppress them. You would too; we have all been conditioned to react this way.

From this understanding, I could begin to put the pieces together into a composite whole. I was able to go back and reverse engineer my earlier experiences with Freddie, and develop a system that became the blueprint for my own healing. I have since shared it successfully with thousands of others; this was the birth of my Breath Alchemy Technique!

BODY AWARENESS

I have had many clients who have told me that they have tried virtually everything in an attempt to reduce their stress levels to more manageable levels; yet nothing has worked well. Why has effective stress management been so confusing? Why are so many people like you confused about how to do this? You wouldn't be reading my book if you weren't a little confused. But it's okay if you feel that way because it makes total sense; up until now it hasn't been so simple.

I was confused about it too, as I continued to experience increasing levels of pain and frustration. I felt like I had fallen into a very deep rabbit hole; all my efforts to climb out only seemed to throw me deeper into what had become a bottomless pit. But once I found out what I'm about to share with you, I began to realize that I wasn't as much to blame as were the teachers and books; the fact is that most of what we have been taught and thoroughly conditioned to believe is directly contrary to what really works!

A new client who was burning out in a major way, came to me recently—after reading *Nothing in This Book Is True, But It's Exactly How Things Are*—for a series of Skype coaching sessions. He told me of his traditional background, how he was taught the rules of society and set out to master his life experience through their use. And twenty-five years later, he said, it almost killed him. It was in a search for a way out of the tremendous pain that he had accumulated in his physical body as a result of playing that game that he was led to seek me out.

My friend went on to tell me that as a lawyer, he was deeply immersed in an adversary system and felt stuck. He began to tell me of his frustrations. "I was trained for many years to deal with a body of laws. It's virtually impossible to master them," he said. "They're changing all the time, and no two judges or lawyers ever have the same opinion on something that is written in black and white, which you would think would be so simple, but never is." He told me how his desire to serve other people through this medium was hindered quite a bit by the gross uncertainty of the experience.

I began to tell him about a body of law that is certain and unchanging, "universal laws," as I call them. I told him that these laws or principles work on a 24/7 basis; they never take a vacation. "And as you well know," I said, "you are deemed to know the law and you had better know it for your own good. Ignorance of the law is no excuse!"

Universal laws are relatively simple; if we could take our consciousness and wipe it clean and start from scratch, one day would be enough to learn them. And since you have no resistance to them, you could master them instantly. And it's simpler than that, because part of the human condition is that we resonate with them naturally; so, it would be very easy.

"The practical problem that you're faced with," I told him, "is that in almost every instance, it is directly contradictory to the laws that you and I experience in our daily lives. In order to master these laws, you have to be willing to give up those principles and guidelines that you have been trained to believe are true. And in so doing, instead of trying to push the river, you learn that the river of life flows by itself."

I focused on only three of these universal laws—the Perfection Principle, the Resistance Principle, and the Harmonizing Principle—because they are the cornerstone of my Breath Alchemy Technique. I told him that mastery of these laws will not only alleviate his distress, it will also completely transform his life. The same is true for you. Here are these three principles:

> **The Perfection Principle:** You are perfect, but there are barriers that keep you from experiencing and expressing that perfection. You are a perfectly functioning hologram of the One Infinite Creator; yet when we became our mind, we successfully blocked our connection to Source.
>
> **The Resistance Principle:** Resistance leads to persistence. If you try to resist or change something, it will become more solid. The only way to get rid of something is to just let it be. That doesn't mean to ignore it. Ignoring is actually a form of rejection or resistance. To ignore stress, anxiety, or anger is a very common way of trying to eliminate it. To let something be means to observe it, stay in touch with it, but make no effort to change it.
>
> **The Harmonizing Principle:** The re-creation of an experience, thus re-experiencing it to completion, makes it disappear.

"You say that trying to change something makes it persist," my friend said. "But I thought people were taught to learn to control their emotions. Doesn't that mean trying to resist and change them?"

"Yes," I said. "Look, I know it's a paradox, but the effort to control or change something absolutely ensures its persistence. If you're angry and begin to get angry at your anger and try to change it, your anger will persist. If you're feeling tense and try to relax, you'll continue to be tense. If you are feeling stressed out, you will continue to feel stress as long as you're trying to change it. If you have a headache and try to change it, your head will continue to ache as long as you're trying to get rid of it. This is also true for feelings of fear, sadness, guilt, shame, anxiety, impatience, boredom, depression, bitterness, and so on."

He then asked me how change ever occurs. I told him that this is not about change; rather it is about whether something persists or not. If you try to change your tenseness you may change the form of it, but the tenseness will still persist. It will not disappear; the substance will remain the same.

I told him that in order to re-create an experience, you get totally in touch with it; you rebuild it element by element until it is entirely restructured, and the paradox is, it disappears. So, using the example of tenseness, you first have to get in touch with the elements of tenseness. You get in touch with its exact location, its size, shape—and especially—you get in touch with the actual sensation. You tune in to what it feels like in your body.

So, if you will stop resisting the feeling of tenseness, stop trying to change it, and just be with it, observe it, and feel it; you would in fact re-create the experience of tenseness and it would disappear. Trying to change an experience makes it persist. Re-creating an experience—accepting it, being with it, observing it, and feeling it—makes it disappear.

As our discussion continued, my friend gave me an example of how he's learned to control his anger with regard to a fellow partner in his law firm. He told me that he tends to be quite pushy and that his suggestions quite often sound more like orders. He told me how he would really like to stand up to him, in fact punch him in the mouth on occasion. But for the sake of maintaining peace, he swallows his anger and does what his partner wants. So, he told me that he has learned to maintain control and successfully change his anger into something that will permit him to avoid doing something he might regret.

"So, each time you've been trying to resist and change your anger?" I asked him.

"Yes," he replied. "And I have."

"And is your anger persisting?"

"Yes, but I've changed it so I won't do something I will regret."

I told him that he's modified it, but it still persists. He then asked me how to better deal with it. My suggestion was that he stop resisting his anger, stop trying to modify it, and start to just observe it and feel it. I then guided him through a simple process—encouraging him to witness it, be with it, and get in touch with exactly what anger is for him by noticing his bodily sensations, feelings, and attitudes. I asked him to notice what muscles it is affecting, what sensations it produces in what parts of his body. He really needed to get in touch with his exact bodily sensations and feelings in relation to this person. If he allows himself to fully experience it in this way, I reassured him that his experience of anger will disappear and he will be left with a new experience.

I explained how these three universal principles serve as the foundation for my Breath Alchemy Technique, and how Breath Alchemy harmonizes the emotional and spiritual energies in the body. The process can be applied in daily situations as well as in dedicated sessions. Next, I showed him a profound breathing method known as *circular breathing* and told him that the purpose of this breathing rhythm is to give him the experience of coming more fully into the present moment. The result of this, I said, can be a very useful magnification of emotional feelings, physical sensations, and for many people, spiritual feelings. When these feelings that arise from the subconscious are experienced thoroughly and are embraced rather than pushed away, there is a deep feeling of emotional resolution that leaves you feeling calm, centered, present, and very good. I told him too, that this result, called integration, is permanent.

I then guided him through his first Breath Alchemy session. My friend, upon completion of his session, was absolutely amazed at how good he felt. His exact words: "I didn't know it was possible to feel this good!" He has subsequently reported to me that by applying these principles, his relationship with his law partner has magically cleared up. He now calls me his universal lawyer!

Okay, so what does this have to do with healing the inner child, and thus integrating the ascension symptoms that are surfacing as unwanted, stress-causing emotions? The answer in a word is *everything!* In the chapters that follow, I will show you that *all* stress is caused by our resistance to what is, by our habitual attempts to try and swim upstream. I will show you that it's much easier to ride the horse in the direction he's going.

15

Be Here Now

I first heard of the Resistance Principle and the Harmonizing Principle—and how they contain both the problem and the solution to all of our unwanted conditions—way back in 1972. I had some initial success, but it took many more years of putting up with or trying to change my condition before I finally began to get it. These principles, along with my experience with Freddie, became the cornerstone for my Breath Alchemy Technique.

I must also say that to this day I still do not fully understand how Freddie was so spontaneously and completely healed; maybe it was pure luck, maybe my burning desire for his healing and for my own healing was a factor. Whatever the reason, he was a great teacher; he led purely by example and with total humility.

THE LAW OF CAUSE AND EFFECT

There is yet another extremely important universal law that we must not only be aware of, but we must master if we truly wish to be in harmony with life. This principle is called the law of cause and effect.

What you believe about life now is what controls your life. This law says you always get what you want, there are no exceptions. Wanting is defined as both conscious and subconscious, and most of what controls you is on a subconscious level. Wants are a result of beliefs. Many of your beliefs are acquired under circumstances that cause you to suppress them immediately after you adopt them. Therefore, you don't remember where they came from; in fact, you aren't even consciously aware of many of them. Since most of what controls us is on a subconscious level, most of our beliefs, the operating principles in our lives, are on a less than conscious level, and *you have thousands of these beliefs.*

As we go through the life experience, creating things in our lives, it's rather difficult to say, "Oh, I created that," because you are not conscious-mind aware that you did, but we know from the principle involved, and principles are unfailing, that you did.

There is one simple way to use the law of cause and effect—and it's the only way to use it successfully—and that is backward. If you see what you have created in your life, you know you wanted it. Done that way, you will never fool yourself. If you do it forward to backward, there is room for a lot of mischief. You can always say, "In this particular case, I really didn't." And you can very often point to a lot of circumstances so seemingly the fault of someone else, or beyond your control, that you could probably get a hundred people to agree with you that you had nothing to do with it. But that will only misguide you. If anything occurs in your life, you know you created it. Not only did you create it, but you want it to be precisely the way it is. And that includes the status of your relationships, your work and financial situation, and everything else in your life.

Many, perhaps most, people have difficulty with this and seem to be forever looking for exceptions to this rule of law. However, this law says you can have anything you want, and in fact, you get it! That people focus on the one side of it is interesting: it is a function of the way we view the life experience, constantly looking at the troublesome side, the negative side.

Everything that you experience in your life is a projection outside of you, of your state of consciousness, that's all you ever experience. Anything that is less than totally comfortable for you is a result of a subconscious belief that it has to be that way.

We do create everything that happens in our lives, and it's wonderful that it is that way, because as you get in touch with universal principles, as you get in touch with that part of you that is real, you will experience such magnificence that it is beyond the ability of the human mind to describe it.

We tend to believe that we are who we project ourselves to be, and we do a good job of convincing each other that we really are that way. So we get locked into this crazy situation of acting certain ways that are much less than who we really are, and getting the reinforcement from others who respond to us the way we project ourselves. The trick then is to break this; we have to get in touch with the fact that we are not our beliefs. We are not how we act, and other people aren't either. It takes some practice to do this, but here are three tips to get started:

First, recognize that you always get what you want is to say to yourself, "Oh, look what I created." You do this because you know from the unfailing principle that you did create this particular situation even though you may not be conscious-mind aware that you did.

Second, there is no such thing as right or wrong, good or bad, in the physical universe. Everything that happens is just another event that you singly or in group created. When you judge anything, from an energy standpoint, you lock the energy up tight, and where you lock it is always in the same place, in your physical body. Judge anything, judge anybody, and what you end up doing is creating extraordinary energy blocks in your body that you carry around as pain. The only solution is making peace with the judgment.

Our society has a tremendous investment in, and has taught us well, to judge virtually everything in life. We are literally taught that we cannot go through life unless we evaluate, judge, and analyze everything that happens to you. Unfortunately, the truth is exactly the opposite. Not only is it the opposite, but the very act of judging is so counterproductive that you cannot get on with your life when you do it; it is a total block.

So, we must learn not only not to judge anymore, but also to release all of the judgments we presently have. There is no substitute for it; there are no shortcuts. The simplest way to start is in the present, because that's the only time that exists anyway. Whatever you experience in the present moment in your life is true for you for all times. If you notice whatever's going on in your life—any particular person or people that you are having difficulty with—just deal with those situations. They represent, for you, all of the other people that you might have problems with.

You do it very simply, but you have to watch out for one big trap, one of the biggest traps in the Universe: if you look to figure out the "why" of anything, you are in deep trouble. There is another principle involved here that you must watch out for; it is called the Law of Increase. What you focus on expands. If you focus on the "why," and you invariably ask "why" when you have a problem, what you will get is more of the problem. Principles work all of the time; you can't sneak around them. So no judging of others, no judging of yourself either, as that is equally counterproductive; and that's something we tend to do quite a bit. Also, no judging of the events and circumstances in your life.

Third, this is a critical step. How would you like to feel? Since we all want to feel good, the answer is pretty obvious. To do it, you have to make friends with the Harmonizing Principle.

There are actually two ways to use the Harmonizing Principle: one way is to integrate the situation you have the negative feelings about by choosing a positive context for it, and the other is to integrate the unpleasant feelings themselves into your sense of well-being. Either one of these approaches will work, however, there are some significant advantages to working at the feeling level. Feeling is in the moment—it is immediate, and thinking is not. You can feel the integration as it's taking place. With mental processing on the other hand, it might take a while to figure out what's good about the situation. And then, it's not always clear if you have done enough to produce the desired result.

Another problem is that the mind you are trying to change is always the same mind that is directing the process. It may appear to be reformed, yet it is quite capable of tricking you into falsely believing that you've resolved the situation, and you're left with positive thinking. That only creates an even thicker barrier between your conscious mind and your subconscious mind by plastering over the unresolved feelings. Therefore, it is extremely useful to know that if you make peace with the feeling by shifting the context in which you are holding it, the mental context (the situation you were making wrong) will also shift.

THE ESSENCE OF BREATH ALCHEMY

Keeping the above in mind, let's take a look at the essence of Breath Alchemy. Breath Alchemy is the practical application of the Harmonizing Principle. It is a system that enables you to achieve emotional resolution with regard to any stressful situation, working at the *feeling* level. It enables you to relieve yourself of the burden of negativity that you have carried due to suppressing emotions from any part of life. It does so by going well beyond symptom masking and quick fixes and harmonizes the distortion in the base state.

Breath Alchemy is *also* a technique that enables you to make a creative breakthrough with regard to any situation that you are dealing with in life. Once you learn how to use the Breath Alchemy Technique, you can use it *by yourself* anytime, anywhere, while engaging in any activity.

Breath Alchemy is a kinesthetic process; that means it is a feeling-level system for eliminating negativity. All of the problems that you have in life come from your own negative contexts that interfere with your ability to have your ideal relationship with the things that are happening in your life. All negative contexts come from insisting that reality should be different from how it is.

I'm sure you have noticed by now that reality is not the way it "should be," reality is the way it is. In order to eliminate the source of your distress so you can be more creative and at peace with your life, it is necessary to find a more useful relationship with the reality of your experience. Breath Alchemy is a way to do that without engaging in a lot of mental head trips. You don't need to have a cognitive understanding of what you are dealing with using the Breath Alchemy Technique; you can do it entirely at the feeling level.

And one more thing: Breath Alchemy is not about the past, it *is* about the present moment. All that matters about the past is what you are currently carrying with you from the past. From past experiences, you do have some traces of trauma or negativity that are still influencing you from the subconscious level and influencing your feelings. These can have a profound impact on the way that you make your decisions, on your behavior, your habits, and on your feelings.

All that matters is the feelings that you are carrying with you now, and you can best get access to those in the present moment. The analogy I like is that if you pack a lunch and go on a hike, you don't have to go back to the moment you put your lunch in the sack in order to eat your lunch. You get access to it best in the present moment; the same thing is true of all of your emotions.

So, this is not a regressive process to take you back to your birth, or your early childhood, or really to anything. Quite the opposite, this is a process of coming more fully into the present moment than you usually do, and letting yourself *feel* the present moment more richly and honestly than you have typically been doing.

MAXIMIZING YOUR ENJOYMENT OF THE PRESENT MOMENT

Breath Alchemy is really about maximizing your enjoyment of the present moment. And with that in mind, I would like to have you try a process. This is very simple; it's a process of maximizing your enjoyment of the present moment. I suggest that you close your eyes; notice what your body feels like and notice that the present moment is indeed enjoyable, at least to some extent.

> Focus in on the enjoyable quality of the present moment, and make up your mind to enjoy the moment even more.

Really open up to the pleasure that's available in the present moment, and enjoy it now, even more.

And now enjoy it even more.

Good, now double the amount that you're enjoying the present moment.

Now enjoy the present moment infinitely.

Alright, now, if you're like most people, what happened for you at *some* point during that process was that you reached the point where it seemed like no matter what you did, that's just as much as you can enjoy the present moment. You reached what seems to be the limit to how much you *can* enjoy the present moment.

Well, what does that limit feel like? Or put another way, what is it that is limiting your ability to enjoy the present moment? Whatever that limit is, that is something that you can focus on and have a vivid experience of and find a new way of relating to, so that you can *expand* your ability to enjoy the present moment to include whatever it was that was placing that limit there.

That is the essence of how Breath Alchemy works. What you do is find what feeling is limiting your ability to enjoy the present moment and you apply the Breath Alchemy Technique to that feeling, so that you can include that feeling in what contributes to being you; and you can expand your ability to enjoy the present moment.

Now, doing this does more than simply expand your ability to be present; it does do that. It does, in fact, expand your ability to be peaceful; but it also has a profound effect on your mind. All of the feelings in your body that cause stress and limit your enjoyment come about from insisting that something that you are contemplating should be different from what it is.

Any time you compare the reality of the present moment to what I call an "imaginary standard," you create negativity. You create a withdrawal from the reality of your situation that creates the illusion of limitation and reduces your creativity and your effectiveness. And it creates an unpleasant feeling in your body that limits your ability to enjoy the present moment.

If you change your mind about that, the feeling that you have about it will change at the same moment. But more important for understanding how Breath Alchemy works, if you change your relationship to the feeling itself, that will change how your mind relates to the situation at hand. That change of relationship to what you're dealing with—or that change of context—both resolves the emotion that you are having *and* gives you a creative breakthrough.

All creative breakthroughs come from shifting from a context in which you're insisting that something should be different from how it is, into a context in which you're focusing on what *is* currently there that you can use as a resource. This allows your natural creative process to flow, enabling you to find the solution based on what *is* there.

And so, in every case, the result of Breath Alchemy is embracing reality in a new and more useful way; and it is done entirely at the feeling level. So, Breath Alchemy is about maximizing your enjoyment of the present moment, thus enabling you to find relief in any stressful situation. You might then ask, "How do you do that?"

The answer will be revealed in the following chapters, so stay tuned!

16

The Building Blocks of Breath Alchemy

As mentioned in the previous chapter, Breath Alchemy is about maximizing your enjoyment of the present moment. The answer to how one does this is through application of the skills known as the Five Step Harmonizing Method of Breath Alchemy. The Five Steps are the Harmonizing Principle in action.

FIRST, A BIT OF HISTORY

Breathwork has gone through major changes as it has evolved over the years. Originally, in 1974, it began as a very valuable but often painful and cathartic process involving intentional over-breathing with a forced exhale, which created hyperventilation (modern circular breathing *never* involves hyperventilation). This often, but not always, ended with a "release" and a blissful feeling of completion. The Five Step Harmonizing Method completely transforms the process of breathwork. These steps were initially developed by Jim Leonard; he called them the Five Elements.

I can best illustrate the significance of this breakthrough discovery by sharing my earliest experiences of rebirthing, as it was exclusively called back in the day. In February of 1979, I took a weekend workshop on relationships co-led by two friends of mine. At one point they told us we were going to do the "breakthrough process." This is the name they decided upon after their initial introduction to rebirthing in a weekend workshop just one week earlier.

With no previous training, and very little understanding of the process, suffice it to say that they were in no way qualified to teach us. They described and demonstrated what they called a connected breathing rhythm and then told us to lie down and begin breathing in that manner. They offered no other explanation.

Their description instantly triggered a red alert in my mind. I knew it would cause hyperventilation, and I thought that was dangerous. So, I lay down on the floor along with the rest of the group (there were about ten of us), but because of my extensive belief system and fear surrounding hyperventilation, I decided not to breathe that way.

Then my friend, the co-leader, looked at me and saw I wasn't breathing. Of course, he instructed me to breathe as directed. I said, "No, it's hyperventilating and that's dangerous." He said, "No, it's okay, breathe." I decided to breathe only when he was watching me. Since there were ten of us, he would only be noticing me about ten percent of the time. When he watched I breathed; of course, I was fighting and resisting it all the way. It felt scary and awful. The moment he looked away, I stopped. And so it went for what seemed like an eternity. I breathed just enough to make myself sick. I felt dizzy and nauseated. It took me a few hours to recover.

But since I was totally committed to finding a way to heal myself, I continued to pursue rebirthing as a possibility. One month later, I found myself in a two-day rebirthing workshop given by two of the most qualified teachers of the day. Well, that turned out to be as bad or even worse than my initial experience. So circular breathing is not just a straightforward automatic thing; in the absence of the Five Steps, it can be very problematic indeed!

Jim Leonard researched what happened in the moment of "release" wondering what exactly caused the bliss and why such a blissful result often happened only after dreadful discomfort. What he found was that at the moment of release people finally surrendered to the feelings they had been fighting. He theorized that if a person could possibly surrender sooner, there would not be so much struggle, and the technique could be more efficient. From that, he developed the Five Elements, and a whole new possibility for breathwork began to emerge.

Because of my unshakeable resolve to find a true healing method, I went on and received more training in rebirthing. It was not, however, producing the consistent results that I was looking for, so I went searching for answers. I found what I was looking for out of my decision to work closely with Jim—who I had known and befriended a few years earlier—and his wife at the time, Anne Jill Leonard. What I learned from him, in my view, is the most significant of all the teachings that I have gathered from the many instructors I have worked with over the years. Learning the Five Elements, and the Five Step Harmonizing Method I created from that, has completely transformed my life, and it can do the same for you.

It wasn't until late 1987 that I fully committed myself to mastering his technique. I took the first of several trainings from Jim and Anne beginning in March 1988. He was extremely generous in his willingness to share his time and expertise with me; and for that, I am eternally grateful. I went for numerous private sessions, and though it took some time and patience to undo the bad habits I had acquired from earlier experiences, I finally began to create some serious healing. I was beginning to get my life back!

THE FIVE STEP HARMONIZING METHOD

Breath Alchemy is really *one* process; however, it can best be taught by describing it as five component skills called the Five Step Harmonizing Method of Breath Alchemy. In the course of maximizing your enjoyment of the present moment, anything that is standing between you and the ability to enjoy each moment infinitely will come to your attention.

And you can apply the technique to whatever that is. The Five Steps then are ways of relating to the present moment. Every moment feels like something. Another way to put that is, in every moment there is some pattern of energy that is most prominent. So to engage in the Five Steps, this is what you do:

1. **Circular Breathing:** You breathe in the way that most enables you to have rapport with that feeling.
2. **Complete Relaxation:** You relax in the presence of the feeling, rather than taking action to make it go away.
3. **Awareness in Detail:** You tune the feeling in. It is asking for your attention, so you give it your attention.
4. **Integration into Unity:** You find a way to relate to that positively; you find a way to accept the feeling as it is, rather than insisting that something else should be your present moment experience.
5. **Do Whatever You Do, Willingness Is Enough:** Whatever your response to the feeling is, it's alright; everything leads ultimately to integration anyway.

So you don't have to do the first four steps perfectly. And you won't. That's good news, that you don't have to do it perfectly. There is a huge margin for safety in the Universe. You can screw up badly and still survive, as you have probably noticed. The fifth step applies to life.

It's important though, to realize that the Five Steps are not steps that you do sequentially. Instead, you do them all simultaneously because Breath Alchemy is just one process, it's not five separate processes.

The Five Steps, when used together, will give you the result called integration. It is so called because you integrate something into your sense of well-being. Everyone has a sense that certain things contribute to their well-being. But they also think that there are other things that detract from their well-being.

So, Breath Alchemy is about focusing on something that you think has been detracting from your well-being and, by applying the technique, you integrate that into your well-being so that it is obvious to you that it does contribute to you positively. Doing that eliminates stress and all other forms of negativity at the source. It also calms and centers you, leaving you feeling more creative and more effective.

It is absolutely essential to realize that the Five Steps are skills; they are not just a model of what happens automatically in the Breath Alchemy system. All of the Five Steps are skills that you have some degree of mastery with already, just because of your life experiences. At the same time, they are skills that you can keep getting better at forever.

BREATH ALCHEMY WORKS AT THE FEELING LEVEL IN YOUR BODY

The experiences you have in life are what they are; however, what they mean to you and the effect that they have on you—whether they bring on peace or distress, and whether they empower you or disempower you—all of that is a function of how you relate to them.

You can learn to change how you relate to things; so if you discover that you are relating to something in a way that makes you feel unhinged or disempowered, you can develop a skill for changing your relationship to it so that you will benefit from it. And that's really what this is about.

That sounds sort of intellectual, but this technique is not intellectual at all. Breath Alchemy produces its results at the feeling level in the body. You notice your feelings about what's there, and you change your relationship to the feeling; that's the most efficient method for changing your relationship to what the feeling is about. There will be a lot more detail forthcoming.

I am using the word *feeling* in its broadest possible sense, and that is the term that I will use most often in conjunction with this. What I mean by that is anything you feel in any sense of the word *feel*.

It was Aristotle who proposed the limiting idea that we have five senses; we actually have more than five senses even if you don't talk about extrasensory stuff. If you just talk about your physical senses, there are lots more than five. For example, it is a totally different sense by which you perceive heat than by which you perceive pressure.

In Aristotle's system, all kinds of things would be included in the sense of touch. Some of that seems pretty weird, because how do you know when you've had too much coffee to drink? You feel it, and it's not because you're touching each cup of coffee; you feel it inside. Or how do you know when you're angry? It's not because you feel your fist touching someone's jaw, you feel it inside.

I use the word *feeling* to include all of that. It includes your emotional sense, your literal sense of touch, your biochemical sense, your intuitive sense, and all those kinds of things. I sometimes also use the word *kinesthetic* to mean all these things. That word has not always been broadened to include everything in the feeling sense, but that's the way it is used in neuro-linguistic programming, and it is used here in the same way.

- It means the feeling of fear.
- It means the feeling of tiredness.
- It means feeling worried.
- It means feeling like you drank too much coffee.
- It means feeling an itch.

NO NEED TO LABEL

The physical sensations that go with an emotion would only be called an emotion if you were labeling it, otherwise you might just call it tension. It could be that what anger is like for you is that you get tight in the chest and tight in the arms and the jaw. If you know why you are angry, like if your boss is there yelling at you, it's easy to label it as anger. But if you have those same physical sensations and you don't have any reason to attribute it to anger, you might just call it tightening of the jaw or tension.

The technique works equally well either way, there is no real benefit to labeling the feelings that come up. The word *feeling* is especially apt because what matters in this process is just to feel whatever is there; labeling it as an emotion doesn't make any difference.

It can, in fact, be a distraction because people tend to label feelings in order to avoid having contact with them. They start to focus on the label and the corresponding narrative, instead of the feeling itself. As soon as you describe it you have taken a step away from reality; the label is only a conceptual representation of the sensation. So, what I mean is the thing itself that you are actually perceiving—the feeling itself.

That is significant, especially when we are dealing with the feeling realm, because of this tendency to label a feeling. For instance, if you get tension across your chest, you might call it discomfort, or you might call it anger. If so, it will be a blanket statement in your mind, it will be firmly rooted, and your reaction to it will be based on the label. If it's unpleasantness, you will act on it like you have to withdraw in order to avoid the unpleasant feeling. And because of that lack of contact, there is not a lot of flexibility—not much, if any, sense of getting benefit.

This is about opening your senses to what you are experiencing now, and that is the feeling itself. Keep reading and I will explain how this is done.

JUDGMENT

In chapter 11, I said that all of the problems we have in life come from judgment, from insisting that reality should be different from how it is. I also said I would unpack this in a future chapter; now is the time to do that.

I have given the details on the veiling, why it was necessary, and that it was successful in that it created violation of free will, which in turn created movement and creativity. However, we have reached a point where it is no longer useful or necessary because it also locked us into our polarized mind, which sees good and evil but not wholeness. As such, the mind is in a continual state of judgment. It looks out at a world that it perceives as separate from itself, and compares what it sees to the "ideal" that is held in the mind. If the situation at hand does not live up to the ideal standard, it is judged as bad or wrong. The same type of judgment is made about other people if we do not agree with their behavior.

Now, take a moment to look at all the times you have judged someone or something. Yes, it is a countless number of times; we are stuck in judgment. Whenever you do this, there is the judgment itself—you have decided that the person or the situation at hand is bad and wrong for not measuring up to the ideal held in your mind; furthermore, there is usually a high degree of emotional charge connected with the judgment. Then there is an instantly created energetic component; you can call it a bodily sensation, or simply a feeling. Because the mental component is making the person or situation wrong, the corresponding sensation can only be an unpleasant feeling.

We then do our utmost to avoid feeling that unpleasant pattern of energy, so our breathing becomes inhibited, and we do whatever we can to distract ourselves (see my previous discussion on suppression). That sensation, in turn, lives in the body as unresolved, stuck energy. So, we lock the energy up tight; yet emotions are energy in motion. Every time there's an energy that wants to be in motion, and you are stuck in judgment, or make-wrong, that energy has nowhere to go, so it stays in your body. Eventually that stuck energy will start popping out in undesirable ways like stress, anxiety, tension, frustration, guilt, shame, aches and pains, stiff joints, and arthritis, and so on. I will simply say that this unresolved emotional trauma living in the body as stuck energy is the source of *all* illness and disease.

What we do then, whenever we judge, is lock ourselves into the resistance principle. This is the one that says resistance leads to persistence. We have unwittingly agreed to an ever-increasing diet of what we don't like and do not want. That in turn reduces us to just going through the motions and living life conceptually. We are eating the menu!

CONTENT AND CONTEXT

Breath Alchemy is about harmonizing with the reality of your experience, whatever your experience is moment by moment. Let's take a moment now to look at the relationship between *content* and *context*. By *content,* I mean "the thing itself" or "reality itself." The thoughts in your mind, as well as the sensations in your body and the circumstances in your life are all content. *Context* is "the container in which you hold the content;" it is your relationship to what you are experiencing.

Your mind does not relate to the content of your reality directly. Rather, it perceives reality through the lens that is the context in which you are holding your experience. In the unawakened state, we see the present through the eyes of the past, from our conditioning; these traumatic incidents and the beliefs we have formed about life from them become the unwitting filter—or context—through which we see life. We are living mechanically in our belief systems, rather than in our experiences. It's as though we put on a pair of very dark glasses and then forgot that we're wearing them—everything in life will look dark— everything we see and experience is shaped, molded, and formed by the lens through which we are unknowingly looking, and we think that's the way life is.

When you realize that your context determines how the content of your experience affects you, you are now opening the doorway to consciously creating your life experiences. Knowing that the circumstances in your life (the content) affect you only as a function of the context in which you hold them is very empowering.

A negative context is a judgment; it is any context in which you compare the content to an imaginary standard and tell yourself that reality should not be the way it is—that it should be the way you are imagining instead. It is nonacceptance of what is, and it keeps you stuck in resistance, which equals persistence. You have let your subconscious mind choose it for you, which usually means contaminating fresh, new situations with stale, old negativity. You are looking at life through the filter of your unquestioned, unexamined past conditioning. Whenever you are holding an experience in a negative context, you are never in the present moment, because a substantial part of your mind is off in something that is totally imaginary and has nothing to do with reality.

A positive context is any context in which you are letting the reality of your experience be the way it is, rather than making it wrong because it doesn't conform to your mind's imaginary standard of how "it should be." It puts you into the present moment, and into your personal power. I assert that in the absence of judgment, or make-wrong, all experiences are empowering and pleasant; that's a big statement to make right now, but it is so because it aligns you with the Harmonizing Principle. This, in turn, allows for emotional resolution.

All it takes to integrate the make-wrong is to feel the feeling in detail. All you need is the physical feeling component of the experience and to shift context with that, so you can have a thorough experience of the actual sensation. You will then discover your innate ability to transmute the feeling that had been unpleasant into your sense of well-being. It now becomes a source of pleasure and is clearly contributing to your aliveness. As soon as you do that, you have integrated at every level and throughout all of your senses. It is called kinesthetic processing; it is done entirely at the feeling level.

BENEFITS OF KINESTHETIC PROCESSING

If you process with words, with affirmations for example, one word comes after another; that's the nature of words. What that means at least, is that it is time-consuming, it takes time to process with words;

whereas it only takes a moment to feel something, you can stay completely in present time and feel something. So, one of the benefits of processing at the kinesthetic level is that it is immediate.

You can run sentences through your mind that lie to you for years at a time, and perhaps you have noticed that you have been doing that. With feelings, you can pretend that you are not feeling anything, you can do that. But if the feeling is there, there is an inherent honesty to it; you feel the feeling that is actually there. It is a more honest sense through which to process than with thoughts; it is inherently grounded in reality.

You can feel when the integration takes place. With affirmations there can often be a sense of, "I have done ten pages of affirmations with this for ten days, is that enough?" It's not always completely clear. But when you are focusing on a feeling in Breath Alchemy, you can feel when it transforms and becomes a pleasant feeling. There is no question about when the integration takes place.

When you are feeling, you can feel the whole pattern at once. For example, if you are grieving the death of a loved one, the feelings that come up are very complex. You might feel glad, sad, mad, guilt, or more. You can feel all of it at once. If you were to verbalize, you could not adequately describe the feeling fast enough. And yet within a split second you can feel the entirety of the feeling; and as the feeling evolves, you can feel it in entirety. So you aren't just dealing with the sadness; you are dealing with the whole complex feeling. And by making peace with the whole complex feeling, you are making peace with all of it all at once. It can be extremely effective because of the multiple levels that are affected.

There are only about fifty words in the English language for feelings, and yet there are hundreds of thousands of patterns of energy that people experience all the time. Words are not very precise in dealing with feelings. With sadness for instance, it feels totally different to feel sad thinking you have done a poor job at something than it does to feel sad about somebody dying. It's a totally different feeling even though they would both be labeled with the same word. Words are a very inefficient method for processing feelings. *Feeling* them works much better. That's why they are called feelings—they are meant to be felt.

For all of those reasons, I think that you are best off learning a kinesthetic process for eliminating make-wrong from your life; there are some substantial benefits to it compared to any kind of mental processing.

INTEGRATION

Integration means that you shift to a positive context regarding something that you had been holding in a negative context.

Because of suppression, integration usually involves two components: You bring the feeling out of suppression so that you are contemplating it consciously. Then you shift from a negative to a positive context.

Roughly, the first three steps of Breath Alchemy deal with the first component of bringing the feeling out of suppression, and the fourth and fifth steps are about the shifting of the context. Those two things together comprise integration.

Breath Alchemy is an extremely efficient method for causing integration. Everyone has experienced integration many times—when experiences that started off seeming bad wound up being obviously good. But for most people, integration takes place rather haphazardly; most people have things they still don't feel good about after twenty years or so. And there may well be some things even from birth or childhood that they haven't felt good about their whole lives. This means that most people spend more time suppressing than they do integrating.

It is greatly to your benefit to learn how to bring about integration at will, to take responsibility for causing integration. That is what this technique is about. If you go about your life with the assumption that you will integrate your emotions about whatever happens, it makes it much easier to plan; it is much easier to stay on purpose with your life.

If you assume you are going to be traumatized for life if you go into a business and the business fails, it makes it very hard to start an endeavor in anything worthwhile. But if you know that even if the business does fail, you will learn some valuable things that will make you better at business forever after, it makes it very easy to take the chance. That's the best attitude to have, and that's true for almost any process in life.

This is different from being compulsively positive. There are some ways you can change your relationship to things so you enjoy or get benefit from them, ways that make them "right." But there are also equally important contexts that don't make it right. Acceptance doesn't necessarily make it right; it just makes it okay. Sometimes a neutral context, where you are allowing something to be the way it is, even if you don't initially like it, is better than a positive context.

To put it a little bit differently, it is always to your benefit to be aware of the benefits you get from everything. But it is not useful to be positive by ignoring reality, for instance, by going into a new business venture with very positive thoughts like "I'm sure I will always succeed at everything no matter what I do," and "I don't really need customers because God is the source of my supply," or "I don't need to do any selling, I don't like selling anyway." If you are doing this, you are ignoring an important part of reality, and that won't work to your benefit. But instead, if you focus on the reality of your experience and find a positive and empowering way to relate to it, that's useful. That's of actual benefit.

So if you leave the third step out of Breath Alchemy, you wind up with positive thinking. Putting the third step in there is absolutely essential. That is what allows you to integrate things and to come into better and better relationships to reality. It is important to have reality in that formula.

THE BREATH

Most people are breathing less than they should be; this is a result of judgment—or make-wrong, as I like to call it—and the attempt to distance yourself from the unpleasant feelings that it produces. I will refer you back to the topic of suppression in chapter 12. Sub-ventilating is exhale-oriented breathing and it anesthetizes the body. In exhale-oriented breathing, you slowly push the exhale out, and after a long pause, inhale a small amount of air—almost as an afterthought. It is literally holding your breath, and it greatly restricts your intake of life-enhancing prana and oxygen. The energy in your body that wants to be in motion has nowhere to go, so it stays in your body. Eventually that stuck energy will start popping out in undesirable ways, as you have probably noticed.

Inhale-oriented breathing is pulling firmly, yet smoothly and evenly on the inhale and relaxing on the exhale. Your breathing becomes efficient because you are using all your energy for the inhale. You don't have to exert effort on the exhale because relaxation and your natural muscle contractions will do it for you.

Additionally, you are filling the cells with oxygen; your cells greatly prefer oxygen to carbon dioxide. Paul Bragg, author of *Super Power Breathing,* says in his book that we are slowly committing suicide because of the way we live and breathe. According to Bragg, shallow breathing starves the body of vital oxygen and causes premature aging. Bragg notes that oxygen-starved people go to bed tired and wake up tired. They suffer from headaches, constipation, indigestion, muscular aches and pains, stiff joints, aching backs, and the list goes on.[1] Medical research shows that over 90 percent of the body's energy is produced by oxygen, and that the more oxygen we have in our system, the more energy we produce. Our ability to think, feel, and act comes from the energy created by oxygen.

When you are breathing efficiently, you are breathing prana and oxygen. This combination keeps the body clean—it flushes the circulatory, nervous, and respiratory systems as well as the aura or energy body. It cleanses psychic dirt, negative mental mass, physical tension, physical illness, and emotional problems out of human consciousness.

The breathing used in Breath Alchemy allows that stagnant energy to move again. It creates a wavelike motion of energy that moves through your body. That energy is life-force energy, or prana—it is the energy of life, and as such, it is the purest and most powerful healing energy in the Universe. It has been called different names in different cultures. In Chinese energy systems, it is called *chi*. The Japanese call it *ki,* and all through the Eastern part of the world there are words for this energy. But no matter what you call it, it is Source energy.

The breath is the vital link between spirit and matter, between pure Source energy and the physical universe. There is a life-force energy that we are flowing in, that's flowing into us and through us, and that sustains us. Breathing is like our umbilical cord to our true mother, which is this energy of universal life. Breath is that vital link between spirit and the body, it is a way of bringing heaven onto earth. It is the link between the spiritual and the material.

With circular breathing, the inner and outer breath merge. The outer breath is the lungs and physical breathing; the inner breath is the flow of life-force energy or prana. In a Breath Alchemy session, they join: your outer breathing joins with an internal rhythm, the internal rhythm of connecting to Source.

AN OVERVIEW OF HOW BREATH ALCHEMY WORKS TO CAUSE INTEGRATION

The breathing enhances your awareness of the aliveness streaming through your body. Circular breathing creates a wavelike motion of the energy in your body that enhances your ability to feel that energy. If you've never done this before, you have no idea what I'm talking about; but if you have, you know that when you breathe like this, you start to feel all that energy in your body.

When you start to feel the enhanced energy of aliveness streaming through your body, it will feel 99 percent pleasurable and 1 percent weird. Now, the percentages might vary somewhat, but basically it's 99 percent pleasurable because it fundamentally feels good to feel your aliveness. The 1 percent weird is because whatever emotions you have been suppressing will come to your attention now that you are running more energy through your body. This is the healing aspect of the prana: it is bringing up the packets of stuck energy that you have been suppressing due to judgment.

So, if you have been suppressing emotions in your chest and you start the circular breathing, you will feel them gradually emerging in that area. All it takes then is focus on the feeling by tuning it in, and then changing the way you relate to it in order to accomplish integration.

When the feeling first starts coming up, it might seem mildly weird and pretty interesting. If you don't give it your attention and you keep breathing, it will get more and more intense, just like anything in life. Eventually it can reach the point of being intense discomfort. You can decide when you are going to focus on it and embrace the reality of it. You can stay in denial until it gets really intense, or you can very intentionally focus in on the feeling when it is still subtle and integrate it there. You do that by giving it your attention when it first appears as the most prominent feeling.

More intensity does not produce more results. That is very important. This was a theory that was held about breathwork at one time, but it does not work out that way. This also differs from the theory of primal therapy, where they say that a feeling has to come back to the same level of intensity as when it was first experienced. That is just plain false.

The amount of intensity with which you experience something is a separate function from the make-wrong. That has to do with how much juice you are putting into the make-wrong at the present moment. Some people can become wildly upset if they go into their donut store and find they are out of their favorite donuts. You may not think of that as a big deal, but a person can make it as big a deal as they choose to. And other people are able to integrate very big things in their lives relatively easily. You may have noticed that on a given topic, some days you will be very intense about it, and other days you will still be aware of those feelings, but it just won't be so intense.

You can learn to adjust the breathing to bring it to the perfect intensity and comfort level so you can integrate easily on a very subtle level. Some people like intensity; others like calm and mellowness; you can adjust the breathing to give you the level of intensity that suits you best. Integration does require having a thorough experience of the feeling. A thorough experience is not at all the same as an intense experience.

With that said, sometimes it is to your benefit to make the feeling more intense. That doesn't mean that more intensity is always better. There is always that happy medium, and I will give a music analogy. Suppose you are listening to music on your stereo and you know there are piccolos, but the music is real soft and you can't quite hear the piccolos. It is to your benefit then to turn up the volume so you can hear all the nuances that are there. In that situation, turning up the volume will enhance your enjoyment of the music.

That doesn't mean that the louder the music is, the more enjoyment you will get—it just doesn't work that way. If you have a powerful amplifier and speakers that can handle it, and you turn the volume all the way up, at some point, even for those who love loud music, you will be dealing with the overwhelming intensity and pain from the extremely high volume, and you will start missing the subtle nuances in the music then too. You will have less enjoyment. So there is some ideal range in music for maximizing your enjoyment, and the same thing is true in Breath Alchemy.

It is possible to make the energy in your body so intense that you will have a harder time integrating, because you start missing the details of what's coming up, and you're dealing with just the overwhelm of it coming up so intensely. In that situation, it is then to your benefit to take smaller breaths for a while until it gets to a level of intensity where you can easily give it your attention.

There is no difference between changing the context in which you hold your feelings about something and changing the context in which you hold the thing itself. If you are truly at peace with your feelings about another person, that is exactly the same as being at peace with that person; there is no difference. If you are out of harmony with that person in some way, you will have corresponding feelings that you will similarly be out of harmony with.

If you make peace with your feelings about something, that's the same as making peace with the thing itself. You experience another person through your feelings about that person. So, when you make peace with your feelings, you are also making peace with your experience of that person. That is why you can process completely at the kinesthetic level.

WHAT SESSIONS MIGHT BE LIKE FOR YOU

The only way to truly experience the life-transforming experience of Breath Alchemy is to begin with proper one-to-one instructions in the form of coached sessions. Trying to learn it on your own is like trying to learn how to play a piano without getting any lessons. Yes, you will get a sound when you hit any of the keys, but it will probably not be the sound of harmonious music. Nor can you learn Breath Alchemy from people who teach other breathing techniques; that would be like trying to learn how to cook by going to a dance instructor. All sessions are geared toward your particular needs; they are private and are conducted on Skype, so no matter where you live, I am as close as your computer.

Each Breath Alchemy session has a twofold purpose: the first is to experience a completed energy cycle that leaves you feeling calm, centered, present, and very, very good; the second is that each session is also a lesson in how to give yourself unassisted sessions. You already have everything you need to transform your life, and it is all contained within you. My job is to show you how to access your inner healing capabilities, and then how to use them to harmonize the spiritual and emotional energies in your body to create emotional resolution so you can be truly present in your life. After a few coached sessions/lessons, you will be able to guide yourself to completion.

When it's time for your first session, I will show you the circular breathing rhythm and teach you how to use it in a way that is free-flowing, rhythmical, and intuitive. Then I will show you how to use the Five Step Harmonizing Method so you can be in harmony with the increased energy flow and the sensations in your body as they arise.

I will coach you throughout the actual session, I can tell when you go out of any of the Five Steps, and I will offer suggestions to get you back on track. This will facilitate your letting go and bringing you into the present moment without expectations, and without trying to make anything happen. My presence and guidance throughout the session will allow you to go much deeper and receive far more benefit. As you continue to trust and let go, you will find yourself in the flow of the Five Steps. You are now connecting to Source through your Higher Self; the session happens automatically at that point.

At first, the breathing will probably take most of your attention, and then at some point you will realize that the breathing is very natural, and as you continue to relax and let go, your breath will begin to breathe you. Then you can let yourself be entertained by a concert of sensations as you put all of your attention into the feelings in your body.

The breathing will give you an enhanced awareness of the energy in your body, and that could feel like almost anything; it could feel like tingling, or itching, or an emotion, or it could feel like some strange buzz between your ears, or just purely physical sensations. There's no predicting what it could feel like.

Just about every week something occurs in someone's session that I've never seen before, and I've coached a lot of sessions. There are not many things that have kept my attention for thirty-four years, and this keeps my attention very fully, probably because it's so different every time, and definitely because of the results it produces. You will never have two sessions that are alike.

During the session, you keep expanding your acceptance of the sensations as they appear so you can get as much pleasure as possible from every moment. The satisfaction you gain from each moment is what causes the healing in this technique. It means you find a way to derive enjoyment from things you previously thought were in opposition to your well-being. As soon as you succeed at doing that, you have integrated, and something else will come up.

So that's what it's like from an experiential point of view. Integration is different at different times too. Each pattern of energy feels different when it's activated, and is different when it integrates. In general, one of two things will happen when something integrates: either it will become a permanent source of pleasure, or else it will disappear.

Your breath is an example of something that becomes a permanent source of pleasure. As you discover and then master your innate ability to transmute ill-feeling, stuck energy into pleasurable sensations, you have created a new muscle memory, and you will quickly realize that breathing is indeed pleasurable. An example of a feeling that disappears when it integrates is tension. When you integrate tension, it disappears and you are left with a profound feeling of relaxation. A headache is another example of a previously intense sensation that completely disappears when it has been integrated.

Emotions transform, but they do not go away. If you start off with negative feelings about something, you don't wind up having no feelings about it, you wind up having positive feelings about it. I don't recommend going into this technique with the intention of making your feelings go away about something. Breath Alchemy is not about that.

In your session, whatever has been interfering with your ability to fully enjoy your aliveness comes to your attention, feeling by feeling, and is transformed. After an hour or so of integrating the feelings, there comes "completion"—the magical moment when there are no more blocks against maximum enjoyment of the moment, and you feel profoundly ecstatic.

You will experience integration differently at different times: sometimes you will feel more energized and alive and present and connected. Sometimes you will have a profound sense of relaxation, and sometimes you can feel the emotional energy you had been experiencing as unpleasant suddenly become a big source of pleasure. Other times, something will cease to be an issue so completely that you'll forget it ever was an issue, and you notice that you have more freedom to be; things that were troubling you have just cleared up.

In general, whatever gets integrated in a completed Breath Alchemy session stays integrated—that is, unless you make the same thing wrong again, which you can do. Nonetheless not all your judgments will get integrated in one session or even in several sessions. The reason for this is that you most likely have many thousands of judgments, or make-wrongs, suppressed in your subconscious mind. However, every integration feels wonderful, and every integration makes the next one easier. This process will give you a new paradigm for dealing with stress as it comes up in the moment; you will quickly become less judgmental because you are eliminating the root cause of your judgments, and whenever you do get triggered, you have a newfound skill for restoring inner peace and presence in your life.

The effect of Breath Alchemy over a period of time is that layer after layer of suppressed negative emotions get resolved, never to trouble you again. You become much more alive and present, as your inner light is now shining brightly. You are now living from your true self and are connected to Source. You have restored your mind back to its proper role of faithful servant to your consciousness, and life has become an exciting adventure.

FREQUENTLY ASKED QUESTIONS

How long does a session last?
There is no prescribed length. Usually, coached sessions last from sixty to seventy-five minutes. Sessions are never done by a clock, it is important that you continue until you have reached a point of completion, regardless of the time it takes. Almost all sessions are somewhere between one and two hours. Generally, after your skill level increases, the sessions become shorter.

What kind of changes can I expect?

Since Breath Alchemy eliminates judgments at their source, you can expect greater relaxation in formerly stress-producing situations; freer-flowing creativity; willingness to take action to resolve situations you have felt stuck in—and to do so with clarity and confidence, and a greater feeling of presence and connection with friends and loved ones.

How long should I keep doing Breath Alchemy?

This is not a quick-fix solution; once you learn it, Breath Alchemy becomes a lifelong process that you can use whenever and wherever you wish to transform former stress-causing situations into harmonious experiences. It is a technique you can use to increase your enjoyment of life and your effectiveness for as long as you walk this Earth.

How often should I do Breath Alchemy?

One coached session per week will keep you in a balanced state of integration even after you have learned to give yourself unassisted sessions. Then, as you learn to "listen" to your body, you will receive instant feedback on when and how often to give yourself a session.

Can I do Breath Alchemy on my own?

Yes. Most people find that they can learn most quickly and easily with a few guided sessions with me. I can teach most people how to do Breath Alchemy sessions on their own in five to twelve coached sessions. I will also teach you the 24/7 aspect of Breath Alchemy by giving you some simple daily techniques for shifting any experience from a negative context to a positive context.

Is Breath Alchemy dangerous?

Breath Alchemy is dangerous only to your misery. The technique consists of the Five Step Harmonizing Method, and each of the steps is completely safe. Circular breathing, as I teach it, never involves hyperventilation and is therefore safe. Sub-ventilating, on the other hand, is very dangerous to your long-term health and sense of well-being. It is completely safe to relax and tune in to the feelings in your inner body. It is safe to find a context of acceptance for your feelings, as doing so will allow you to integrate their energy into your sense of well-being. It is also safe to know that as you trust and let go, your inner guidance will take over and literally do the session for you.

How do I know if I integrated something?

Since Breath Alchemy works at the feeling level, as you develop the skill of awareness in detail you come precisely into the present moment. From there, you can feel the moment-by-moment subtle changes in the feeling as its energy is literally transmuting in your body. You will notice an undeniable feeling-level shift in your body. You don't *think* integration, you *feel* it.

Will I know what I've integrated?

Sometimes you will have a clear understanding of what has been resolved; other times it will be purely a feeling-level integration. You do not need to have a cognitive understanding of what it is because when you have integrated at the feeling level, you have integrated on all levels and throughout all of your senses. So sometimes you just notice that you have more freedom to be; things that were troubling you have just cleared up.

Do you have a different experience every time?

Yes. Things that get integrated tend not to come up in sessions anymore, unless you make them wrong again. But if your session goes through to completion, you are unlikely to put the make-wrongs back again. So yes, it is different every time.

Is integration permanent?

Yes. Making the sensations in your body wrong and trying to keep them suppressed requires effort. Your mind and body seek peace; since Breath

Alchemy creates a new paradigm for dealing with unresolved experiences, it becomes natural for you to continue to relax in the presence of stressful situations as they come up in your life.

Will integration give me an irresponsible attitude about things that matter?

Absolutely not! The resolution of sensations that you have been struggling with leaves you with an abundance of newfound creative and inspired energy, so you can be truly present in life and devote yourself to the values and causes that matter to you. Your increased self-reliance and sense of purpose will empower you to create your life as you want it to be.

Will integration change my emotions?

Integration transforms your experience of your emotions. It changes the negative effect they have had on you, so instead of suppressing them or acting them out by blaming others, you will be able to consistently use them to your benefit. Fear, for example, transforms into alertness if a threat to your safety is involved. It transforms into excitement if you have an irrational fear, such as the fear of public speaking. Sadness integrates into gratitude, and anger into intention and determination. So, if anything, you will feel your emotions more.

How will I know when my session is complete?

Whatever has been interfering with your ability to fully enjoy your aliveness comes to your attention, sensation-by-sensation, and is transmuted—it is integrated. You will feel calm, peaceful, and alert. If you are feeling energized, relaxed, and very good, then your session is complete.

How do I get started?

All Breath Alchemy sessions are conducted on Skype. Prospective clients begin with a free thirty-minute Discovery Call. The purpose of the call is to create a vision for your life that will inspire you to take the first step to move ahead, identify the true source of your stuckness so you can shift from frustration to focused action, and get crystal clear on your next step to moving ahead with clarity, precision, and confidence.

• • •

After we have talked about all of the above, if we both feel that it makes sense for us to work together, I will share with you what that would look like.

Your mission, should you choose to accept it, is to discover and master your innate ability to transform your fears and doubts into powerful, purposeful, life-enhancing guidance systems in twelve weeks or less, so you can move ahead with clarity, precision, and confidence.

17

Igniting Your Inner Light

Life is either a great adventure, or nothing.

HELEN KELLER

Have you experienced times in your life where you felt truly inspired and connected to something pure and powerful, deep within yourself? Moments where things seemed to fall into place and the solutions to problems appeared almost magically—where you knew just what to do and good things happened at almost every turn?

Unfortunately, not only did those moments probably not last very long, you probably don't even know why they happened when they did, and have no idea how to make them happen again. Well, I'm here to tell you that in those moments you were actually connected to your truest self. And I will also tell you that it's possible to live every moment of your life from that exhilarating place of confidence and clarity.

Can you imagine what that would be like, to be able to be your truest self in every moment—relaxed, focused, and self-assured—effortlessly attracting abundance, excitement, and joy into your life? It wouldn't matter where you lived, how much money you had, what you did for a living, or who your friends were; you would feel deeply happy and content, ready to face every day with a real smile, and no longer at the mercy of your doubts and fears.

The key to catching the wave to total transformation and living life as a true adventure in these accelerated times is to learn how to include and embrace all facets of your life—the so-called bad as well as the good. This makes it possible to integrate and thus be in harmony with absolutely everything in your life.

The first idea I want to share with you is that existence itself is fundamentally valuable. People don't always think about it that way. Sometimes people think that their own existence is valuable only when they are content and getting what they want in life. I disagree. I think that to have even the potential of experiencing joyfulness or of getting anything that you want is of infinite value. Regardless of how you think you came to be—if you accept and internalize the *Law of One* truth that you are a sub-sub-Logos and thus, a perfectly functioning hologram of the One Infinite Creator, or if you think you came about through biological evolution, or from anything else—it is an absolute miracle that you exist.

With any experience that you ever have, the most important thing is that you exist to be having the experience in the first place. People don't always think of it that way; people are accustomed to existing, so they take that for granted. Yet that is the most significant part of any experience. If that same thing was happening and you didn't exist to be experiencing it, it wouldn't seem significant to you at all.

So why is it that people don't go around continually blissing out on the miracle of their existence? I realize that's true, but why is it? The answer is because of make-wrong: they are so busy insisting that reality should be different from what it is that they don't let themselves have the benefit and pleasure that's available in the experience that they're actually having. That keeps them from having the moment-to-moment experience of the miracle of their own existence.

All suffering is a result of judgment, or make-wrong. In any moment you have the opportunity to be grateful that things are as good as they are, or at least that they're not worse than they are. That is available in every single moment. It is only by insisting that things should be different that suffering comes about.

Even if you have the physical sensations of pain, whether or not you suffer from it is a function of context. A Breath Alchemy definition of pain is a feeling that you are making wrong, experienced intensely. That includes both physical and emotional pain. When people do something about pain, and they don't know about Breath Alchemy, they tend to act on the intensity. If you take an aspirin for a headache, that doesn't mean you're no longer making the headache wrong, it means that you have done something to experience it less intensely. The idea is to make it fade out.

If you've ever had deep-tissue work, you may have had the experience that you could hold the sensations during the session in a context where it is very unpleasant, where you tend to tense up and resist it and wish something else was happening. On the other hand, if you relax and let the person into your tissues, which requires trusting the person, then it can still be intense, but not necessarily painful. It can actually even feel good.

Another example is if as a child, you got a series of shots. At some point you may have realized that if you didn't struggle and make it wrong quite so much, it still wouldn't be one of your favorite pleasures, but it would at least be better. Women who have given natural childbirth, without anesthetics, commonly experience the same thing; that they have the choice to go with the sensations, in which case, it will still be intense, but it's not nearly as painful as if they are making it wrong and resisting it. There are lots of times where you can have experiences like that; making changes in life can be like that. If you resist the changes, you can be miserable, and if you go along with the changes, it will be alright.

So suffering is a result of make-wrong, and both are things that happen in your mind and your body, and you are not your mind or your body. You can tell you're not your mind by learning to watch your thoughts as an impartial observer. You do this by listening to the voice in your head as often as you can. You want to pay particular attention to any repetitive thought patterns—the old endless loop recordings that have been playing in your head perhaps for many years. As you observe your thoughts, you will begin to feel a conscious presence—your truest self, your Higher Self—underneath the thought. The thought then loses its power and quickly subsides because you are re-creating it instead of energizing it through identification with it.

There are two ways that everyone relates to time; one way is that the present moment is all that exists—momentary time. Another is where the future and the past and the flow of time are considered to be real—linear time. The mind has linear time, and your Higher Self has only momentary time. You can tell this is true because even when your mind is contemplating the future or the past, you still have only a present-moment experience of your mind doing that. All direct experience happens in momentary time, so your true self has only momentary time.

There is no direct experience in linear time; in linear time the present moment does not exist. By the time we receive data through any of our senses, the experience that originated the data has already become part of the past. I will refer you back to chapter 11 for the details.

The mind is able to make comparisons because of its linear-time capabilities. When you compare two things, you have to shift back and forth between them, and while you are contemplating one, remember what the other one was like. Linear time is absolutely required for making any type of comparison. So, the mind is capable of making comparisons whereas your Higher Self is not.

Make-wrong in every case is a comparison. It means you are comparing what you are actually experiencing to an imaginary standard of how you think it should be, or how you wish it was. So, the mind is capable of make-wrong, and your Higher Self is absolutely incapable of making anything wrong because it only has momentary time.

In the absence of comparison, *everything* is experienced as perfect—and I'm not using the word *perfect* in any weird way. *Perfect,* as defined in the dictionary, means "having all the characteristics and components that normally pertain to a thing of its kind." How broadly or narrowly you define *kind* is a function of context. For example, how many legs does a perfect three-legged dog have? It depends on what you compare it to; a perfect three-legged dog obviously has three legs. You could see that dog as incomplete; it is missing a leg. And yet, it's perfect at being what it is; it's a perfect three-legged dog. If it had four legs, it would be a totally imperfect three-legged dog.

All phenomena are in the realm of "entertainment" for the Higher Self, the real you. Your mind and body are reading these words and contemplating their meaning. Your Higher Self has no interaction with anything other than just experiencing it; it is the space in which all manifestation occurs.

Unity is the context in which everything is allowed to be perfect in its own right, rather than being compared to how it should be. It is the *only* context that is available to your Higher Self, but one of an infinite number available to the mind. Why is this not the context the mind always chooses? *Because of make-wrong!* All other contexts available to the mind are a function of make-wrong.

All of the stress, in fact, all of the unpleasantness that you experience with anything is a result of comparing it to an imaginary standard. The pleasure that you get in contemplating it is an inherent quality of the thing itself. The displeasure is not an inherent quality; it is a function of comparing it to how you think it should be. Integration, unity, bliss, and pleasure are your natural states, and in the absence of make-wrong, anything can be experienced as pleasurable.

As an example, you could pick something totally ordinary and mundane, like a rock. It is quite possible to have a pleasurable experience contemplating a rock; do you remember the "pet rock"? If you tell yourself it ought to be a gold nugget, then you will be unhappy with your experience of your rock. But in the absence of any comparison, if you just let it be what it is, the truth is that there is no limit to how much pleasure you can get from contemplating it.

Or you could just close your eyes and be in your space. There is pleasure inherent even in that; there is pleasure inherent in experience and existence itself. So, suppose you are closing your eyes and going into your space; if you start listening to that nagging "inner parent" in your mind that's telling you that you should be getting things done, then you can have all kinds of displeasure just sitting there. But that displeasure is a result of comparing it to what you think you should be doing instead. The pleasure of just existing is inherent in sitting there. The displeasure of thinking you should be doing something else is a function of comparison.

This is true for the rock also. If you are panning for gold and you get a pan full of ordinary rocks, you will throw them out. But if you don't do that, if you're panning for rocks, you will say, "Wow, look at all these great rocks!" Pleasure is actually inherently available in any experience. Displeasure in every case is a function of comparison to an imaginary standard.

In truth, every experience is infinitely beneficial and infinitely pleasurable. You will only connect with that consciously if you allow yourself to. You can take something that is infinitely beneficial and pleasurable and make it wrong. Country and western songs commonly make love wrong; many people make God wrong. You can make anything wrong; that is an eternal option that goes with having a mind. But in the absence of make-wrong, you can realize that you can get infinite benefit and pleasure from any experience.

You don't have to do anything to experience unity, pleasure, and bliss. You have to do something to *not* experience it—you have to put up a barrier of make-wrong between you and the experience. That barrier effectively shuts out the pleasure and benefit that's available in that experience.

You could say, then, that the purpose of Breath Alchemy is to expand the context of unity in your mind to include all things—to increase your ability to enjoy things as they are, to be in harmony with the reality of your experience, *whatever* your experience is moment by moment—rather than insisting that it should conform to some imaginary standard.

You, meaning your true self, are always in a state of unity, whether you like it or not. A corollary to this is that, regardless of anything that exists in your reality, either you are enjoying it, or you are enjoying not enjoying it, or you are enjoying not enjoying not enjoying it. An example of enjoying something is easy, whatever any of your favorite pleasures are, you engage in them because you enjoy doing so. An example of enjoying not enjoying something is sharing with a co-worker how bad and wrong your boss is; you are both enjoying making him wrong. As an example of enjoying not enjoying not enjoying something, suppose you reach a point in your life where you no longer enjoy having sex. Well, you're probably not glad that you are not enjoying sex, however, you're glad that you're not glad that you're not enjoying sex. And that's as far as you need to go to get to the truth about your continual state of unity.

So, you are always in a state of unity. It's all your Higher Self knows. It's up to you and how you relate to things whether you enjoy them or not. It is an opportunity that is available to you in every moment—to acknowledge and consciously experience the unity that is always there.

Therefore, *there is nothing suppressed in anyone but suppressed bliss.* We don't often see it that way. We speak of suppressed fear, sadness, and anger. But where did that fear, sadness, or anger come from? It came from an experience that, in truth, was infinitely beneficial and pleasurable and then finding fault with it, making it wrong for not being what you had in your mind instead. Depending on how you made it wrong, you got anger, sadness, or fear or some combination of those. If you made that feeling wrong, you then suppressed it.

As soon as you have a Breath Alchemy session and enhance the energy flow in your body, the anger, sadness, or fear comes back to your attention. As soon as you've found a way to accept the feeling as it is and feel it in detail, as it integrates, it turns right back into bliss, which it has always been. If you remove the comparison in your body, it turns right back into bliss. It is only the comparison that has separated you from that reality in the first place. So, there is nothing suppressed in anyone, but suppressed bliss.

THE HEART

We live in a time that can be deeply moving, but first, you must be listening with your heart. On this planet, thoughts and ideas—using the mind—have been considered to be most important. This leads us directly into polarity consciousness and judgment. If you identify only with your mind, and you think that you are your limited identity, then you will defend your mind to the death because that is your identity. If that is gone—if your sense of identity is gone—it's like death. Remember, the mind is a survival machine; it needs to be right.

When you listen with your heart, you can begin to find a common language that is beyond right and wrong, good and evil.

Researchers at the HeartMath Institute have established that the most powerful electromagnetic field in the body is the heart.[1] There are more nerves going from the heart to the brain than coming the other way.

If the heart, brain, and the central nervous system are in coherence, the person goes into a much higher level of awareness. If that is broken with incoherence, then you come out of that high state into a much lower level of consciousness.

The heart has now been shown to have its own innate intelligence (far more than the brain), its own nervous system, called the "heart brain," and it has been found to have a sensory organ that decodes and encodes information. The heart is a gland as well as an organ and secretes hormones that connect with the pineal and pituitary glands, which are part of the third eye.

We feel intuition, intuitive knowing, through the heart and the heart chakra vortex. The brain thinks; the heart *knows*. It is true innate intelligence, not memory or thinking—it is knowing. The heart generates sixty times the electrical output of the brain and connects through the heart chakra to far higher levels of awareness. This is why intuition knows.

The heart only knows unity and oneness, and it is thus able to take us beyond the illusory walls of limited perception. In the Infinite, there is no time, no place, no divisions, no sense of *us and them*. Infinite consciousness is the only truth—everything else is the imagination of that consciousness made manifest in infinite forms.

A mind society looks like the one that we are experiencing; it is based on control and manipulation of our perception, and when you take it as far as we have, it gets pretty weird. A heart society is one of love, truth, beauty, trust, harmony, peace, incredible levels of awareness, creativity, and insight.

The right brain is our connection to the all that is; it is holistic, intuitive, experiential, and knows only momentary time—the eternal now. It is able to intuit the oneness, like a four- or five-year-old looking up at the night sky. The left brain sees dots and does not connect them. It is logical and locked into linear time, so it is never in the present moment. We need both however, and we need them harmoniously working together.

When the mind (left brain) truly sees unity, an integration takes place and a relaxation occurs. The corpus callosum opens up, and communication takes place between both sides of the brain. That opens the doorway to the heart.

A SHIFT IN IDENTITY

As I have said previously, you are a perfectly functioning hologram of the One Infinite Creator; you are a smaller version of the whole. Your Higher Self is your personal connection to Source; it is still there, and it only knows and experiences the Unity of Being. It is one with the energy moving through it from Source; this is the energy of unconditional love, joyfulness, inner peace, creativity, inspiration, and compassion. It is in a constant state of bliss.

However, if it has to pass through an unquestioned, unexamined filter that is tinted with the unresolved emotional trauma of your inner child, it will and can only be a distorted reflection of that. That means you are using your infinite power of creation to continually re-create a world that mirrors those limiting belief systems that have become the unwitting context through which you are experiencing life. You become a powerless victim, continually looking to your circumstances to see if your life has turned out yet. You know when you get the right job, or when you get the right relationship, then everything will be okay. That is totally negating your powers of creation; the reason the circumstances are not lining up as you would like is because you are creating them exactly that way; they can only be consistent with the unwitting context through which you are creating life.

Do not underestimate the power of context; it is the filter through which you perceive and experience your life. Therefore, it is incumbent upon us, if we truly wish to heal our severed aspects so we can see and experience wholeness again, to create a powerful and purposeful context for our lives. You must change your identity so it is consistent with your true nature, and that is oneness with Infinite Creator. You are a spiritual being having a human experience!

Let that be the conscious context through which you experience life. That shifts you from a powerless victim to a co-creator. You then use that as a place to come from; now your experience is not conceptually or circumstantially derived. Your experience of life ceases to be a function of your circumstances, of your concepts, of what you believe. And it begins to be a function of, a reflection of, what you're generating, what you're creating from your own *being*.

So now you don't go to the relationship with your mate trying to get love out of it. It's like you go to the relationship having created a context of love; and the relationship becomes a place in which to experience and express the context that you've created. You shift from just getting by at work, to using your job as a place to discover whatever it is that's needed and wanted, and you produce it. You don't wake up in the morning hoping to just make it through the day, you arise with the inner glow of your Higher Self shining brightly; you shift from just going through the motions to living your life as an exciting adventure! The circumstances in your life are now becoming consistent with the Divine perfection that is coming through you from Source.

Now, I caution you, this is not positive thinking; you cannot create in opposition to anything. If there's something in your life that you are struggling with and are trying to change, you can't create resolution in opposition to that thing. You can't say, "It's horrible, but I'm going to make it ecstatic." This is not "act as if," this is not pretend, this is not going through the motions.

You can, however, include anything in what you create. So, to create from a context of wholeness does not mean that any particular thing has to be in your life. There can be any circumstance or any condition presently existing in your life, and as long as you're willing for that circumstance or that condition to be included, it now shifts from having been an unwitting context that kept you stuck, to mere content, and you can transmute its energy back into wholeness. You can do that using the Five Step Harmonizing Method.

THE SPACE OF NO-MIND

Integration, or transmuting energy as I like to call it, is a result of expanding to include all aspects of your life and of discovering your innate ability to transform previous limitations into powerful, purposeful internal guidance systems that are clearly contributing to your full aliveness. This creates a gap between your thoughts and puts you precisely into the present moment. And by doing this you are aligning yourself with universal principles and matching your energy with the energies directly from the field of all-possibility—those high-frequency energies of love, kindness, inspiration, passion, joy, and so on. You have created the space of "no-mind," and as such, you have shifted from the black-and-white world of living mechanically in your belief systems, to a world of living color with holographic surround sound. You wake up every morning feeling truly inspired and connected to something pure and powerful, deep within yourself; your life has become an exciting adventure!

The following is a quote from George Bernard Shaw's play *Man and Superman,* "This is the true joy in life, the being used for a purpose recognized by yourself as a mighty one . . . the being a force of Nature instead of a feverish selfish little clod of ailments and grievances complaining that the world will not devote itself to making you happy."[2]

And this captured by Shaw's biographer Archibald Henderson:

I am of the opinion that my life belongs to the whole community, and as long as I live, it is my privilege to do for it whatsoever I can.

I want to be thoroughly used up when I die, for the harder I work, the more I live. I rejoice in life for its own sake. Life is no "brief candle" for me. It is a sort of splendid torch, which I have got hold of for the moment; and I want to make it burn as brightly as possible before handing it on to future generations.[3]

18

Your Entrance
Requirement

SOCRATES AND SUCCESS

Long ago, a young man asked Socrates, the ancient Greek philosopher, the secret of success. Socrates told the young man to meet him near the river the next morning, and he would reveal it to him.

The young man barely slept that night, as eagerness and curiosity kept his mind from drifting into the night's slumber. And as soon as dawn struck, he was out the door, making his way to the river. When he arrived, Socrates asked the young man to walk with him into the water.

Puzzled, yet curious beyond words, he walked into the river, fully clothed, and ready for his master's big reveal—the secret of success itself! What he discovered wasn't exactly what he had in mind, for within a matter of seconds, he found himself being held under the water by Socrates.

At first, he thought it was an exercise in seeing what others miss, so he opened his eyes under the water. He was greeted only by the darkness and the cold.

As his air began to run out, the young man started to panic. "Ah ha!" he said to himself, trying to keep his composure. "Do not panic! That must be my master's lesson for me!"

Yet his newfound calm in the face of disaster soon dissolved into absolute terror as his air ran out completely. The young man struggled to get out but Socrates was strong and kept him underwater until he started turning blue.

After what seemed like an eternity, Socrates pulled the drowning boy from the waters, as he panted furiously for every ounce of air he could muster.

"WHY?" screamed the boy, once he could gather the tiniest bit of his strength back, as his heart slowly stopped pounding out of his chest.

Socrates looked at the boy, smiled, and simply asked, "What did you want the most when you were under the water?"

The young man replied, "Air!"

Socrates said, "That's the secret to success. When you want success as badly as you wanted air, then and only then will you get it."

NO EXCEPTIONS TO THE LAW OF CAUSE AND EFFECT

The law of cause and effect, as presented in chapter 15, is an extremely important universal principle that we need to be aware of, so let's briefly revisit it. It says you always get what you want; there are no exceptions to this. But you might be saying, "You've got to be kidding, why would I want all this chaos in my life? I just want all this to go away!"

Okay, I hear you; however, you must remember too, that *wanting* is defined as both the conscious and subconscious mind. And the mind is analogous to an iceberg, in that 90 percent of it is beneath the surface. That means that there is some deep-seated subconscious belief that wants the undesirable situation to be exactly the way it is. Wants are a result of beliefs; many of your beliefs are acquired under circumstances that cause you to suppress them immediately after you adopt them. Therefore, you don't remember where they came from. So, most of our beliefs are on a less-than-conscious level, and you have thousands of these beliefs.

Furthermore, there is a payoff for every so-called unwanted condition; there is a payoff for being a victim. You get people to care, to feel sorry for you, to help you. There is however, also a price to pay—things like love, happiness, health, and self-expression.

In universal terms, what you currently believe is creating your life. If you're noticing that any of that is less than perfect for you, your intention to change it must be 100 percent. Because the way it presently is, is the way you 100 percent want it to be now.

Nothing less than 100 percent intention to have it different will be strong enough to overcome the embedded subconscious belief system that is creating the condition—remember the payoffs. In universal terms, 99.9 percent equals zero. So, if you can't feel it, taste it, be jumping up and down about it, it isn't enough. And the law of cause and effect tells us that until you achieve the result, you know you don't want it. Having and wanting are simultaneous; the only way you know you really want it, is when you have it.

INSPIRATION UNIVERSITY

In 1980, I joined an intense training program, along with thirty-two other aspirants from all over the United States and Europe. The training, led by Leonard Orr, began in March and continued throughout the year.

Inspiration University was its name, and I will always remember the neat black-and-white poster with a photo of planet Earth taken from space, with the caption in big bold letters that read "Inspiration University Campus." Leonard has an interesting imagination, I thought.

This was a time when, even though I was coming from a total commitment to find a way to heal myself from a crippling low-back injury and I saw breathwork as a possible tool to aid in my healing, I joined primarily as an attempt to keep my then relationship alive. Unlike my partner, who came to the program with very high intention, I saw no possibility of me ever becoming a teacher of breathwork, or any other form of transformation. I was there for healing.

In looking back, it seems strange to me that even though I had to pull out my life savings of $1,000 to join—$1,000 in 1980 would be like $10,000 or so today—I still entered the training with less than total intention. I guess I was really committed to keeping our relationship together, and to finding out if breathwork could help me.

Anyway, back to the training, we met every single day in March from 10:00 a.m. to 10:00 p.m. And yes, it was intense—intensely boring much of the time, with far too little valuable information coming from Leonard. We did our breathwork sessions three times weekly by pairing up with a partner and trading guided sessions. That meant that most of the sessions were coached by instructors who were not totally qualified; I was a glaring example of that.

The month of April was given to us as a time for reflection and putting into practice whatever it was that we were learning. So, what was I learning? Well, it certainly wasn't breathwork; I felt totally incompetent when it came to guiding a person through a session, so I let that go.

What I was grabbing onto was a document created by Leonard, called *The Prosperity Consciousness Consultation.*

THE PROSPERITY
CONSCIOUSNESS CONSULTATION

I had first met Leonard in March 1979, when I, along with a friend named Ila, ventured across the bay and into San Francisco to 301 Lyon Street to a place called the Theta House. We went to the "Money Seminar," as Leonard called it. Once there, and after paying our $15 entrance fee for the evening, we were led up a narrow, winding staircase that finally took us to the attic that was filled with about seventy to eighty eagerly waiting participants.

Finally, Leonard made his appearance, and what an appearance it was—I would soon discover that being on time was not one of his main attributes. Anyway, into the room came this guy with a completely shaved head, who was wearing a green sweater with $$ signs all over it. Then he sat down while saying nothing and had his assistants pass out a document called *The Prosperity Consciousness Consultation*. As Leonard continued to just quietly sit there, the participants were asked to read portions of the consultation aloud, until we came to a section entitled "Negotiation."

I sat in utter amazement as Leonard gave everyone the opportunity to come up and pay him anywhere from $1 to $100 extra. The line was long! "We had already paid our $15 entrance fee," I thought, "so why would anyone want to stand in line just to pay more?" Here was a guy who said virtually nothing the entire evening, who had the participants deliver the seminar to him, and then sat there with a big smile on his face as people patiently waited for their chance to pay more. That ranked as one of the weirdest things I had ever seen.

I decided I had to go back to a future seminar, just to see what it was like to stand in line and wait for my turn to hand a bill or two over to Leonard. As I waited in a seemingly endless line, I became overwhelmed with emotions, and was barely able to even look at him as I forked over an additional $20.

Now as we fast-forward to April 1980, Leonard gave me the job of sharing this consultation with others. He told me that if I gave it to nine people a week, he would pay me $100 for the week. So I did, and I quickly discovered that the only way I could venture into it was to make it perfectly clear that there would be no exchange of funds, that we were just doing it for entertainment.

"BOB, COME TO EUROPE"

As the calendar turned to May, we reconvened as a group for two weeks at Leonard's 680-acre training center in the Sierra Nevada mountains.

Upon returning to Theta House in San Francisco for the third and fourth weeks, I remember clearly a life-altering individual consultation I had with Leonard. We were scheduled to go to Europe beginning in June to participate in his scheduled breathwork training seminars. We were to spend two weeks in each country, beginning in England, to act as Leonard's chief assistants.

As I arrived for my scheduled meeting with Leonard, I was certain that I wanted no part of Europe. I had latched on to a dear elderly woman named Mildred, who had in her possession some rather useful healing hands. She quickly became my "security blanket," as I visited her on a regular basis and actually felt some lower-back relief for the first time in years.

But the real clincher, I felt, was the fact that I had only enough money for a one-way ticket to London. How could I possibly go to Europe on that basis? What would happen to me if I did? Would I ever get back home again? Any reasonable person would agree with me, right?

So, I was *not* going to Europe, and I told Leonard why. He said little if anything in response. Then he looked at me, he smiled, and said very softly, "Bob, come to Europe." In that instant, I knew with total certainty that I was going to Europe—one-way ticket and all. For the first time in this program, I was coming from 100 percent intention.

On that trip, I was given the job of delivering the *Prosperity Consciousness Consultation* to the entire seminar. That was vintage Leonard, giving it to the guy who was virtually broke. So now I'm teaching prosperity consciousness to others, and suddenly the tables were turned. I was given the opportunity, on a repeated basis, to discover just what it was like to sit up there while the participants read the consultation to me, and then to see what it felt like as people lined up to pay me extra.

I'm not sure quite what it was, but somehow in spite of all my doubts, an inner light began to glow as I began to see the possibility that I could become a teacher of some form of personal transformation.

Was I challenged on that trip? Oh, just a bit . . . every moment of every day. Was it comfortable? Oh yeah, about as comfortable as sitting in a dental chair with the Three Stooges yanking at your teeth. Was it necessary for my spiritual growth? Well, had I not gone, nothing else would have happened!

But I would still have my books out there, you might be thinking. Not so fast; my books happened as a direct result of my becoming a breathwork coach. It began when a guy named Richard called me on a fateful day in October of 1992. He was calling to book a session with me. He must have liked what he received because he ended up coming for thirty consecutive weeks.

We got to know each other pretty well in those days, and though he owned a publishing company, I had no interest in approaching him about a possible book. My interest centered around the fact that he was the publisher for Richard Hoagland's book, *The Monuments of Mars: A City on the Edge of Forever*. And since Hoagland's work had already presented itself to me in the form of a fascinating video called *Hoagland's Mars: The NASA Cydonia Briefings,* I continually pressed Richard for more information. I also gladly shared with him all my findings regarding Mars, UFOs, the Secret Space Program, and more.

Then of course, Richard called me one fine day and completely shocked me by asking if I would be willing to write a book. So, none of the rest would have happened if I had not rediscovered 100 percent intention in one brief, shining moment, thanks to Leonard!

19

Connecting
to Source

We see ourselves as living on Earth in a human body, yet we also exist multidimensionally. Our higher level, our Higher Self, has Higher Selves connected to Higher Selves, and on and on, until the waveform level of universes is transcended. If we can reconnect, we get clear guidance from within, we are present in life and are able to live in a manner that seems impossible to us now. Reconnecting is not channeling; it is just reconnecting the severed aspects of ourselves.

When we became identified with our minds, we perceived ourselves as separate entities. We were perfectly veiled from our truest self, our connection to Source. Since the mind is polarized, it is in a constant state of judgment, as discussed. Yet, in truth, there is no such thing as a polarity. I will give some simple examples, such as black and white having the middle or unifying component of gray; up and down having center; and for hot and cold, there is lukewarm. You could go on and on with this; the point is, polarity is all a function of our perception where, in our separate state, we often don't connect the dots to see wholeness.

We have three components too: Higher Self, Middle Self, and Lower Self. When we are perceiving reality from our mind, we are living from our Middle Self. We are cut off from Source and our true identity. As such, we see the present through the eyes of the past, which is analogous to driving down the highway of life and steering with the rearview mirror. We then wonder why we have so many accidents. A life lived out of the past is going to be a life in which you're going through the motions. You can do it better than you did it in the past; you can do more or less; you can do more of the good stuff and less of the bad stuff than you did in the past. And you can even try to do it differently. But it's all derived from the past, different *in relation* to the past—you are still trying to overcome the past. It's possible to complete the past in a way that allows you to be truly present in life, and it is only in the present moment that you have access to your Higher Self.

Drunvalo Melchizedek once told how his inner guidance described the connection to the Higher Self. He said suppose you are on a river in a canoe; it's a beautiful day, and you're having a great time paddling down the river. All of a sudden, the Higher Self comes in and says to take your canoe over to the shore and carry it through the woods. That might seem rather inconvenient, and you might wonder why. Inconvenience, however, means nothing to the Higher Self. Yet, if you have learned to follow the Higher Self without hesitation, you will take your canoe out of the water even though it makes no sense to you at the time—in retrospect you will understand.

Even though the Higher Self isn't all-knowing, it certainly has a greater perspective than we do. In this story, the Higher Self was able to fly a few hundred feet above the ground and see beyond the bends in the river. It was able to observe a five-hundred-foot waterfall beyond the next bend!

The question becomes: How do you connect with your Higher Self? As I have previously stated, in order to heal our severed aspects so we can live from our true self, we must first go down and heal the Lower Self, the wounded inner child. In so doing, we rediscover our childlike innocence and can begin to live in the present moment.

For me, it was something that just seemed to happen. I didn't plan it, I didn't ask for it, I didn't even know there was such a thing. It began when I moved to California and discovered the wonderous magic of the Redwood forests. I spent much time hanging out in nature, and as a result, I rediscovered my childlike innocence and the present moment. So, I was beginning to heal my wounded inner child, but only on a surface level. There was still a long way to go, and that would come later.

THE INNER VOICE APPEARS

While in Europe in the summer of 1980, I heard much talk of Babaji, the immortal yogi master referred to in Paramahansa Yogananda's classic book *Autobiography of a Yogi*.[1]

I learned that Babaji had materialized a new adult body in 1970 and that he spent most of his time in his Herakhan ashram near the city of Haldwani in northern India. While in Europe I met quite a few people who had gone to India to find him. They all had stories to tell, ranging from just interesting to incredible. One friend told of being caught in a rainstorm with Babaji. When they reached shelter, her clothes were soaked and Babaji's were completely dry, even though he was beside her in the same rainstorm.

I heard how he materialized his body out of a ball of light to Leonard and others, which inspired them to go to India to find him. I also heard that to demonstrate his mastery of yoga, he stayed in one position for forty-five days without moving. He sat motionless, no food, no water, nothing, for forty-five days.

I was struck by a quote from him: "If you come to me with doubts, I will give you every reason to be doubtful. If you come to me with love, I will show you more love than you have ever known." I knew it was important to remain open to the possibility that Babaji was all that everyone said he was. I knew that if I closed myself down to that possibility, my experience would only be consistent with my doubts.

So I remained open. As a result, I began to feel an increasing personal connection to him. My entire European experience was a continual lesson of letting go and trusting. As previously mentioned, it began with having only enough money for a one-way ticket to London, plus some loose change. That meant I had to earn my way as I went, teaching others what I was learning myself, as I was learning it. That gave me a pretty fair idea of what it was like to be in the void. My old world had fallen apart, and the new one was not yet in place.

I remember arriving in Stockholm, Sweden with my traveling companion at 2:00 a.m. We knew no one and had nowhere to go, so we decided to find the site of the current rebirthing training. When we arrived, we saw a note on the front door telling us that no one was there, that the seminar had been moved to a farmhouse in the country many miles away. We were alone.

Then at 3:00 a.m. one person just happened to be walking by; she also spoke English. When we asked her if she knew the whereabouts of the training, not only did she know, she gave us directions to get there by bus, and she also let us sleep in her apartment that night.

I felt the presence of Babaji and knew that as long as I kept trusting and letting go, I would be safely guided to wherever I needed to be and to whatever I needed to learn. I have had a personal relationship with him ever since and can feel his presence whenever I call upon it. An inner voice, an inner communication, began spontaneously while I was in Sweden. I was in the midst of chaos, confusion, and turmoil, yet present in this chaos was an inner voice that suddenly appeared telling me that everything was okay. That voice stayed with me throughout the trip. Chaos and confusion were still present, but somehow I had a shifted relationship to them. I felt an inner calmness, like being in the eye of the hurricane.

Then came mid-August, four of us had separated from the main group and we were in Amsterdam. I don't remember where Leonard was. Because I was away from the group, I no longer had a source of income. I didn't even have enough money to get back home, and I was becoming desperate. I wanted to go home more than anything!

A friend told me of a possibility: there was a courier service, DHL, that offered free transportation to New York in exchange for your luggage space. I called them and was told that there was only one free trip a day, but I could be placed on a waiting list. There was no possibility, they said, of an opening for at least two months.

The news was most depressing. Here I was stranded in Amsterdam, with no idea how or if I would ever get home. For some reason, I decided to call DHL back the next day. This time I was told of a situation that, as they said, "never happens." There was a last-minute cancellation for that day, and if I could get to the airport right away, I could get the flight. I never moved so fast in my life. I said, "Thank you, Babaji," and was on my way!

When I got to New York I discovered that the airlines were in the midst of a price war, and I was able to get from New York to San Francisco for $99. When I got home to the West Coast, I felt I had failed in the sense that I would not be going to India to meet Babaji. But it didn't matter, I was so happy to be home. As it turned out, while the rest of the group went to India to meet Babaji, I went home to meet him.

Back home, the inner voice not only continued, but began to take on a different form. This ties in directly with the spontaneous healing experiences I had with my cat Freddie. Throughout it all, I felt a deep inner knowing; it was as though Spirit had an important learning experience for me and was guiding me every step of the way. I reached a moment with Freddie that arose spontaneously; I suddenly saw, knew, and felt with total certainty that there was no reason whatsoever that he could not and would not be totally and completely healed. And in that moment of pure presence, Freddie was instantly healed—first from paralysis, and then, a few weeks later, from the infected eyeball that looked like a piece of raw meat. Both times we were sitting in my backyard patio in very similar positions. It all felt and seemed perfectly natural and normal to me.

I suspected deeply that it was Babaji working through me, and I soon received confirmation that it was indeed so. I had earlier purchased an 8.5 × 11-inch poster of Babaji from Leonard; I recall sitting in my room and meditating on all that had transpired. Then I suddenly and spontaneously began to merge with the likeness of him in the poster. I silently asked, "Babaji, was it you?" That was code for asking about the inner guidance, ranging from when the voice first appeared, to the instant and complete healings of Freddie. Suddenly his image became animated, like a cartoon character; he danced around and smiled at me. Confirmation was given and received. And no, I wasn't on some psyche- delic trip, I was completely sober.

I had no name for it at the time, I had never heard of the term Higher Self, but looking back, it is clear that Babaji was acting as a con- duit to show me my inner powers. It was a huge lesson, and from it I was beginning the process of learning to follow the Spirit within rather than external authority.

This experience was so powerful that it took many years for its full significance to sink in. I originally thought it was just Babaji coming through me for whatever reason; I was missing the fact that he was jump-starting the process of discovering my own inner powers. I also delayed my full understanding as I continued to spin my wheels for another seven years. When I began working with Jim Leonard in 1988, I discovered the full healing and transformative power of breathwork when it is done properly. I was now getting the deep-seated healing of my wounded childhood. One day in 1991, I was in the midst of yet another major episode with my back, however, this time was different. I began to see it as a racket, and you know all racketeers' payments are under the table: they pay and get paid under the table. I now clearly saw the payoffs from being helpless; I got people to wait on me, to care about me, and to take care of me, and so on. What it was costing me, however, was my life!

In that moment of insight and clarity, I shifted from helpless victim to conscious co-creator, and the inner voice appeared for the first time since the Babaji experiences eleven years earlier. It said very clearly, "I don't have to do this anymore!" My back, after fifteen years of struggle, finally began to heal.

BE A MASTER

The things you do in your life are completely logical, based on your picture of reality. It is the one place where you have maximum leverage in terms of creating change in your life, as well as on the planet itself. One of the major elements of your picture of reality is your identity. It takes an enormous amount of veiling to create the illusion that you are just an isolated person with no power. If you have been identifying yourself as a lowly, isolated human, you have been turning to outside authority for advice, and you have been living a massive lie.

Remember, you are the entire Universe expressing itself at a single point; it is a holographic projection of your consciousness, and you are creating it all the way out to the most distant stars. The entire Universe rearranges itself to accommodate your picture of reality, so whatever you identify yourself as, it will rearrange itself to accommodate.

Many have held the identity of a struggling human who is trying to learn enough to become enlightened. First you have to get through all your stuff in order to get to enlightenment. Students are taught to solve problems; that means you are continually confronted with what isn't working and what you don't want. The Universe will notice this and give you more of it.

But the old concepts are dying—the ones that say you must struggle and suffer and do it alone in order to become enlightened. What if you were to switch that around to declare yourself as a magnificent being of light already, and you happen to be channeling yourself into this dimension to raise the planet's vibratory rate and create the critical mass necessary for ascension?

You have to start with no evidence that this is real; you take a stand and declare it—I am a Master! You are a spiritual being having a human experience! You shift the context by shifting the questions you ask of your experiences. Ask: How does this contribute to the greater good? How does this contribute to the creation of heaven on earth? rather than: What am I supposed to learn from this?

Shift your way of measuring reality from beliefs and outer circumstances to it *is* so because *you say so.* Your word then becomes law in your universe, and now manifestation is instant. Visualize your idea of perfection and begin to use that as your measurement of what's real. What if you suddenly became fascinated with your vision of perfection, with a shift into fourth density, and the fire of purpose burning in your heart? And you said, "I am here to live as a Master, and to co-create heaven on earth." If you took a radical shift in your identity, and then in the context in which you hold your reality and in how you measure reality, the Universe would have no other choice than to give you a radically different reality. Follow your Spirit without hesitation; the shift will happen naturally and organically.

You are an extraterrestrial, multidimensional master; in the higher worlds you are a Christ-consciousness being. Remember who you are and bring that love, light, and wisdom down here to assist the planet in its transition. Be a conscious master co-creating heaven on earth.

We are creating this reality moment by moment, whether we are aware of it or not. If we are not conscious of it, we will create reality through the eyes of the past, from old patterns that are reflections of unresolved emotional trauma from childhood. If we are conscious of it, we create in a way that is increasingly consistent with our true nature as interdimensional spiritual masters who are having a human experience.

You must burn with the fire of purpose because anything less pure than that position will come to your attention. If you are operating at anything less than 100 percent intention, you will be stopped when these fears and doubts come up. If you act with purpose, then when the same fears and doubts do come up, they will seem unimportant, and you will move right through them. In fact, you will transmute their low vibration into life-enhancing energy so you can move ahead. If you are not burning with the fire of purpose, and you are doing it because someone suggested it or it sounded like a good idea at the time, then you are still following outside authority, and your reason for proceeding is not big enough.

The entire planet, and everyone on it, is in the throes of this change. We are all mutating—Mother Earth is in transition, and so are we individually. Some of us are more aware of this than others. It means we get to experience the joy of having more light flow through us and also the inconvenience of having our old world dissipate before the new one is completely together. The old world within us is dying and crying out "Save me!" The new world within is calling, and if we are burning with the fire of purpose, we will embrace it and we will be allowed to enter.

The DNA codes in our bodies are mutating, and if we resist, it can get pretty rough. No one will be able to avoid having their old world fall apart. If you try to go back to your old way of being, it won't work anymore. If you begin to identify as a master here to co-create heaven on earth, you are moving in the direction of the transformation and therefore helping it. You will be able to find your way more easily.

We used to get our security from being a servant to form; if we followed the rules of society, we got a payoff. Now we are being asked to follow the Spirit within us instead of outside rules. Furthermore, we are being asked to follow Spirit without hesitation.

We no longer have lifetimes on this planet to resolve our karma; this is it. Breath Alchemy clears up unresolved experiences from all periods of life, from before birth right up to present time. Integrating dysfunctional patterns allows you to get on with it, so you can do what you came here for, so you can come from your truest self and live your sacred purpose.

Follow your Spirit without hesitation, and everything you need to know will be revealed to you in your own unfoldment. If you follow outside authority in these accelerated times, everything you get will be too late, and probably not of much real value to you. It will be a day late and a dollar short.

There are many millions of extraterrestrials here on Earth at this time. Some have been here for a very long time: they have been holding the space for the evolution of the planet. An ET is anyone whose point of origin, in all that is, is somewhere other than planet Earth. You can be a human as your point of origin or an ET, but either way, it's time to become aware of your spiritual essence.

Who cares if you are an extraterrestrial or not? You still have to live here and pay your bills. The value in knowing whether you're an ET or not is in expanding your picture of reality. Your identity, your sense of who you are, is the major element in your picture of reality. If you identify yourself as a human being, then you are a being who has lost your spirituality and must somehow regain it. It's not true, but it's consistent with playing the game of hide-and-seek. If you identify yourself as an ET, then you are a spiritual force channeling itself through this human embodiment to serve the planet in the most appropriate way. Which would you prefer?

We live in a time that can be deeply moving, but first you must listen with your heart. When you begin to listen with your heart, you can begin to find a common language that is beyond right and wrong, good and evil. It is the language of the Higher Self, your connection to Source.

20

The Shift of
the Ages

We are in the process of an accelerated spiritual evolution that is unprecedented in the known Universe. Ancient prophecies and astrological theory together agree that we are living at a moment of great transition and change, but the rate of change that is occurring is something that has never been known before and was not anticipated by our most prescient sages.

The old world is dying and crying out to be saved; a new world is emerging and we are all being drawn into it. This new world offers incredible possibilities: a shift in the very nature of our consciousness and of the dimensional structure of the region of the world in which we live; a promise of "ascension" to a way of being where all the old conflicts melt away, and where harmony, love, and joy are the constant bases of our existence.

But the passage to this new world seems fraught with struggle and disorientation. It doesn't seem that we are very well prepared to make this shift. Unresolved emotional trauma, intentions, and personal histories lie dormant within us; and if they are not dealt with by each one of us, we will resist the coming changes. Resistance will cause us great suffering and prevent us from embracing the possibilities that are open to us. For some, a stubborn resistance may prevent them from entering into the fourth dimension.

"It was the best of times, it was the worst of times," wrote Charles Dickens about the years of the French Revolution. It seems that there is a cosmic law at play, that where there is great hope there is also great danger; that where we seem on the brink of disaster, unimagined benefit may lie just around the corner.

A FORK IN THE ROAD

We have reached a fork in the road. Are we going to awaken to our true genius and potential as infinite consciousness and ascend as one planet? Or are we going to remain trapped in our limited identity and continue on the karmic wheel of reincarnation? The choice is between the mechanical mind that keeps you in separation, and the intuitive heart that connects you to all that is.

If we don't change our direction, we're likely to end up where we are headed, and because we have been so spiritually ignorant, it's going to take major Earth changes to wake us up. In that version of ascension, the vast majority of people will not be here for the disaster. They will be transported by an interstellar rescue plan. Corey Goode said in the Secret Space Program that it was common knowledge that certain ETs come in and rescue people who are unready for ascension and take them to another third-density planet. Courtney Brown also saw this scenario in his remote-viewing sessions: he witnessed humans from Earth who were time-traveled and dropped off on a third-density planet in the Pleiades. Many Native Americans believe that most of the people of Earth will die and then travel back to the stars where they came from. From there, it is believed that their transformation will be easier. Only the most evil people will stay with the Earth as the changes hit; they will be consumed, as they have a huge karmic debt to pay.

Those who are living from the heart and are connecting to Mother Earth will stay here as the planet transforms. There's a new energetic configuration for the Earth, and people who are ready are able to stay with it as it upgrades into the higher frequency of fourth density.

The Native Americans call them the people of One Heart; they say we will become literally one people, breathing in unison. From there, we will begin to transform into a new humanity.

We will be led through an amazing series of consciousness movements and experiences as we enter into fourth density. We already know all of this on a very deep, inner level, for the pathway is already recorded in our DNA.

At that point, we will have a light body, we will be able to levitate, we will be able to lift objects with our mind, telepathic communication will become the norm, you and I will remember our past lives, and we will never again have a break in memory. We will also discover that whatever we think is the instantly manifested reality. It is imperative, then, to stay in love and see beauty all around you, and that is what you will create. If however, you go into fear, whatever you fear will manifest. That is a clear signal that maybe you were not yet ready to ascend; if so, you will be returned to a third-dimensional world to complete your karma and finish your growth process.

It is so important to be fearless and to know that you are One with the Infinite Creator. When you know that, the transformation will be easy; it will also be extremely pleasurable. The bottom line is we must be balanced on Earth or the planet will go through the pole shift and solar flash.

THE HUNDREDTH MONKEY EFFECT

The Japanese monkey, Macaca fuscata, *has been observed in the wild for a period of over thirty years.*

In 1952, on the island of Koshima, scientists were providing monkeys with sweet potatoes dropped in the sand. The monkeys liked the taste of the raw sweet potatoes, but they found the dirt unpleasant.

An eighteen-month-old female named Imo found she could solve the problem in a nearby stream. She taught this trick to her mother. Her playmates also learned this new way and they taught their mothers, too. This cultural innovation was gradually picked up by various monkeys before the eyes of the scientists.

Between 1952 and 1958, all the young monkeys learned to wash the sandy sweet potatoes to make them more palatable.

Only the adults who imitated their children learned this social improvement. Other adults kept eating the dirty sweet potatoes. Then something startling took place. In the autumn of 1958, a certain number of Koshima monkeys were washing sweet potatoes—the exact number is not known. Let us suppose that when the Sun rose one morning there were 99 monkeys on Koshima Island who had learned to wash their sweet potatoes. Let's further suppose that later that morning, the hundredth monkey learned to wash potatoes.

Then it happened!

By that evening almost everyone in the tribe was washing sweet potatoes before eating them. The added energy of this hundredth monkey somehow created an ideological breakthrough!

But notice. A most surprising thing observed by these scientists was that the habit of washing sweet potatoes then jumped over the sea—colonies of monkeys on other islands and the mainland troop of monkeys at Takasakiyama began washing their sweet potatoes![1]

The above story is from Ken Keyes Jr., the creator of the Living Love method. It came from a book written in 1981 that was not copyrighted, called *The Hundredth Monkey*. This was during the height of the Cold War when the nuclear threat was very real. Ken asked people to reproduce it in whole or in part, to distribute it with or without charge, in as many languages as possible, to as many people as possible.

On a personal note, I met Ken at one of his workshops in the early 1980s. He was wheelchair bound with polio, but that didn't slow him down one bit. He was a shining ball of light; he loved everyone, and the reverse was true also.

THE HUNDREDTH HUMAN

Drunvalo Melchizedek told the story of an experiment conducted by scientists from Australia and England. They created a photograph that had hundreds of human faces hidden in it. Yet, it took training and concentration to see more than just a very few faces. They took the photograph to Australia and selected a group of a few hundred people for their experiment. Each person was given a certain amount of time and was asked to identify as many faces as they could. Predictably, they only saw a few—maybe six to eight faces.

Then the photo was taken to England, where it was shown on a closed-circuit BBC television station. Each of the faces was carefully revealed and shown to the British audience. Just a few minutes later, the photo was shown again in Australia to a new set of people. Suddenly, they could now see most, if not all of the faces.[2]

THE GLOBAL GRID

The mechanism for this transference of ideas works the same way for monkeys as it does for all sentient beings because there is a global energy field—let's call it a grid—that connects not only humans, but all species.

Every single life-form on the planet has a grid—an electromagnetic, geometrically shaped energy field—connected to it. Even if that species exists on only one spot on the Earth, its grid extends around the whole planet. These grids subtend an average of sixty feet from inside the Earth to about sixty miles above it. If you were to see them superimposed over each other it would look like a light, white-blue haze coming off the Earth.

In Nothing in This Book Is True, But It's Exactly How Things Are, I gave the details on how the grid that will enable us to move into fourth density was created.[3] It began 13,200 years ago, when three ascended masters—Thoth, Ra, and Araragat—went to the Giza Plateau in Egypt.

They were beginning to consciously manipulate the internal energy flow of the Earth in such a way that it ultimately would dramatically alter the flow above the Earth. This is a process known as geomancy. This they hoped, would result in the synthetic creation of the fourth-density grid, which would, in turn, give us the vehicle to move into the next higher level of awareness.

So this trio made a hole aligned directly with the axis of the old, now inoperative, Christ grid. Then they laid out three pyramids, a major project of geomancy. Subsequently they situated 83,000 sacred sites throughout the planet. These were created totally on the fourth-dimensional level. Then over a period of thirteen thousand years they drew humans from every race and all walks of life to build the requisite church here and pyramid there to establish an operational pattern of this grid on the third dimension. All the sacred sites on the planet are laid out in either logarithmic or Fibonacci spirals, mathematically connected and delineated back to that single spot at the Great Pyramid at Giza in Egypt. A man by the name of Carl Munck conclusively proved this to be true. The positions of the sites are given in the geometry of their construction.

This is from Drunvalo Melchizedek's book *The Mayan Ouroboros*. The following is quoted directly from the book:

> Going further, what if you study upwards of 250 Sacred Sites and find that the longitude relative to Giza and the exact latitude are encoded into every single one? Even if there were only 10 sites involved, you would have ruled out coincidence. And Carl Munck has discovered that you can find the exact longitude relative to Giza and the latitude, down to several decimal places, encoded into every single one of the 250 Sacred Sites that he has studied!
>
> In proving that the placement of the Sacred Sites he's studied could not have occurred by chance, Munck has also proved that the people who built them must have been able to view our planet from outer space! It would have been literally impossible for us, today, to verify

the accuracy of these ancient builders' calculations before we ourselves had satellites!

So Munck is giving us proof that there was a much higher technology in ancient times than classical historians have assumed. Besides that, the overwhelming implication is that the Sacred Sites—at least the ones that Munck has visited—were planned and executed by the same mind or agency. They were all built according to a single plan.[4]

Drunvalo Melchizedek—in *The Ancient Secret of the Flower of Life,* Volume 1, tells us that the new grid, after 13,200 years, was completed in 1989. Then after twenty years of fine-tuning, it became a fully functioning, living energy field. Without this grid, ascension would not be possible. However, with it, the Shift of the Ages and the birth of a new humanity is in full swing.

REACHING CRITICAL MASS

When a certain critical number achieves an awareness, this new awareness can be communicated from mind to mind. Although the exact number may vary, the hundredth monkey effect shows that when only a limited number of people know of a new way, it may remain the consciousness property of these people. But there is a point at which if only one more person tunes in to a new awareness, a field is strengthened so that this awareness is picked up by almost everyone!

The Shift of the Ages is the awakening of humanity's heart; it is the movement from the polarized mind to the heart, which is connected to Source and only knows Unity. This transformation of consciousness, the greatest one ever recorded, first became apparent in the mid-1960s and has been building momentum ever since.

The shift is a collective transformation consisting of the sum of each individual's step into the new reality. Each person, in their own time, is moving forward into a stage of consciousness that brings a wider vista and an awareness that springs from the heart. When the primary attention of enough people becomes focused through their heart chakras, then the hundredth monkey effect will occur.

THE WANDERERS

There are many millions of ETs here on our planet; they are here to assist in the great awakening, and since you are reading this, you just might be one of them. The *Law of One* calls them the Wanderers; their primary function is to help raise the vibration of the Earth. When the *Law of One* was asked, "do the vibrations somehow add, just as electrical polarity or charging a battery or something? Does that also aid the planet, just the physical presence of the Wanderers?" they stated:

> This is correct and the mechanism is precisely as you state. You may, at this time, note that as with any entities, each Wanderer has its unique abilities, biases, and specialties so that from each portion of each density represented among the Wanderers comes an array of pre-incarnative talents, which then may be expressed upon this plane which you now experience so that each Wanderer, in offering itself before incarnation, has some special service to offer in addition to the doubling effect of planetary love and light and the basic function of serving as beacon or shepherd.[5]

The "doubling effect" is such that for each additional person calling upon love, there is an exponential increase in the amount of love and light that the angelic beings—the vast majority of ETs are angelic beings of light—can beam into our planet. Each person who is raising their vibratory rate by healing their inner child and who is putting out for the planet to be a more loving place, raises the contribution of these beings exponentially. The ETs on Earth, as they stay in love, are increasing exponentially the amount of light on this plane. When the dark side, by contrast, attempts to keep us in fear, pain, rage, revenge, betrayal, terror, jealousy, and so on, their actions only count as one vote.

Then there is a massive wave of psychic children that began in 1972. The first "super psychic" child was discovered in China in 1974. You can read about it in a book by Paul Dong, called *China's Super Psychics*. He tells how this child could see with his ears, mouth, tongue, nose, hands, or feet better than you and I can see with our eyes. They have many other abilities, all of which are equally mind-blowing.

Now, the percentages of children being born who are not from here is most likely close to 100 percent. They bring with them memories and knowledge of advanced consciousness, which is exponentially adding to the "doubling effect."

WHAT WILL IT TAKE TO CREATE CRITICAL MASS?

Let's begin by taking a look at some of the characteristics of an ascension-ready person. There is a shift in identity that is inclusive of the fact that you and I are perfectly functioning holograms of the One Infinite Creator; we are spiritual beings having a human experience. Our inner light is shining brightly, and we are truly present in life. Now we are coming from an unlimited inner supply of joyfulness, inner peace, creativity, inspiration, compassion, unconditional love, and fulfillment rather than looking to our outer circumstances to try to find it. Our relationships, livelihood, and friends now become a place in which we live and experience that wholeness that is emanating from within.

Then, the *Law of One,* like all the great spiritual teachings, makes it very clear that the shift each of us needs to make is from service to self—meaning using control and manipulation to get what you want at the expense of others—to service to others. They say if you actually want to help people at least 51 percent of the time, you can still be up to 49 percent manipulative, controlling and evil, but you will still ascend.

You just have to be more interested in helping people than you are in causing them pain and keeping them in fear.

This, in other words, speaks to the importance of shifting from a "you *or* me world" to a "you *and* me world." In the former, the old paradigm, where we are living in a "what's-in-it-for-me world," no one is empowered, and therefore nobody makes any real difference, no matter what they do. Even acts of great courage are coming out of a condition where a meaningful contribution to the whole is not possible. They will merely show up as gesturing or showing sympathy for the less fortunate.

You are familiar with the idea that says if you give someone a fish, that person will be fed for the day. Yet if you teach that person how to fish, he or she will be fed for a lifetime. That is the shift that each of us needs to make, from gesturing to empowerment, that is, from "you or me" to "you and me." This is now inclusive of the whole, and suddenly everyone is empowered to make a difference.

So, what are the rules for functioning effectively in this new paradigm of a world that now works for everyone? Surprisingly, they are very simple; you lead by example, as Gandhi said, "Be the change you want to see in the world." Then you have to find a way to be efficient. It's what Buckminster Fuller calls the trim tab principle. He explained in a February 1972 interview that a trim tab is "a tiny thing at the edge of the rudder" and "just moving the little trim tab builds a low pressure that pulls the rudder around. Takes almost no effort at all'."[6] He went on to offer a metaphor comparing what just one person could accomplish, to that small little trim tab that could change the direction of an ocean liner.

> So, I said that the little individual can be a trim tab. Society thinks it's going right by you, that it's left you altogether. But if you're doing dynamic things mentally, the fact is that you can just put your foot out like that and the whole big ship of state is going to go. So I said, "Call me Trim Tab."

The truth is that you get the low pressure to do things, rather than getting on the other side and trying to push the bow of the ship around. And you build that low pressure by getting rid of a little nonsense, getting rid of things that don't work and aren't true until you start to get that trim-tab motion. It works every time. That's the grand strategy you're going for. So I'm positive that what you do with yourself, just the little things you do yourself, these are the things that count. To be a real trim tab, you've got to start with yourself, and soon you'll feel that low pressure, and suddenly things begin to work in a beautiful way. Of course, they happen only when you're dealing with really great integrity.[7]

So, to be a trim tab you simply start from where you already are, none of the circumstances in your life need to change. You take a look around—whether you are at home, at work, with friends, or wherever you are—and discover what's needed and wanted, and you produce it. Anytime you feel unclear about your next steps, or feel a bit out of sync with your highest path, ask yourself this simple question: How may I serve? What is it that's needed and wanted that I can produce?

When you ask yourself this question, and then consciously quiet your mind, open your heart, and look inward allowing your inner guidance and inspiration to appear, you will receive an answer. It will likely be something simple and small to start, but when you listen, trust, and act upon your inner guidance, your next step will appear, and then the next. And by continuing to stay present, with the intention to serve with love in a way that you enjoy, a way that is truly in the highest interest of all, you will discover the magic of it. Because one step at a time, you naturally come into alignment with your highest path and timeline.

You are now making a difference in a "you and me world," shining your light and aligning with your highest, awakened light and radiant truth. So ask yourself today, "How may I serve in a way that I love and enjoy that is in the highest interest of all?" And then be sure you listen and act upon the guidance you receive.

THE GREAT AWAKENING

Are we creating this necessary critical mass, and are we doing it in a way that alleviates the need for severe Earth changes, such as the solar flash? In a word, yes. Remember, in the same way that heart attacks, cancer, and other illness and disease are a direct result of our individual imbalances, earthquakes, volcanoes, tsunamis, hurricanes, tornadoes, and the like are the result of our collective disharmony.

We are living in the midst of a great awakening, where the collective darkness is being brought to the surface in order to be transmuted into the light of the higher-dimensional energy that is enveloping and affecting us all. What we are living through now, this collective dark night of the soul, is absolutely necessary; we must be shown, not just told, how we have been controlled and manipulated by a malevolent group of psychopaths for a very long time. We are also seeing how their time is up: that level of evil and corruption cannot survive in these accelerated times.

As they are removed from the scene, we will be given a level of freedom that we could previously barely imagine. What if your car battery could also provide all the energy for your entire home? What if you could put a thousand pounds of garbage in a machine and hours later get pure, drinkable water and usable fuel as we transition into free energy? What if we evolved the automobile and added antigravity technology making it a gas-free hover car?

If this advanced technology were to come into mainstream use, we would live in a world with far less pollution, less environmental stress, and more safety and protection. We would be stepping into the golden age. We would be creating the perfect bridge that would allow us to transition into fourth density in an orderly and organic way.

Let's return to the *Law of One* and the pole-shift prophecies of Edgar

Cayce. They compared these Earth-change prophesies to the availability of different goods in various stores, and said Cayce was looking at only one of many items in the store—that item is akin to a pole shift. There are many timelines and many probable futures where we go through a catastrophe. But they say that there are other things that Edgar did not see that are equally important.

> We speak of these possibility/probability vortices when asked with the understanding that such are as a can, jar, or portion of goods in your store.
>
> It is unknown to us as we scan your time/space whether your peoples will shop hither or yon. We can only name some of the items available for the choosing. The, shall we say, [Akashic] record which the one you call Edgar read from is useful in that same manner.
>
> The value of prophecy must be realized to be only that of expressing possibilities. Moreover, it must be, in our humble opinion, carefully taken into consideration that any time/space viewing, whether by one of your time/space or by one such as we who view the time/space from a dimension, shall we say, exterior to it will have a quite difficult time expressing time measurement values. Thus prophecy given in specific terms is more interesting for the content or type of possibility predicted than for the space/time nexus of its supposed occurrence. . . .
>
> Given the amount of strength of the possibility/probability vortex which posits the expression by the planet itself of the difficult birthing of the planetary self into fourth density, it would be greatly surprising were not many which have some access to space/time able to perceive this vortex. The amount of this cold cereal in the grocery, to use our previous analogy, is disproportionately large.[8]

What they're saying is that the planet needs to evolve; it needs to become heaven on earth, a true paradise. The Cabal is playing the biblical satanic role of pure evil. Their time is up; there is nothing more to be gained from this evil. They are a mirror and outward projection of our inner unresolved traumas. For example, there's incest and molestation going on in people's homes, and the victim of this is supposed to act like everything's okay—you don't talk about it, it's all hidden. Another example is an abusive relationship where the abuser keeps control by never letting go and admitting their wrong behavior.

That's the individual level, which then iterates into the collective level where the Cabal is hidden. Because we have evil in our own lives, it iterates out into the world as a reflection of what the Cabal really represents. Once we learn to break away from the abusers in our own lives, and we actually do that, we are holographically healing the planet. We are saying to the collective bad guys that their services are no longer required.

When their time has expired, we have the possibility of a golden age—true prosperity, no more hunger, free energy, antigravity, and a pollution-free environment. There is, then, a possibility where we don't have the Earth changes:

We may note at this point while you ponder the possibility/probability vortices that although you have many, many items which cause distress and thus offer seeking and service opportunities, there is always one container in that store of peace, love, light, and joy. This vortex may be very small, but to turn one's back upon it is to forget the infinite possibilities of the present moment. Could your planet polarize towards harmony in one fine, strong moment of inspiration? Yes, my friends. It is not probable; but it is ever possible.[9]

In this scenario, there are no Earth changes because we have transformed from within. Since Earth changes are an outward reflection of our inner trauma, and since we are healing it, the outward will now reflect that. We have the power to do this; what is happening now is absolutely necessary to awaken the masses and alleviate the need for the solar flash. We appear to be on that optimal timeline.

What if our entire planet is indeed polarizing toward harmony? What if the solar flash on Proxima Centauri on or very near the Mayan calendar end date of December 21, 2012, was a sign that we are progressing in a way that alleviated the need for such an event here? What if it is all unfolding in exactly the way it must in order for us to create the critical mass that will enable most—if not all—of humanity to ascend into the next level? And what if we were doing it in a way that allowed for smoother sailing, where we went through this without Earth changes? What if we could get through this without the really severe stuff?

What if out of our collective shift into a "you and me world," we each made it our personal business to see to it that the Earth is able to shift 21 degrees off axis slowly, without volcanic eruptions or tsunamis or anything. We would definitely notice that it was moving, but it would just be like, "Wow, look at the stars moving in the sky!" That's the positive ascension. If you made it your personal business to see to that, would your life now become an exciting adventure?

LIVING IN TWO WORLDS

For those of us who are staying current with these evolving times, we are literally living in two worlds. The first is the everyday world as we know it; I live in it as though it will always be here; I suggest you do also. That means we have bills to pay, we have families to love and care for, we must also do our best to help the world in whatever way we can.

At the same time, we must prepare inwardly for what we know is coming. We are being given an opportunity to resolve lifetimes worth of karma so we can move into the higher worlds. It is important to embrace our darkness within as it arises from suppression; it is important to realize that we are being given an opportunity to revisit our unresolved issues so we can transmute their stagnant energy into life-enhancing internal guidance systems that are clearly contributing to our aliveness. From that newfound presence, we are in the space of no-mind and are thus connecting to Source through our Higher Self.

The blueprint for this shift can be found in the three universal principles that I presented in chapter 14. By adopting and aligning with those three laws—the Perfection Principle, the Resistance Principle, and the Harmonizing Principle—we are shifting out of mind-based resistance to what is, into heart-based acceptance of the moment where we can recreate and therefore transmute the energy of emotional trauma into our sense of well-being.

I will illustrate this by giving you a very practical example. If you are in a primary relationship, whatever emotions you have been suppressing are going to get activated by your partner; you can count on that. It might seem as though your mate is constantly doing things that agitate and upset you, that he or she is making you angry. So, using anger as an example, if the only way you know how to relate to anger is to make it wrong, then when your partner does something that activates your anger, you are not going to be very loving of them just then. I suspect you know what I mean. You will blame your mate for triggering this emotion that you are resisting, and you will be trying to control their behavior to not activate this emotion anymore.

However, if you know how to integrate your anger, you can be loving even when your anger is activated. If you allow all your emotions to cycle through and be okay with you, and you are able to include all of your feelings in your experience of love, then you can genuinely be unconditionally loving. Otherwise, you can only love with the condition that your mate not set off the emotions you are choosing to resist.

Let me state for the sake of clarity that because Breath Alchemy works at the energetic level, it is effective for anything you can feel. That includes a huge list of possibilities, ranging from headaches to stress to fatigue, with many stops in between. Any sensation that has been bothering you can readily be transformed or integrated using the Five Step Harmonizing Method described in previous chapters.

Breath Alchemy is also an extremely efficient method for integrating emotions. It does so in the most direct way possible; you simply focus on the emotion, the actual sensation, and find a positive way of relating to it. Each emotion is made of energy, and the energy it contains is held away, as a separate entity, until you integrate it. Once you integrate the emotion, its energy merges back into your overall aliveness. In the same moment, you gain the lesson the emotion has for you.

Fear, for example, integrates into excitement and alertness. Anger integrates into intention or determination. Integrating guilt enables you to forgive yourself and others so you can move on. Shame is much more complex because unlike guilt's message that you made a mistake, the message behind shame is you *are* a mistake! Furthermore, since we live in a shame-based society, all your emotions will be bound with shame. Therefore, there will be an integration of shame every time you integrate an emotion. Integrating shame-bound emotions is one of the most important keys in reclaiming your childlike innocence, which is essential in the process of reconnecting with your Higher Self and your natural divinity.

When you have reconnected your severed aspects, you are living from your heart and not from your mind. It becomes a natural expression to experience and express your wholeness in the form of service to others, and to do it in a way that empowers them to make a difference. Loving and helping people remember who they are and being of service to the world is the only outer purpose that creates character. This will assist you greatly as you journey into higher consciousness.

When you are connected in this way, you create a vibration within you that is recognized by Mother Earth. As the dimensional shift takes place, you will be taking the most exciting journey of a lifetime. Mother Earth knows you and will protect you under all circumstances, and you will become part of the One Heart beings that will begin the journey beyond the stars and into the higher worlds.

As I said in *Nothing in This Book Is True,* "The Christ-consciousness grid has been fully formed and birthed. It is now alive and conscious; it is a living energy field around the Earth, and this changes everything.

In every instance, whenever a grid has become a living entity and connected to its planet, it has always gone to the next level. Mother Earth has made a conscious decision to move into the higher worlds of the fourth density and beyond. We are now in a heart-based energy field; when you connect to it, a new possibility opens up. This means that our spiritual acceleration will quicken dramatically—there is nothing left to stop it.

It also means that sometime, perhaps soon, the entire cycle that we are now on will disappear in a single day. In its place a whole new world will be birthed—one based not on the mind, but rather on the heart. We are right on the edge of the emergence of this world. Everything is in place; the grid is alive and functioning; yet most of the world continues in its old pattern, thinking this is the way it will be forever, hardly imagining that something incredible is about to occur.

This is a time of great celebration as we move out of the darkness and into the light. It means that the veils will be lifted, we will remember and live our intimate connection to all life, we will be allowed to reunite with our cosmic brothers, and to move about the Universe. This is the birth of a new humanity; we will completely redefine what it means to be human!

Notes

Because hyperlinks do not always remain viable, we are no longer including URLs in our resources, notes, or bibliographic entries. Instead, we are providing the name of the website where this information may be found.

CHAPTER 1. LIFTING THE VEIL

1. Knapp, *UFOs: The Best Evidence.*
2. Corso, *The Day after Roswell.*
3. Richards, *Above Majestic.*
4. Cooper, *The Secret Government.*
5. Cooper, *Beyond a Pale Horse,* 201.
6. David Wilcock, "The Great Awakening," Ascension Mystery School (website), 2020, online video course.
7. Dwight D. Eisenhower, Farewell Address, January 17, 1961, accessed on C-SPAN (website).
8. Miles, "Alternative Three," episode on *Science Report.*
9. Richards, *Above Majestic.*

CHAPTER 2. WHAT'S GOING ON?

1. Richards, *Above Majestic.*
2. Cooper, *The Secret Government,* 15.
3. Frissell, *Something in This Book Is True,* 15.
4. Frissell, *Nothing in This Book Is True, But It's Exactly How Things Are,* 232.

5. Frissell, *Nothing in This Book Is True*, 232.

6. Knight, *Change*.

7. Scallion, *The Earth Changes Report*, 3.

8. Cooper, *Behold a Pale Horse*, 168–69.

9. Cooper, *Behold a Pale Horse*, 169.

10. "What Are the Sustainable Development Goals?" United Nations Development Program, UNDP (website), accessed September 10, 2022.

CHAPTER 3. THE GREAT YEAR

1. Cruttenden, *Lost Star of Myth and Time*.

2. Cruttenden, *The Great Year*.

3. Frissell, *Nothing in This Book Is True, But It's Exactly How Things Are*, 31.

4. White, *Pole Shift*, 149–50.

5. Melchizedek, *The Mayan Ouroboros*.

CHAPTER 4. CONTACT IN THE DESERT

1. Nikola Duper, "Clarifying the 'Friendship' Italian Contact Case," *Open Minds* (website), November 5, 2009.

2. Cesana, *UFO Secret*.

3. Duper, "Clarifying the 'Friendship' Italian Contact Case."

4. Duper, "Clarifying the 'Friendship' Italian Contact Case."

5. Wilcock, "The Great Awakening."

6. Williamson, *Road in the Sky*, 161–62.

7. See Williamson, *Road in the Sky*, 169, 172.

8. Walt Rogers, *The Brown Notebook*. LL Research (website), accessed September 12, 2022.

9. Rogers, *The Brown Notebook*.

10. Rogers, *The Brown Notebook*.

11. Rogers, *The Brown Notebook*.

12. Rogers, *The Brown Notebook*.

13. Rogers, *The Brown Notebook*.

14. Rogers, *The Brown Notebook*.

15. Rogers, *The Brown Notebook*.

16. Wallace, *Space Story and the Inner Light*, 4.

17. Wallace, *Space Story and the Inner Light*. 4.

18. Wallace, *Space Story and the Inner Light*. 5.

CHAPTER 5. THE SOLAR FLASH

1. "ESO Discovers Earth-Size Planet in Habitable Zone of Nearest Star," Jet Propulsion Laboratory, NASA (website), April 24, 2016.

2. "Proxima Centauri's No Good, Very Bad Day: Flare Illuminates Lack of a Dust Ring; Puts Habitability of Proxima B in Question," Carnegie Science (website), February 26, 2018.

3. Daniel Strain, "Humongous Flare from Sun's Nearest Neighbor Breaks Records," *CU Boulder Today* (online newsletter), April 21, 2021.

4. Michael Salla, "Impending Solar Flash Event Supported by Scientific Studies and Insider Testimony," Exopolitics (website), January 7, 2019.

5. Salla, "Impending Solar Flash Event Supported by Scientific Studies & Insider Testimony."

6. Bob Frissell, "The Flower of Life Workshop: Igniting Your Inner Light," Bob Frissell (website), 2016.

7. *Law of One* (website), Session 2, question 2.

8. Santos, *Fatima in Lucia's Own Words*.

9. Cooper, *The Secret Government*, 11.

10. David Wilcock and Danion Brinkley, *The Path of Light*, Los Angeles, 2020, online video course.

11. Santos, *Fatima in Lucia's Own Words*, 8–9.

12. Santos, *Fatima in Lucia's Own Words*, 22.

13. Wilcock, *Awakening in the Dream*, 297.

14. Frissell, *Nothing in This Book Is True*, 185–86.

CHAPTER 6. COSMIC HISTORY

1. Richards and Goode, *Cosmic Secret*.

2. Hoagland, *Hoagland's Mars*, vol. 3, *The Moon/Mars Connection*, video.

3. Richards and Goode, *Cosmic Secret*.

4. Richards and Goode, *Cosmic Secret*.

5. David Icke, *The Lion Sleeps No More*, David Icke Books, 2010, DVD video.

6. Icke, *The Lion Sleeps No More*.

7. Icke, *The Lion Sleeps No More.*

8. Icke, *The Lion Sleeps No More.*

9. Icke, *The Lion Sleeps No More.*

10. Vasin and Shcherbakov, "Is the Moon the Creation of Alien Intelligence?"

11. Wilcock, "The Great Awakening."

12. Richards and Goode, *The Cosmic Secret.*

13. Wilcock, "The Great Awakening."

14. Salla, *The U.S. Navy's Secret Space Program & Nordic Extraterrestrial Alliance,* 111.

15. Frissell, *Nothing in This Book Is True,* 7.

16. Wilcock, *The Ascension Mysteries,* 394–95.

17. Wilcock, "The Great Awakening."

18. Icke, *The Lion Sleeps No More,* 414.

19. Wilcock, *The Ascension Mysteries,* 375.

20. Brown, *Cosmic Voyage,* 85–86.

21. *Law of One* (website), Session 6, question 10.

22. *Law of One* (website), Session 6, questions 11–13.

23. *Law of One* (website), Session 10, question 1.

24. *Law of One* (website), Session 10, questions 4–5.

25. *Law of One* (website), Session 10, question 6.

CHAPTER 7. THE DARK SIDE

1. Tom Beisner, "Thomas Jefferson's Top 10 Quotes on Money and Banking," Whitlock Co. (website), November 2, 2009.

2. "Ann Delap: Cabal Video Series Parts 1–10, with summaries," February 16, 2020, Public Intelligence Blog of Robert David Steele.

3. Rothschild quote in "Monetarists Anonymous," *The Economist* (website), September 29, 2012.

4. Janet Ossebaard, *Fall of the Cabal* video series.

5. *Liberty in the Balance: America, the FED and the IRS,* video.

6. Peter Schiff, "Nixon's Folly Is Your Gain," Schiff Gold (website), August 2021.

7. "The [CB]/[DS] Move Forward with Infrastructure," X22 Report (website), Episode 2549a, August 10, 2021.

8. Lauren Von Bernuth, "Operation Mockingbird: The CIA's History of Media Manipulation," Medium (website), April 10, 2018.

9. William Colby, "Church Committee Testimony," April 1976, *American History TV,* C-SPAN (website), April 25, 2016.

10. "The Spread of Disinformation and How We Respond," NAACP (website), accessed September 21, 2022.

11. Ossebaard, *Fall of the Cabal* video series.

12. Ossebaard, *Fall of the Cabal.*

13. Ossebaard, *Fall of the Cabal.*

14. Ossebaard, *Fall of the Cabal.*

15. Shenali D. Waduge, "Three Corporations Run the World: City of London, Washington DC and Vatican City," Sinhalanet (website), May 31, 2014.

16. Richards, *Above Majestic.*

17. Waduge, "Three Corporations Run the World."

18. Lynch and Granger, "What Happened to the Hominids Who May Have Been Smarter Than Us?"

19. Igor Gontcharov, "The Story of Elongated Skulls and the Denied History of Ancient People: An Interview with Mark Laplume," Ancient-Origins (website), updated December 19, 2014.

20. Richards and Goode, *The Cosmic Secret.*

21. Niall McCarthy, "The U.S. Cities with the Highest Homeless Populations in 2020," *Forbes* (website), April 16, 2021.

22. James Fetzer, "Proof That the Pandemic Was Planned and with Purpose," *Principia Scientific International* (website), September 30, 2020.

23. Torsten Engelbrecht and Konstantin Demeter, "COVID19 PCR Tests Are Scientifically Meaningless," Off Guardian (website), June 27, 2020.

24. Center for Disease Control and Prevention, "CDC Novel Coronavirus (2019-nCoV) Real-time RT-PCR Diagnostic Panel," FDA.gov (website), July 21, 2021.

25. Bill Wood, "Looking Glass Project," Odysee (website), March 22, 2021, video.

26. Wood, "Looking Glass Project."

27. Wood, "Looking Glass Project."

28. Wood, "Looking Glass Project."

CHAPTER 8. WHEN WE WERE ONE

1. Wilcock, "The Great Awakening."

2. *Law of One* (website), Session 82, questions 18–19.

3. *Law of One* (website), Session 82, question 22.

4. Michelle Holt, Tobey Wheelock, Carla Rueckert, and anonymous, "A *Law of One* Glossary," s.v. "polarization," *Law of One* (website).

5. *Law of One* (website), Session 17, question 2.

6. *Law of One* (website), Session 82, questions 21, 29.

7. Watts, *The Book: On the Taboo against Knowing Who You Are,* 12–13.

8. *Law of One* (website), Session 77, question 17.

9. *Law of One* (website), Session 85, question 19.

10. *Law of One* (website), Session 85, question 19.

11. *Law of One* (website), Session 4, question 20.

CHAPTER 9. THE HOLOGRAPHIC UNIVERSE

1. Bill Hicks quote, Anonymous Art of Revolution (website).

2. Shaza Oliyath, "Morpheus Quotes from *The Matrix*" (1999), Kidadl (website), last edited July 4, 2022.

3. *Law of One* (website), Session 1, question 0.

4. *Law of One* (website), Session 27, question 15.

5. *Law of One* (website), Session 27, question 16.

6. Frissell, *Nothing in This Book Is True,* 171–80.

CHAPTER 10.
CATCHING THE ASCENSION WAVE

1. Newton, *Journey of Souls.*

2. Brinkley, *Saved by the Light,* 10.

3. Brinkley, *Saved by the Light,* 10.

4. Brinkley, *Saved by the Light,* 2.

5. Brinkley, *Saved by the Light,* 13–14.

6. "Dannion Brinkley," The Twilight Brigade (website), accessed September 16, 2022.

7. *Law of One* (website), Session 4, question 20.

8. Melchizedek, *The Ancient Secret of the Flower of Life,* vol. 2.

CHAPTER 11. MIND MATTERS

1. "Ramana Maharshi Quotes," Stillness Speaks (website).

2. Rhinehart, *The Book of Est,* 174.

3. Albert Einstein, quoted in Walter Sullivan, "The Einstein Papers: A Man of Many Parts," *NY Times* (website), March 29, 1972.
4. Werner Erhard, "Creation, A Matter of Distinction," San Francisco, 1983, audiotape.

CHAPTER 12. DIGGING DEEPER

1. Richards and Goode, *The Cosmic Secret.*
2. "Albert Einstein Quotes," Brainy Quote (website), Brainy Media Inc., 2022.
3. Selye, "The Nature of Stress," 1985.

CHAPTER 13. SHINING THE LIGHT ON THE DARKNESS WITHIN

1. Leboyer, *Birth without Violence,* 15.
2. Ray, *Loving Relationships,* 32.
3. Ray, *Loving Relationships,* 32.
4. Bradshaw, *Healing the Shame That Binds You,* 41.

CHAPTER 16. THE BUILDING BLOCKS OF BREATH ALCHEMY

1. Bragg, *Super Power Breathing,* 8–39.

CHAPTER 17. IGNITING YOUR INNER LIGHT

1. See the HeartMath Institute (website).
2. George Bernard Shaw, *"Man and Superman: A Comedy and a Philosophy,* xxxi.
3. Archibald Henderson, *George Bernard Shaw, His Life and Works: A Critical Biography,* 503–4.

CHAPTER 19. CONNECTING TO SOURCE

1. Yogananda, *Autobiography of a Yogi.*

CHAPTER 20. THE SHIFT OF THE AGES

1. Keyes Jr., *The Hundredth Monkey.*
2. Melchizedek, *The Ancient Secret of the Flower of Life,* vol. 1, 107.
3. Frissell, *Nothing in This Book Is True,* 84–89.
4. Melchizedek, *The Mayan Ouroboros,* 119–20.
5. *Law of One* (website), Session 65, question 12.
6. Buckminster Fuller, "A Candid Conversation," 15.
7. Fuller, "Candid Conversation," 15–16.
8. *Law of One* (website), Session 65, questions 9–10.
9. *Law of One* (website), Session 65, question 12.

Bibliography

Bradshaw, John. *Healing the Shame That Binds You.* Deerfield Beach, Fla.: Health Communications, 1988.

Bragg, Paul. *Super Power Breathing.* Goleta, Calif.: UNKNO, 1995.

Brinkley, Dannion. *Saved by the Light.* New York: Harper Collins, 1994.

Brown, Courtney. *Cosmic Voyage.* New York: Dutton, 1996.

Cesana, Luca Trovellesi, dir. *UFO Secret: The Friendship Case; Extraordinary Case of Mass Alien Contact.* Cinedigm, 2012. DVD.

Cooper, Milton William. *Behold a Pale Horse.* Sedona, Ariz.: Light Technology, 1991.

———. *The Secret Government: The Origin, Identity, and Purpose of MJ-12.* Self-published, 1989.

Corey, Caroline. *Connecting to Source.* Omnium Foundation, 2006. Compact disc.

Corso, Phillip J. *The Day after Roswell.* New York: Pocket Books, 1997.

Cruttenden, Walter. *The Great Year.* Directed by Robert Ballo. Binary Research Institute, 2003. DVD.

———. *Lost Star of Myth and Time.* Pittsburgh, Pa.: St. Lynn's Press, 2005.

Dong, Paul, and Thomas Raffill. *China's Super Psychics.* Boston: Da Capo Press, 1997.

Ehrlich, Paul. *The Population Bomb.* New York: Sierra Club-Ballantine, 1970.

Fetzer, James. "Proof That the Pandemic Was Planned & with Purpose," *Principia Scientific International* (website), September 30, 2020.

Frissell, Bob. *Nothing in This Book Is True, But It's Exactly How Things Are.* 25th anniversary ed. Berkeley, Calif.: North Atlantic Books, 2019.

———. *Something in This Book Is True.* Berkeley, Calif.: North Atlantic Books, 2019.

Fuller, Buckminster. "A Candid Conversation with the Visionary Architect/ Inventor/Philosopher R. Buckminster Fuller," *Playboy* 19, no.2, February 1972.

Grossinger, Richard. *The Return of the Tower of Babel,* Opera Jupiter (substack), November 6, 2022.

Henderson, Archibald. *George Bernard Shaw, His Life and Works: A Critical Biography,* Cincinnati: Stewart & Kidd Co., 1911.

Hoagland, Richard C. *Hoagland's Mars.* vol. 1: *The NASA-Cydonia Briefings.* UFO TV, 2000. VHS video.

———. *Hoagland's Mars.* vol. 3: *The Moon/Mars Connection.* Directed by Bill Cote. 2000. VHS video.

———. *The Monuments of Mars: A City on the Edge of Forever.* Berkeley, Calif.: North Atlantic Books, 1993.

Huxley, Aldous. *Brave New World,* New York: HarperCollins Publisher, 1984.

Icke, David. *The Biggest Secret.* Isle of Wight, UK: David Icke Books, 1999.

———. *Human Race, Get off Your Knees: The Lion Sleeps No More.* Isle of Wight, UK: David Icke Books, 2010.

Keyes, Ken, Jr. *The Hundredth Monkey.* N.p.: Good Press, 2020.

Knapp, George, narrator. *UFOs: The Best Evidence.* Las Vegas: KLAS TV, 1989. VHS video.

Knight, Christopher, and Alan Butler. *Who Built the Moon?* Illustrated ed. London: Watkins, 2007.

Knight, J. Z. *Change: The Days to Come.* Yelm, Wash.: Ramtha Dialogues, 1986. VHS video.

Leboyer, Frederick. *Birth without Violence.* New York: Alfred A. Knopf, 1976.

Lévi-Strauss, Claude. *The Raw and the Cooked: Introduction to a Science of Mythology,* Vol. 1. New York: Harper Colophon Books, 1970.

Liberty in the Balance: America, the FED and the IRS. Pasadena, Calif.: Mosaic Media, 1993. Video.

Lynch, Gary, and Richard Granger. "What Happened to the Hominids Who May Have Been Smarter Than Us?" *Discover,* December 27, 2009.

Melchizedek, Drunvalo. *The Ancient Secret of the Flower of Life.* Vol. 2. Flagstaff, Ariz.: Light Technology Publishing, 2000.

———. *The Mayan Ouroboros.* San Francisco: Weiser Books, 2012.

Miles, Christopher, dir. "Alternative Three," episode on *Science Report.* Anglia TV (UK). Aired June 20, 1977. Video.

Newton, Michael. *Journey of Souls.* Woodbury, Minn.: Llewellyn Publications, 1994.

———. *Memories of the Afterlife.* Woodbury, Minn.: Llewellyn Publications, 2009.

———. *Wisdom of Souls.* Woodbury, Minn.: Llewellyn Publications, 2019.

Orwell, George. *1984,* London: Arcturus Publishing Ltd., 2021.

Ossebaard, Janet. *Fall of the Cabal Video Series,* Rumble (website), assessed in 2021.

Ray, Sondra. *Loving Relationships.* Berkeley, Calif.: Celestial Arts, 1980.

Rhinehart, Luke. *The Book of Est.* New York: Holt, Rinehart and Winston, 1976.

Richards, Roger R., dir. *Above Majestic.* SBA Media, 2018. Video.

Richards, Roger R., and Corey Goode, dirs. *The Cosmic Secret.* SBA Entertainment, 2019. Video.

Ross, Gary, dir. *Pleasantville.* Larger Than Life Productions, 1998. DVD.

Salla, Michael. "Impending Solar Flash Event Supported by Scientific Studies & Insider Testimony." Exopolitics (website), January 7, 2019.

———. *The U.S. Navy's Secret Space Program and Nordic Extraterrestrial Alliance.* Pahoa, Hawaii: Exopolitics Consultants, 2017.

Santos, Maria Lucia. *Fatima in Lucia's Own Words: The Memoirs of Sister Lucia, the Last Fatima Visionary.* N.p.: Keep It Catholic & Keeping It Catholic KIC, 2015.

Scallion, Gordon-Michael. *The Earth Changes Report* 2.4. Westmoreland, N.H.: Matrix Institute, May 1, 1992.

Selye, Hans. "The Nature of Stress." *Basal Facts* 7, no. 1 (1985): 3–11.

Shaw, George Bernard. *Man and Superman: A Comedy and a Philosophy.* New York: Brentano's, 1903.

Timms, Moira. *Prophecies and Predictions: Everyone's Guide to the Coming Changes.* Santa Cruz, Calif.: Unity Press, 1980.

Tompkins, William. *Selected by Extraterrestrials.* Self-published: CreateSpace Independent Publishing Platform, 2015.

Tzu, Sun. *The Art of War,* Trans. Ralph D. Sawyer, with Mei-chün Lee Sawyer, New York: Basic Books, 1994.

Vasin, Mikhail, and Alexander Shcherbakov. "Is the Moon the Creation of Alien Intelligence?" *Sputnik,* July 1970.

Wallace, Baird. *Space Story and the Inner Light: A Series of Articles.* Grosse Ile, Mich.: Self-published, 1972.

Watts, Alan. *The Book: On the Taboo against Knowing Who You Are.* New York: Collier Books, 1966.

White, John. *Pole Shift: Predictions and Prophecies of the Ultimate Disaster.* Virginia Beach, Va.: A.R.E. Press, 1980.

Wilcock, David. *The Ascension Mysteries.* New York: Penguin Publishing, 2016.

———. *Awakening in the Dream.* New York: Penguin Publishing, 2020.

Williamson, George Hunt. *Road in the Sky.* null, 2011. First published by Neville Spearman, 1958.

Yogananda, Paramahansa. *Autobiography of a Yogi.* Commerce, Calif.: Crystal Clarity Publishers, 1980.

About the Author

Bob Frissell is the founder of the Breath Alchemy Technique and has been teaching for thirty-four years. His books are regarded as underground spiritual classics. In addition to *Nothing in This Book Is True, But It's Exactly How Things Are,* he is the author of *Something in This Book Is True,* and *You Are a Spiritual Being Having a Human Experience.*

His three previous books—having sold in excess of 700,000 copies—are published in twenty-five languages and are available in more than thirty countries. As a result, he has given his two workshops—"The Breath of Life" and "The Flower of Life"—throughout North America, as well as Europe and Australia.

As an avid lover of music, it pleases Bob greatly to know that musicians have credited the ideas presented in his books as a source of inspiration for their own creative work. This list includes Tool (band), Danny Carey, and Gojira (band).

In his books, he details from a big-picture perspective the enormous infusion of higher-dimensional energy that is dramatically raising the vibratory rate of the planet and everyone on it. He also gives the details of the personal transformation that we must make if we are to survive and thrive, so we can catch the wave into higher consciousness in a way that enables Mother Earth to reach critical mass and become lit from within.

He is, therefore, on a mission to help as many thousands of men and women as he can to open up to their unlimited potential by discovering that the resolution to any unwanted condition lies within them!

Bob gives private Breath Alchemy sessions on Skype, along with Fast-track coaching consultations. He has been a featured speaker at the Global Congress of Spiritual Scientists in Bangalore, India, the Fourth Annual Symbiosis Gathering at Yosemite, The Prophets Conference in Tulum, and many New Living Expos. He has also appeared on numerous talk shows, including: The Jeff Rense Program, Red Ice Radio, Far Out Radio, and has been a three-time guest on Coast to Coast AM.

On a personal note, he is a nature enthusiast. Bob loves hiking; and all manner of cats, squirrels, ducks, wild turkeys, deer, and redwood trees catch his eye. He lives in Sonoma, California.

You can contact him at his website, BobFrissell.com.

Index

Page numbers in *italics* refer to illustrations.